# The
# EdTech Book

## The World's First Crowdsourced Book On EdTech

Alessandro Di Lullo, Janos Barberis, Tamas Haiman

# Acknowledgements

Dear all,

It's more than a pleasure to be able to produce this book. As you know, a book is always something that is weeks, months or years in the making, and it is an incredible opportunity. We wrote it when the world of education was shifting and transforming, though we never believed that it would have an impact beyond the readers that now have access to it. It's had a substantial impact on SuperCharger as a team, whom have now utilised the content of this book to build the fastest growing EdTech Accelerator in the world.

Of course, opportunities are only possible because of people, and we therefore wanted to use this part of the book to thank our team. Georgia Hanley has been leading this project, and Sofia Daley has been providing invaluable feedback. We also want to thank the authors who have provided all of their inside expertise and decades of experience in a succinct manner, in order to make the readers better teachers, parent, policy-makers and investors. Thank you to the whole SuperCharger team for their efforts and support of this project. Finally, we wanted to thank the startups, who are not only making what SuperCharger Ventures stands for, but also what the future of education is all about.

We hope you have enjoyed this book as much as we have, please do share it as widely as you can.

The SuperCharger Team

# Introduction

The EdTech Book has taken the approach to crowd-source the knowledge of the best subject matter experts on the topic of how education will include technology. With over 50 contributors, we are covering trends around the world, in specific sectors and age groups.

Whilst many industries have been digitised, the education sector has been woefully dragging behind. The COVID-19 pandemic has exposed gaps in the global education industry. Stakeholders started to look at Educational Technology (EdTech) solutions to help their students move from the classroom to online.

Like most changes, people need to educate themselves on the consequences of it and the new tools available to them to perform best. This is precisely what the EdTech Book offers to the reader, awareness of the best practises in edtech from real practitioners, decision makers and founders.

As with everything, starting with a definition is key. EdTech is everything that involves the use of technology in education to improve delivery, impact and user experience. As indicated by this definition, EdTech can take a variety of forms, and can be used for a wide variety of purposes.

In fact, EdTech encompasses everything from language learning apps such as Duolingo and Busuu, to digital tutoring platforms such as BYJU's and Yuanfudao, to Massive Open Online Courses (MOOCs) like Coursera and edX. The last two examples are also an illustration that EdTech is not a new phenomenon, but instead a confirmation that the digitization of the education system is increasing.

When reading the book, you will notice that EdTech is not only limited to online learning, but rather, includes the entire suite of software, hardware and digital tools and services that can help deliver education. Therefore, EdTech can be used for so much more than shifting traditional, in-person classes online. EdTech can make education better, by improving processes in a school. But it can also make education different, by teaching students in the metaverse.

We expect that technology will help educators facilitate learning in new and innovative ways. The technology that EdTech presents can help teachers identify a student's strengths and weaknesses through easily-assessed online tests, and the gamification of education can keep students engaged, for longer. Additionally, the implementation of Artificial Intelligence (AI) can help students customise their syllabus based on their needs and interests.

Historically, technology has evolved to suit the society's needs. It has helped us communicate more effectively with those both near and far, aided our medical development, and spurred economic growth in most countries around the world. When it comes to education, 92% of teachers believe that education and pedagogy will undergo a technological revolution.

Therefore, EdTech is not just about shifting off-line education to on-line. In reality, EdTech is what education is becoming - it will transform the future of how education is taught, perceived, resourced and consumed.

Today, EdTech is one of the fastest growing markets globally. Driven by the fourth industrial

INTRODUCTION

revolution, global spending on education is widely expected to rise from over USD5tn last year to close to over USD7tn by 2025. And, within this market, EdTech is booming.

That's why we created this book. As a reference point, The EdTech book takes a look at all that encompasses the industry. From the history of EdTech to the implementation of governmental regulation, to the future of EdTech in classrooms - the authors in this book share a story of EdTech, whether that is its past, present or future.

# Table of Contents

TABLE OF CONTENTS

# Governments

# Technology

# Future

# 1 COVID-19

# Navigating The Toggled Term: Overcoming Instructional Challenges Presented Now And In The Future With The Online Instructional Infrastructure And Toggled Term Instructional Model

**Matthew Rhoads, Ed.D.**

Technology Trainer at Poway Unified School District and Educational Consultant at The Discovery Source

Education has changed forever. When the COVID-19 pandemic hit in 2020, K-12 schools, districts and higher education institutions worldwide raced to determine how to instruct students within a variety of different educational settings. Across the world, we saw schools having to teach students within online, hybrid/blended, and traditional in-person educational settings with COVID-19 safety protocols in place. As COVID-19 outbreaks occurred and the mitigation of local transmission rates transpired throughout the year, schools and districts had to move between various educational settings to instruct students. As a result, teachers and school leaders had to further integrate educational technology (EdTech) into their instructional design and organisational structures to effectively navigate between online, hybrid/blended, and traditional in-person educational settings to ensure learning could continue amid a pandemic.

This scenario is called the "toggled term." Originally coined by Bryan Alexander (2020), the toggled term represents moving back and forth between educational settings where learning occurs due to increasing or decreasing local COVID-19 case and transmission rates. Throughout 2020 and 2021, especially in the United States, schools, districts, and higher education institutions had to toggle between two or three of these educational settings multiple times throughout the school year. Schools navigated through this toggling process with varying success and longevity (MCH Data, 2021). Unfortunately, in many cases, toggles took longer than anticipated to be implemented and put immense strain on teachers and school leaders who had to learn unpremeditaely, collectively and individually the skills needed to integrate instructional pedagogy and design with EdTech tools within classrooms and schools. Ultimately, instructional and organisational frameworks within school reopening plans for hybrid/blended or traditional in-person instruction that were poorly planned, at times, caused additional toggles to take place. Thus, schools must have a solid blueprint to provide effective instruction and toggle between various educational settings.

As the world navigates COVID-19 and future pandemics, schools face scenarios where students, teachers, and staff experience exposure to the virus. As a result of these outbreaks, students and teachers must quarantine to avoid possibly spreading the virus. Based on the outbreak's size, schools may experience a full temporary shutdown of all in-person teaching on campus, or specific classes and sections could be temporarily shut down. We call temporary shutdowns of all on-campus learning a 'full toggle', which means a shift of instruction from in-person to online learning (Rhoads, 2021). This can occur both ways, as the in-person learning shutdown will eventually be lifted once authorities deem it safe to return to some form of in-person learning. On the other hand, lite toggles occur when only a class or portion of the school must quarantine and shift to online instruction or HyFlex/Concurrent instruction (Rhoads, 2021). As with full toggles, lite toggles can be reversed back to in-person learning once quarantine periods are over and it is deemed safe for students and teachers to return.

To navigate the toggled term, all schools need to have a cohesion between their EdTech infrastructure, instructional design, organisational structures and culture to ensure learning is continuous. Not only will this help schools navigate our current challenges, but it will also create the freedom and flexibility so that teaching and learning can occur anywhere and at any time. Thus, presented here is a framework that demonstrates this cohesion in action to allow schools to toggle between various educational settings seamlessly. With the "Online Instructional Infrastructure" and the "Toggled Term Instructional Model" working in tandem together, this can happen (Rhoads, 2021). The implications of having effective instruction for all students at any time or place establishes an environment where equitable learning can be fostered in an ever-changing world.

## The Online Instructional Infrastructure

All of teaching and learning in education will inevitably be digitised and housed with a foundation of EdTech tools teachers can harness to amplify learning. Even before 2020, this was a trend that was gaining momentum in education before it was even accelerated as a result of the COVID-19 pandemic. To teach students in any setting and toggle between them, an online instructional infrastructure needs to be in place. In practice, this assortment of EdTech tools allows teachers to build an infrastructure to use research-based instructional strategies to educate students pragmatically. Ultimately, EdTech tools' infrastructure must contain seven major categories of tools that teachers and schools can harness to be effective, regardless of whether the setting is online, hybrid/blended, or fully in-person. The seven categories of EdTech mechanisms within the online instructional infrastructure" include a Student Information System (SIS), learning management system (LMS), virtual meeting platform, content creation tools, and student collaboration, engagement, and assessment tools.

| Learning Management System | | | | |
|---|---|---|---|---|
| Google Classroom<br>Canvas<br>Schoology<br>Seesaw | | | | |
| **Student Information System** | | | | |
| Aeries<br>Infinite Campus<br>Synergy<br>Powerschool | | | | |
| **Content Creation** | **Collaboration** | **Engagement** | **Virtual Meeting Tool** | **Assessment** |
| • Google Workspace<br>• Microsoft 365 | • Wakelet<br>• Padlet<br>• Jamboard d | • Pear Deck<br>• Nearpo d<br>• Edpuzz le | • Google Meet<br>• Zoom<br>• Microso ft Teams | • Quizizz<br>• GoFormati ve<br>• Quizalize |

**Figure 1.** *The Online Instructional Infrastructure with Mainstream EdTech Tools* (Rhoads, 2020; Rhoads, 2021).

Each component of the online instructional infrastructure is essential to modern classrooms, regardless of the grade level. LMS' act as the central hub where all content created by a teacher is housed and distributed to students. Alongside an LMS is an SIS, which acts as the data warehouse and informational system, tracking student attendance records, grades, and relevant information related to a student's education. Both LMS and an SIS can also act as a communication hub for teachers to utilise for contacting students and families. Outside of the LMS and SIS, we have tools that allow teachers to build content, host online synchronous virtual class sessions, and tools teachers can use to engage students in learning, provide opportunities for them to collaborate together, and to assess their learning.

With the online instructional infrastructure in place, teachers can then strategically integrate research-based instructional strategies with these tools to amplify student learning. Teachers are the ultimate driving force of EdTech tools because they must be used strategically. Using research from John Hattie (2018) and Marzanzo (2011), teachers can determine which strategies to integrate with their tools to amplify learning. Prominent educator researchers and practitioners such as Doug Fisher, Matt Miller, George Couros, and Catlin Tucker discuss these integrations in their work. Overall, when a teacher is equipped with EdTech tools from each of the components of the online instructional infrastructure and knows how to use them strategically, they can create a variety of learning opportunities that can occur anywhere and at any time for their students.

## The Toggled Term Instructional Model

Once the online instructional infrastructure is in place, schools must strategically utilise that apparatus to enhance education. We can have all the EdTech tools we want, but without strong instructional strategies powered by teachers, our tools will not amplify learning to the degree needed to be effective. However, with both strong instructional strategies that are well-founded with EdTech tools, learning will be amplified within any educational setting. The toggled term instructional model demonstrates how learning can take place in any setting, at any time and incorporate research-based instructional strategies that drive student learning.

Each component of the toggled term instructional model will be discussed and how it can be implemented within K-12 schools and higher education institutions. Figure 2 illustrates the model in action as discussed in the book *Navigating the Toggled Term: A Guide for Classroom and School Leaders,* which demonstrates how all of its elements are working together to provide simultaneous and continuous learning at anytime and anywhere for students (Rhoads, 2021).

| The Toggled Term Instructional Model - An Instructional Model for Simultaneous and Continuous Learning for the Present and the Future | | | |
|---|---|---|---|
| **Asynchronous Instruction Online (24/7) Learning** Online Lectures/Content Screencast Videos, Hyperdocs/Slide Presentations, Visual and Audio Scaffolds & Supports, Interactive Asynchronous Slides, Student Collaboration, Independent Practice, Teacher Feedback & Communication, Gamification, Online Tutoring & Support, and Student Assessment | | | |
| **Online Synchronous Instructional Strategies** Teacher Modelling/ Direct Instruction Teacher Feedback Interactive Slideshows Breakout Discussion Rooms Reciprocal Teaching Think, Pair, Share Student Backchannel Discussion I Do, We Do, You Do Student Collaboration Independent Practice Assessment | **Synchronous Live Online Class Sessions** | **Synchronous In- Person Class Sessions on Campus** | **In-Person Instructional Strategies** Teacher Modelling/ Direct Instruction Teacher Feedback Interactive Slideshows Breakout Discussion Rooms Reciprocal Teaching Think, Pair, Share Student Backchannel Discussion I Do, We Do, You Do Student Collaboration Independent Practice Assessment |
| **HyFlex/Concurrent Instruction** Live recorded class sessions or pre-recorded class sessions or online activities that align with instruction during synchronous live class sessions. These classes can offer interactive or passive learning experiences depending on how a teacher deploys them. | | | |

**Figure 2.** *The Toggled Term Instructional Model* (Rhoads, 2021).

The toggled term instructional model is broken down into four major components: asynchronous instruction online, synchronous live online classes and instructional strategies, synchronous in-person learning and instructional strategies, and HyFlex/Conconcurrent instruction. Each component of the toggled term instructional model will be outlined, as well as how they interact and work together as they are all interconnected. Interwoven into this discussion are integrations relating to how this model utilizes the online instructional infrastructure as its foundation to function within any educational setting at any time.

## Asynchronous Instruction Online & Synchronous Live Online Instruction

## Components

First, the asynchronous instruction online and synchronous live online instruction components will be discussed. For the asynchronous instruction online, it consists of an LMS and SIS, which act as the central hub for delivering instruction and communicating with students. Within this component of the model, several strategies can be integrated tactically to allow for asynchronous learning to take place effectively without being live.

During COVID-19 and moving forward into the future of education, having a major asynchronous online instructional component integrated into any class, regardless of the grade level and content, is essential. It provides opportunities for students to learn both inside and outside of the school day by having all of the classes' resources and tasks hosted online for students to engage with at any time or place. When done strategically, asynchronous learning can be a place where students re-engage in material from the day, receive feedback, extend their learning, and connect with their classmates outside of the physical classroom setting. For the second component, we have synchronous live online classes and instructional strategies to go along with that setting. It is essential that engagement and collaborative tools, in addition to assessment tools, are integrated during the synchronous online live instruction. When planning synchronous live classes, educators need to create digital spaces where students can overtly and covertly engage by integrating instructional strategies that optimise these learning opportunities with the tools being utilised. Overall, both of these components provide the opportunity for classes to not need a physical classroom to be fully functional. Students and teachers now have the ability to have a digital realm for their classroom. Therefore, learning can take place anywhere and at any time for students. This means learning can continue during breaks, weekends, snow days, natural disasters, and during pandemics. Furthermore, as we will outline, asynchronous and synchronous online learning can be immediately toggled to at any time if the infrastructure of EdTech tools and instructional strategies are in place.

## Synchronous Live In-Person & Instructional Strategy Component

Next, the synchronous live in-person and instructional strategies component will be outlined. Within the vast majority of classrooms moving forward, most of the content students will engage with will be digital, even during in-person learning. In a similar manner as with synchronous live online classes, synchronous live in-person classes can use the same array of EdTech tools integrated with instructional strategies that can also be used online. As a result, educators can build their instructional strategy and EdTech tool kit to work for in-person and online synchronous live class settings. For example, within an in-person synchronous live class session, teachers can employ a strategy like think, pair, and share with interactive slides to have students overtly and covertly engage with the slides and their peers. Students can pair up and discuss the topic with each other by moving throughout the room while in a physical setting. If done online, a teacher can create one or two sets of breakout rooms that pair students together to discuss the topic before sharing with the class. Therefore, as illustrated in this example, instructional strategies integrated with EdTech tools can be incorporated within any setting. Whilst they may slightly differ in appearance and execution, they amplify learning in the same manner.

Overall, synchronous live in-person classes can use the vast majority of the EdTech tools within the online instructional infrastructure. Additionally, the instructional strategies utilized that are integrated with the EdTech tools can be used in online synchronous class settings. Ultimately, this is a powerful adaptation of the toggled term instructional model. We can see that students' instruction can move seamlessly back and forth between being online and in-person. This is coupled with the notion that many instructional strategies can be deployed in any educational setting, as long as a teacher understands the instructional sequence of the strategy and how it is combined with the EdTech tools they have selected for their classroom.

**HyFlex/Concurrent Instruction Component**

The HyFlex/Concurrent instructional component will be the last component of the model discussed. Ultimately, what this means is to provide live synchronous instruction simultaneously for students online and in-person. Also, it means providing students with several avenues for achieving the objectives of the class. For example, instead of attending a live class online or in-person, students have an alternative activity they must complete in order to have a similar learning experience that aligns with the synchronous class experience that they are missing. Within the context of the COVID-19 pandemic, the HyFlex/Concurrent instructional model is employed when physical classrooms can only hold a certain threshold of students due to COVID-19 safety protocols in addition to students and families yielding to stay home and learn from home due to safety concerns. To incorporate the HyFlex/Concurrent component of this model to see it work in action, the asynchronous online instruction as well as online and in-person synchronous live class instructional strategies can be integrated with the online instructional infrastructure elements. All students would be on the same virtual online meeting platform and would be using the same LMS, engagement, collaboration, and assessment EdTech tools simultaneously. At the instructional level, this is one of the most difficult instructional models a teacher can employ. They have to manage their EdTech tool interfaces on their device(s) along with having students physically in a classroom as well as studentsonline simultaneously.

In the context of COVID-19, the HyFlex/Concurrent component of this model should only be used temporarily over the course of two weeks at a maximum. The focus, planning, and micromanagement of students in both settings, in addition to various EdTech interfaces at once, has proven to demonstrate burnout (Samee, 2020). For short-term lite toggles, this component of the model works best, as demonstrated above. This keeps students who are already quarantined able to continue participating in class with their peers who were not called into quarantine. Beyond the time it takes for incubation periods for self-isolation, the HyFlex/ Concurrent model has a place in education. Suppose that the course has already been pre-planned and built before the semester begins. In this case, it can be used as a good alternative model for providing instruction to students in a variety of educational settings.

### A Synthesis Of Models Working Together

The toggled term instructional model takes the online instructional infrastructure as the foundation for instruction to toggle between online and blended learning settings when lite and full toggles occur.It also lays the foundation for educational instruction moving forward. It gives teachers and school leaders a framework to provide instruction at any time or place, regardless of the circumstances. In addition, students can engage in learning in physical and online spaces as well as connect with their peers and teachers in an online or in-person setting. Finally, it gives teachers a set of instructional strategies that can be integrated with EdTech tools to be incorporated within any educational setting. This is game-changing, as it takes education and places it within various constructs and settings both inside and outside of traditional brick and mortar school buildings.

### Other Considerations: Beyond Integrating Both The Toggled Term Instructional Mode And Online Instructional Infrastructure - Organisational Coherence

Beyond instructional models and EdTech infrastructure, schools must also consider several elements to help with the systematic processes of full and lite toggles when they are triggered. Schools need to have their organisations in the position to execute each toggle. Schools must be flexible, collaborative, focused in their direction as an organisation, have the confidence of teachers and the greater communityand narrow their instructional goals related to 21st-century deep learning (Fullan & Quinn, 2016; Rhoads, 2021). At an organisational level, each of these components allows for the toggled term instructional model to be flexible, reflexive, and adaptable to ever-changing local conditions where the school is located. Schools across the world need to emphasise these organisational facets to navigate the present and be able to adapt to the dynamic conditions of the future.

### Conclusion

Education has become unbound from its traditional brick and mortar setting across all grade levels due to the ever-increasing innovation from EdTech. The COVID-19 pandemic helped propel the inevitable: education that can occur at any time or place with pragmatic instructional designs and strategies, coupled with an online instructional infrastructure. With the EdTech infrastructure, instructional framework, and instructional strategies in place within a school system, education can be effective in-person and online. Additionally, it gives educators the ability to instantly toggle between each educational setting when needed. Beyond the pandemic and into the future, schools and higher education institutions will have the blueprint needed to be flexible, adaptive, and resilient for their students and the local community. Schools will not have to be completely shut down or be constrained to being physically in a school building.

Long term, the implications of using an online instructional infrastructure gives schools and teachers the ability to innovate and transform instruction. Still, there is a great deal of professional development required. The integration of instructional strategies with mainstream EdTech tools remains the final step to effectively using EdTech tools to amplify learning for all students. Therefore, besides focusing on the development of new EdTech tools, there must be long on-going professional learning in the form of coaching, mentoring, self-paced instruction, and teacher professional learning networks to ensure this happens (Abiloch,

Hararda, &Fontichiaro, 2013). Organisationally, schools must invest in this moving forward. To effectively toggle, teachers and school leaders must have the ability to integrate the online instructional infrastructure's basic elements with the toggled term instructional model at the school's instructional and organisational level. Thus, having the ability to utilize both models in tandem is central to navigating the present and future of education. To further facilitate this tandem of frameworks working together, school leaders and policymakers will need to invest heavily in developing a culture of professional learning and collaboration within schools to ensure all students receive effective instruction that is integrated with EdTech tools to amplify learning, regardless of the educational setting (Fullan & Senge, 2010; Fullan & Quinn, 2016). Ultimately, schools that are able to overcome this challenge will be successful now and in the future, as the world of education continues to innovate and change at an immense pace.

# 2 Schools

# EdTech For Schools

## Danish Sayanee

Author and Principal Investor of TeachPower

The term EdTech refers to the fusion of education and technology. When education and technology merge, they benefit a lot of parties, including teachers, learners, parents, and schools. The main purpose of merging education and technology is to help teachers and learners improve their performance and make them life-long learners. It helps the teacher to move from a role of teacher to facilitator. The integration of technology and education has shown some promising results in the learner's performance. Technology has made its place, not just in big multinational companies or offices, it can be easily seen in small classrooms too.

To have a clearer understanding of the fusion of education and technology, we first need to look back at history. Usually, people view EdTech as a relatively new concept. But, looking at history, we learn that it's a much older concept than people might think, with people expressing themselves through art, sketches, drawings, and paintings. A caveman expressing himself through drawing on the cave is a prehistoric example of educational technology.

Additionally, oral communication is one of the oldest forms of communication. People used to pass on knowledge, news, and history from one generation to another through oral communication. It is quite evident in Socrates' method of speech, which is even still used today, where individuals teach by asking different questions related to the topic.

People also used to write on stones, walls, wool, rocks, and leaves. In 15th century Europe, the printing press was invented for the very first time, which made it very easy for writers to write and for readers to read. As printing increased, formal education increased all over Europe.

At the beginning of the 1920s, the British Broadcasting Corporation (BBC) started to broadcast educational programs for schools. In 1924, the first adult education broadcast was on *Insects in Relation to Man*, and in the same year, J.C. Stobart, the Director of Education at the BBC, inspired 'a broadcasting university' in the journal *Radio Times* (Robinson, 1982). In education, television was first used in the 1960s by both schools andadult education in general.

The British government set up an open university, which integrated courses from the British Broadcasting Corporation (BBC) and was opened to all the students. Whilst radio broadcasts catered to oral communication, television showed documentaries, adding images to words. The integration of education and technology spread quickly around the world and was adopted by many developing countries.

By the 1980s, satellite broadcasting was also being used. In 1983, India launched its very own satellite named 'INSAT', which delivered educational television all over the country, and was translated into the various languages of the local community. Even today, India is using tele-education in the parts of the country where people are not able to afford education for children.

Suddenly, in the 1990s, the value of creating and dispersing videos dropped as internet accessibility increased. This led to cost reductions, which in turn, led to the development of the lecture system. This phase of technology ensured that the masses could access videos with a reliable internet connection.

In 2002, recorded lectures and videos were made available for learners free of charge by the Massachusetts Institute of Technology (MIT). In 2005, YouTube was born and was later bought by Google in 2006. YouTube increased access to educational videos that could be easily downloaded and merged into online courses. Later, universities used it to make voice-over lectures, solving multiple equations with the help of pictures. Apple's creation of iTunes also meant that various videos and resources could also be easily downloaded, free of cost.

After programmed learning made its way across the world, computer-based learning was beginning to be introduced. With computer-based learning, the individual was not required to serve as a medium for dispersion of learning, meaning that technology had finally started to take over.

In the 1980s, we were introduced to Artificial Intelligence (AI), with its main focus on teaching arithmetic. A huge chunk of investment was employed to this cause - but results were not as expected, and were, in fact, highly disappointing.

In 1970's New Jersey, blended learning was being experimented within the new Institute of Technology. These attempts primarily used NJIT's internal computer network, through which they integrated physical classrooms with online discussion platforms and named it "computer-mediated communication" or CMC (Hiltz andTuroff 1978). In the 1980s, a software developed in Canada, named CoSy, set up online threaded group discussion forums. The UK's Open University offered various courses which integrated this online discussion feature using CoSy. With approximately 1200 students registered, it is known as the first "mass" open online course.

Later, in 1991, the World Wide Web was launched, allowing users to create link documents, videos, audios, and other digital resources. Once launched, many search engines were created, including Google,the world's most popular search engine.

The web allowed the creation of the first learning management systems (LMS) like WebCT. Through LMS, online classes are easily implemented, with assignments created and allocated to learners. They also provide a discussion platform for both teachers and learners, easily enabling an exchange of knowledge. In 1995, the first online courses using LMS were created and were presented through PowerPoint slides and pdfs. These resources could easily represent text, graphics, pictures, audio, and videos to cater to student needs. Soon, learning management systems became one of the main platforms to conduct online classes. Soon after came the time of social media, which includes various sections of technology, including YouTube videos, blogs, mobile phones, wikis, tablets, FaceTime, Skype, Twitter, Facebook, Instagram, and Botim. Today, social media is a big part of a millennial or Gen Z's life. Formal education has become integrated with all these applications, allowing collaborative learning to take place. Education has always adopted and adapted to technological advancements.

However, it has been observed that teachers of both developing and developed countries are still reluctant towards using technology in their classrooms. There can be several reasons for this reluctance. For instance, there are many teachers who do not understand the importance and benefit of technology, or the opportunities that come with its implementation - so they don't use it in their classrooms. Another reason, which is the most common, is that, whilst schools may buy certain gadgets or applications for teachers, they actually fail to teach them how to use it. As a result, they fail to integrate the technology into their classrooms.

Until teachers are made comfortable with technology, they will never be able to implement it in their classrooms. Often, a lack of guidance and inspiration is why teachers are not able to integrate technology into their curriculum. Even if teachers *are* provided with the relevant training, this is not always sufficient, especially if no-one helps them understand *why* it is important to use these products in the classroom. Perhaps it could be argued that just being familiar with the tool is not sufficient, as the teacher needs to also be equipped with the adequate pedagogical digital skills in order to teach.

Hence, teachers are often left with unanswered questions by the end of the training session. These unanswered questions have become a leading cause as to why teachers are unable to equip themselves with the much-needed technological skills.

One fear that teachers face is that today's learner is more in touch with technology than they are themselves. So, due to their lack of confidence, they believe they might lose control of the classroom. Additionally, they fear that they won't be able to gauge the interest of learners in lessons which do not include technology integration. One of the major concerns is, even if teachers are tech-savvy, they prefer to use applications which work offline - as internet connections are not good enough to support their teaching.

Just placing technology in the classroom is, quite simply, not good enough. It is crucial to train teachers sufficiently, in order for them to use it effectively in the classroom. On the other hand, teachers need to keep clear communication lines with the school, informing them of their struggles in understanding. Running away from technology is no solution.

Schools need to be futuristic in their approach and ensure that the curriculum is naturally integrated with technology. And, if possible, must provide strategies so that teachers can easily use them in classrooms.

Even after the provision of these guidelines, not all teachers will be able to expertly implement technology in the classroom, and many will continue to face obstacles. It is essential that teachers are provided with a fair opportunity to learn and explore technology. It is the miracle of technology that allows learning to continue unencumbered and unhampered through all kinds of crises. Technology-supported learning solutions such as LMS and MOOCs allow learners to connect globally and participate in learning activities from wherever they feel comfortable.

What started at the higher education level can now also be seen at a secondary and high school level, with many parents opting to home-school their children through online schools. It is evident that just introducing technology is not good enough - as technology alone cannot fill the gaps of the education system. It is only *teachers* who can realise the full potential of technology and unleash it in their classrooms. It is equally important that teachers are made comfortable whilst using technology, so that they can comprehend the relationship of a user, technology, and resources.

Now, I turn to a framework which briefly explains the understanding of teachers as the complex interconnection between technology, content, and pedagogy. The framework is constructed based on Shulman's work from 1986 to 1987, and explains the pedagogical knowledge for comprehending how effective teaching can be with the help of technology. More approaches have been taken into account that has extended upon Shulman's work, which is related to pedagogical knowledge that revolves around the domain of technology.

This framework puts the spotlight on the pedagogical content, explaining the importance of technological content knowledge to understand effective teaching and technology. There are three areas of knowledge as per the framework: content, technology, and pedagogy.

Content is the subject matter which is taught by the teachers and learned by students. It includes a variety of subjects like poetry, mathematics, literacy, and history. The content and subject matter of these subjects are different from one another.

Technology includes modern gadgets such as computers, videos, smart boards, tablets, the internet, and projectors. Pedagogy explains strategies, methods, practises, and the processes of how learning and teaching take place. More precisely, digital pedagogy explains how strategies, methods, practices, and processes relevant to teaching, learning, and assessing are put into action using EdTech tools. The beauty of any EdTech tool is that it does not isolate the teaching-learning process from the consequent assessment process - it also covers the area of instruction, assessment, and learning of students.

Content, technology, and pedagogy are extremely useful when they are constructed together. For example, when we have content and pedagogy, we can get pedagogical content knowledge. This is quite close to the idea of Shulman's framework. Technological pedagogy includes a depiction of concepts, pedagogical techniques, knowledge of how to make concepts easy to grasp by students and focuses on the learner's prior knowledge. Similarly, if we take technology and content into account, we can construct technological content knowledge, which explains how a teacher's subject knowledge can be implemented in classrooms while integrating technology.

If we look back at the history of pedagogy, we can trace the role of the teacher back to Ancient Greece. Socrates knowledge, which dates to 5 B.C., is also the foundation of many modern schools where students learn in today. In England, schools were established in 597 AD, with King's School in Canterbury, Kent, the first school in England. Today, these schools serve as public schools.

Historically, the curriculums of these schools were very basic and were divided into two sections:

trivium and quadrivium. Trivium covered grammar, logic, and rhetoric whereas Quadrivium covered astronomy, arithmetic, music, and geometry. Lessons were conducted by teachers, and learners used to read the text and explain it. Later, students were assigned questions and were instructed to give descriptive answers. Before getting a master's degree, students would debate about answers to questions with their seniors.

In 1780, churches realised the importance of education, and Ragged Schools, Parish Schools, and Church Schools used to educate children whose parents or legal guardians could not afford to send them to school for education. Students were taught the Bible orally, and classes included between 30 to 40 students. The brightest student in the batch taught the juniors what they had learned, and this legacy would pass from one student to another. In 1846, the government conducted a teacher training program, where teachers would receive certificates after completing their prescribed program.

The term "pedagogical approach" is broadly used in the teaching profession. The term pedagogy means method and strategies of teaching. It includes teaching style, teaching theory, feedback, and assessment. When people talk about pedagogy, they're talking about the ways in which teachers impart subject matter to learners in classrooms. When teachers plan a lesson, they think of a variety of different ways to deliver the concept and content to learners. This decision is based on various factors, including their teaching style, preferences, context, and personal experience. For example, if a teacher is teaching vertebrates and invertebrates to learners, the very first year she might have done this with a book, by reading out-loud to her students. The next year, she wants it to be more innovative and creative, as her experience suggests to her that her students enjoy practical work more.

Now, I will focus on how the pedagogy differs according to its setting. For example, pedagogy should be age appropriate. If we take the early years and primary school teacher into account, they both will have different pedagogies, as their learners are at different levels. An early year's teacher might use a story telling method, whereas a primary school's teacher's method of teaching might focus on a practical activity.

Different pedagogical approaches can be divided into four categories: behaviourism, constructivism, social constructivism, and liberationist.

Behaviourist pedagogy is based on the theory of behaviourism. It is a teacher-centred approach that focuses on the lecture-based method. Now, I will demonstrate what behaviourism looks like in a classroom setting, based on the research of Thorndike (1911), Pavlov (1927), and Skinner (1957).

This theory looks at teachers as authoritative figures in the classroom, who impart their knowledge to learners. This style mostly caters to traditional classroom settings, where students are passive learners. In this particular approach, one can see lecturing, modelling, and repetition.

Next comes constructivism. The term constructivism is primarily self-explanatory. As per the constructivist theory, individuals learn through their experiences and later they reflect on them.

This is a student-centred approach, which is also called "invisible pedagogy". This approach includes project-based learning, hands-on learning, problem-based learning, and inquiry-based learning, based on the pedagogical research of Piaget.

On a large scale, Piaget wrote about "schemas", which is the notion that students come ready to learn and construct their own knowledge. In this approach, the teacher is expected to build activities in which she acts as a facilitator who guides learners. Young children learn through hands-on activities and older children tackle their experiences and ideas. In this approach, lessons cater to different learners and their different learning styles. When using the constructivism approach, teachers often prefer to be outdoors, as opposed to being in the classroom, as they want to engage learners whilst interacting with nature.

Next, we have social constructivism - a combination of behaviourism and constructivism that is both teacher and student-centred. This theory was developed by cognitive psychologist, Vygotsky. Though he built on Piaget's work, his idea differed in that he concluded that learning cannot take place in a social setting. According to Vygotsky, learning is an interlinked process between teacher and student.

When using this approach in the classroom, the teacher divides students into smaller groups and monitors the choice of topics. They can use various pedagogies like questioning method, modelling method, fusion of individual, pair, and whole-class instruction.

Finally, we have liberationists. This pedagogy was developed by the Brazilian educator Paulo Freire, and is a comparatively critical pedagogy. Paulo Freire used to teach illiterate adults how to read in 45 days. The focal point of Paula Freire was to obliterate the two most important obstacles in learning - poverty and hunger. Later, after serving prison time, he released a book named "Pedagogy of the Oppressed". In this work, he talked about how learners were deprived of their human qualities and called for support, unity, and cooperation. In this approach, the student's voice matters and aims to put democracy in classrooms. This approach expects the teacher to be a learner, ensuring that the class discovers subjects in unity. In a liberationist classroom, learners might act as a teacher, and are given complete freedom of selecting and discussing the topic in the classroom. The teacher's role is to provide adequate space for students to explore and learn. Later, they can display their learning in any form, including dance, art, speech, or drama.

Whether it is the liberalist or constructivist approach that the teacher decides to bring into the classroom, the easiest way to implement it is via technology integration. Schools seeking to gain any sort of edge when it comes to both perspective and skill-building need to be able to integrate and utilise technology to its fullest. Educating students on perspective building can become so much easier when one has a SMART board helping students to visualise multiple perspectives simultaneously. Or, when a teacher is implementing a project-based lesson in the class, EdTech tools help to gather, monitor, and evaluate student learning.

The selection process of EdTech is crucial. Nowadays, technology is generally affordable, with many having access to a mobile phone. Additionally, the security of these applications has greatly improved, making it safer for teachers and students to use such platforms to exchange their ideas and construct their knowledge. It is the teacher's responsibility to figure out which EdTech tool will suit her learners and the situation, whilst the school needs to realise that one EdTech tool is not a solution for all.

The generational shift is so visible that we have already begun to see that technology has become a part of the classroom. It is high time that schools accepted it. For a generation that is already born using technology, is it fair to deprive them of it in the classroom? Rather, why not let them bring their own devices, give them the liberty and comfort of knowing that those teaching them know that technology is an enabler, rather than a disabler.

Schools must realise that they are the makers of the future, and if they do not accept technology as a continuous part of their existence, they themselves might cease to exist. Technology is the solution to many problems and its relevance cannot be discredited. Educators need to realise that it is technology that is keeping them organised, efficient and effective in their classrooms. The whiteboard needs to be replaced by a SMART board, while the pen and pencil need to be replaced by laptops and netbooks. Schools, especially in developing countries, need to move away from monopolised manners of schooling and accept that technology-driven education is the solution for the survival of the school, the generation, and ultimately the cause of future economic prosperity. It would be a gross injustice to our learners today to deprive them of the correct, technology-driven education.

# EdTech For Schools

## Tanja Schjellerup

Founder and CEO at Skolen OnlineApS

### School

First, a glance at the word school. Going back to its Greek roots (skhole), we find that it means free time (from practical work) and the possibility for intellectual expansion. Through its own expansion, school has gone from being for the few – the ones who could take free time off – to the many. Still, if we look around the globe today, there are millions of children who are not attending school. The reasons are many, and they differentiate from country to country - from child to child. There are places where children wish they had more free time, away from school, and other places where children wish they could attend school, even for just a day.

How can educational technology play a role? Can it help those who want more free time from school, as well as bring school to those who really want, and need, it?

And, what is in it for schools using technology within their traditional school boundary?

### Educational Technology & Schools

In this technological and innovative world that we live in, it is fair to ask whether traditional school boundaries constrain educational options, especially if they continue to prevent educational technology from being an integrated part of learning solutions for their students.

If the goal is that everybody should learn the same curriculum, and not get the opportunity to dive into their own competencies and interests, then the answer would be no.

If the goal is that everybody should be able to strengthen their knowledge and broaden their experience, then the answer would be yes.

If everybody is taught and educated to know the same, then the question that arises would be; when should anybody learn something new?

The word education has its origins in the Latin word *education*, related to *educere;* to bring out or lead forth. Exploring its meaning, we find that it is "to promote the intellectual and cultural development of the individual and, at the same time, to encourage the learning of new concepts and skills"(Education, 2022). Schools provide guidance on how to improve skills, as well as how to acquire and expand one's own understanding. Schools are supposed to be a place to learn. To learn is to widen your understanding, it is to get to know how to question specific subjects as well as to learn how to acquire and obtain an ability to do something. And teaching, which arises from the Old English *tæcan* meaning 'to show, point out or demonstrate', (Edustaff, 2022) is done by an educator in charge of presenting different educational resources, and encouraging students to learn from it.

EdTech and its means provide the possibility for an even wider intellectual expansion than before. It is an opportunity to take school back to its roots, as students can dive into self-chosen subjects to help expand their knowledge and skills. That is, if the school allows the students the freedom of self-study through guidance.

The easier it is to find subjects and learning materials that match the students, the more differentiating it is. Various educational technologies, such as access to Mixed Reality, AI & adaptive learning, programmable robots, interactive techs, and online learning possibilities help make access to learning more equitable. These technologies that enter modern schools not only offer the possibility to differentiate the teaching of students but can also reasonably be seen as tools to make it easier to modify and diversify the process of studying.

For the student who gains more from an individualised schedule, flexible learning could be the answer. Flipped classrooms, online courses and self-study are merely some ways to strengthen individual skills and self-discipline, as well as preparing for future online study or work.

Collaboration between schools and teachers – nationally as well as internationally – is an open door for any teacher wanting to teach their students about other countries' cultures, as well as an opportunity to let students collaborate on real world situations via technological solutions. It can enrich students' interaction, engagement, learning and thinking skills, in addition to increasing the flexibility and diversity of their educational experience. It also has a secondary positive side effect of providing students the chance to gain pen pals or distance online friends.

Just because it is possible though, it does not, and should not, mean that all learning must be done online. Educational tech toys, as well as physical learning kits, are both examples of offline solutions and hands-on experiences that teachers can use to educate their students. There are many educational options that teachers can use to provide their students with access to interactive learning – both inside and outside the classroom – some more expensive than others.

With current and emerging offline tech, teachers have multiple varieties to choose between, especially in the English language (though more languages are quickly catching up).

Introduced to a playful, gamified or life-like virtual world, students, and especially the ones who are not inclined to book-focused study, will discover new ways they can use the skills that they have learned in the classroom.

Gamification incorporates game design in educational environments. It is no longer just about earning badges or points by completing tasks. The more innovative the education sphere gets; the more games will be a part of it. The list consists of traditional online and virtual reality games, as well as old fashioned board games and most likely, future games that are not even yet designed.

Incorporating learning into games, instead of the opposite, will provide students with information, facts, and problem-based obstacles which have been designed and built as an integrated element of the game's story. Seamless integration means that students may not even consider it a part of their education, with access to games helping to boost student engagement and motivation. The right games can help students improve skills such as problem solving, creating innovative solutions to overcome challenges or use existing knowledge in new ways.

Online laboratories that use simulations enable low-cost access to experiential learning. It also offers flexible access and is not constricted by a timetable, location, or a strict budget. These virtual or remote laboratories give teachers and students a chance to work with matters that would almost be impossible otherwise. Another area that could prove beneficial for learning are virtual field trips. This would allow students to enter areas of the world that no longer exist or are extremely remote or inaccessible, as well as providing the opportunity to glimpse into an unknown (but still quite predictable) near future of the world. These educational devices could also be used as an innovative tool for students to design their own visions of future cities, infrastructure, agriculture, or possible designs for not yet thought of solutions.

Teachers that are able to both locate and access the right learning tools will be able to tailor the EdTech to individual students' learning capabilities. The more a teacher knows their students, as well as the variety of EdTech options that are available to use in class and lessons, the better the teacher can educate and guide each individual towards their own learning path and style. Personalized learning allows the student to receive challenges that are entirely based on individual learning abilities. This approach helps students gain confidence alongside improving their own academic skills.

It is without doubt that access to both on and offline technological educational tools have altered schools' boundaries. Schools, teachers, and students are on the tip of the iceberg with regards to full use and integration of the various EdTech solutions within the traditional school setting. Meanwhile, even attending school has changed for students. New learning possibilities are emerging, giving them the ability to choose a different kind of learning path. Online Schools for K12 students are rising with different setups. All with one goal – to present students for learning opportunities.

## The Possibilities Of Open And Unconventional Schools

Many of the future occupations for youngsters under ten will be those that do not exist yet. Previously, the student and young adult situation used to be *'earn a degree and get a job'* – but in recent years this has changed. Skills are now, in many cases, considered to be of a higher value than educational background. Multinational companies such as Google, Apple and Hilton are now hiring people based on their skills, rather than their education (Top 7 Companies That Don't Require a College Degree - GeeksforGeeks, 2022). With this, they are paving the way for acceptance of the idea that skills are not only learnt in the common institutionalised school that has, in many countries, been mandatory since the 18th century. The process of learning is much older than mandatory governmental educational institutions. It ages back to human evolution – we are built to learn. And ultimately, this learning ability, including the capacity to self-educate, has given us many inventions.

In areas where companies do not feel that their needs are being met by the educational system, they have already started taking matter into their own hands. They train their employees themselves via blended and online learning to help strengthen their staff's knowledge and talents.

We should insist on these options for young learners as well. Why should they wait until they are adults before getting access to various sources of learning possibilities that fit their needs and topics that trigger their curiosity?

"There is little debate that the pace of change is accelerating—and with it, the rate at which people acquire the ever-evolving skills and knowledge they need to execute their jobs. Yet, our ability to prepare today's learners for tomorrow's work is hampered by a lack of shared understanding of what people will need to know to be successful in the 2030 work environment" (2022).

**The future of work and learning are inextricably linked together.**

Preparing for a job that might not even exist yet is a fact for many children at kindergarten age worldwide. So how do we best prepare them for an unknown future? One essential skill any child should be taught is both how to learn and how to use what has been discovered. Of course, children should still be taught how to read, write, and understand the basics of mathematics. But, from there onwards, educators should consider providing the students with greater access to real-life situations and hands-on experiences with subjects that spark their interest in investigating the topics, train their ability to think as well as form their own opinions, ask questions, seek answers, and make conclusions.

Additionally, companies may no longer require a college degree to get the job offer. fLaszlo Block, former SVP of People Operations at Google, stated that "when you look at people who don't go to school and make their way in the world, those are exceptional human beings. And we should do everything we can to find those people" (Google & 14 More Companies That No Longer Require a Degree, 2022). But, with educational technology and a growing number of access to the internet, the people that Bock addresses have a chance to be even more exceptional by utilising the learning solutions that are available to use without attending physical school.

Many factors indicate that schools as we know them will, in a few years, be outnumbered by unformalized schools and classes. If traditional schools want to keep students engaged, they might very well have to keep up with the world around them.

**Reach further!**

Children in rural areas – far from any physical school, but who still have access to electricity and the internet, will be able to engage in learning activities with or without a teacher. Yet millions are still lacking access to the web, or even access to electricity. For these pupils, access to educational possibilities will be different.

Learning should be an active process. Offline technological learning kits – some of them even solar powered – should be provided for students in rural areas. Access to AR, MR or VR could give them experiences via Virtual Field Trips or let them explore topics with 'hands on learning' that may be too difficult for them to reach otherwise. Setting up 'pop-up' learning cafés is another possible way of reaching students who do not attend school, be it due a lack of money or a refusal to attend.

The economy of local communities will greatly benefit from multi-sector collaboration between EdTech companies, municipalities, governments and international organisations, who will provide diverse learning solutions both within and outside of schools. Children will be able to access different forums of materials and challenges that give children a foundation of knowledge for them to stand on when they grow up.

The more children who have access to the internet, the more can be reached and provided with different learning solutions and opportunities. Access to quality learning is a human right. The world roams with great EdTech solutions. Networking and cooperation between them, as well as the local communities, could make it possible to reach even more children and youth to provide them with learning opportunities via technological solutions with an educational twist.

What is needed is access to learning materials, both on and offline, to educate the students on the basic abilities such as reading, writing and maths, as well as problem-solving, critical thinking, practical work and creativity, all skills which are needed to start their own business, be offered a job, or engage productively in communities – on a local, national, or global basis.

In a small country like Denmark, recent reports and statistics show that at least 14% of students in the 1st-9th grade are absent for more than 10% of a school year. This adds up to approximately 75,000 students who, if absenteeism starts in the early years, could miss an entire academic year in total.

Some of these children do not thrive in ordinary classrooms, possibly due to being sensitive to noise, bullying, or the way in which they are taught. An estimated number of 50,000 young adults under the age of 25 end up with no secondary school education, primarily due to not finishing primary level education. These students are at risk of falling off the edge, ending up with no job or, in the worst-case scenario, living on the streets. This risk will continue to exist if the students are being forced to 'go back to school' instead of listening to the individual students' needs and, in some cases, offer them access to new possibilities. The options exist – the system just needs to work with them, without feeling that their school has failed by not having the right solutions within the traditional boundaries that the students 'fled' from in the first place.

Without having to attend physical school, students can be taught a variety of subjects from teachers all around the world. Diverse learning, distance learning, and home schooling are just some varieties of the different educational paths that are evolving or growing.

This has shown to be highly beneficial for students not who do not thrive in traditional school settings, but still have a desire for learning, evolving, and developing one's own abilities and understanding within different areas. Educational technology provides the opportunity to adapt learning activities to address the unique needs, learning style and pace of the individual student. Thus, giving them a chance to spend more time on subjects they find difficult or challenge themselves within subjects they find easy.

With more companies focusing on soft skills and talents, the goal must be to ensure that each student is able to access learning options that build the skills that are needed in society and asked for by their potential employers.

The flexibility that follows offers students new ways of learning, allowing them access to schooling that suits their demands and schedules. Parents will be able to keep their children connected to education in their national language no matter where they travel, irrespective of time and place.

With the emerging solutions that different providers of educational technological solutions provide, a growing number of students now have a choice – how do they want to study? At traditional school, from home, stationed abroad, as a digital nomad or perhaps a mix of several solutions.

Acknowledging and accepting that education is not 'one-size-fits-all', and that students can learn without attention traditional school with the customary curriculums, might be one of the biggest steps yet to be taken in countries where home schooling or distance learning has not been common for students below the age of 16. It will be one of the most important steps towards equality in education. There is no doubt that technology is continually changing the world.

# A Revolution And Reimagining Of Schooling

## Doug Vass I B.Eng(Chem) I DipEd(Maths)I M.Edtech

Teacher | Edtech advisor | Investor

### The Inflection Vs. The Infection

Globally, education in 2020/21 is at an inflection point, and it depends on which lens you look through as to what happens next. If, like me, you're an optimistic realist, then when you look through this lens at the impact of the global COVID-19 pandemic on schooling, you will likely see that it has rapidly forced education down a path it was already heading. If, however, you choose the other lens, you might focus on all the challenging things that teachers, parents and children had to endure for months on end and can't wait for a return to the good old days (which now sadly only references 2019, and not 1985).

"It's the first time in literally hundreds of years that whole education systems have just been turned off. Effectively, the treadmill has stopped and children have been at home with their parents, their relatives (whatever their situation is) trying to come to terms with how to carry on learning in this new situation." (Sir Ken Robinson, Aug 2020, YT)

SCHOOLS

In this chapter, we will address how 2020 became a watershed moment for education globally, how governments (mostly) and institutions tried to plaster over the cracks that became evident in our schooling systems and what the long-term impact might be. We won't pretend to predict the future; if there is one thing we should have learnt from 2020, it is that nobody can predict the future. However, we will present some scenarios that may just become the 'new normal' in education by 2030.

"As education leaders consider their options in the age of the COVID-19 crisis, they must rethink the conventional wisdom." (McKinsey, Oct 2020)

### The Watershed Moment

From circa March 2020, conventional face-to-face schooling around the globe abruptly stopped. In a toppling domino effect that began in Wuhan, China and rolled on to Italy and the rest of Europe, governments were forced into crisis management mode by an invisible threat, coronavirus, commonly known as COVID-19. Whilst debates continue to rage about when, where and how it began, the initial knee-jerk reactions from governments were to shut down all non-essential services until they could at least gain a better understanding on what they were dealing with. This included schools, mostly because students (aka children), were seen to be contagious vectors that would wipe us all out if left unchecked. Understandably, no government wants the political nightmare of children dying on its watch.

Ironically, as this chapter is being written from Spain in March 2021, almost a year after the crisis began, most schools have been open since the new school year began in September 2020. These schools have implemented strict social distancing measures, compulsory mask wearing for children older than 6, hand sanitising routines on entry, class 'bubble' groups to minimise student mixing, and a variety of other processes that have enabled them to not only stay open but deliver lessons, ensure continuity of learning and prevent the spread of the virus.

"Despite widespread concerns, two new international studies show no consistent relationship between in-person K-12 schooling and the spread of the coronavirus." (Kamenetz, Anya, NPR, Oct, 2020)

However, like many things with this pandemic, governments and nations have had to learn 'on the go' and often, they haven't had the necessary data to make timely decisions, especially when children's lives are potentially at risk. In some countries, like the United Kingdom, schools have remained closed for much longer periods of time due to cases rising as schools re-opened. This may have been a coincidence with wider community transmission and cases also rising due to more contagious variants, but we will never know due to the lack of data collected in schools at the time.

In summary, when you add up what we know and even what we still don't know, some doctors and public health advocates have made powerful arguments for continuity of in-person schooling wherever possible, particularly for younger students and those with special needs.

**Stop-Gap Measures - "Zoom" Band-Aids To Plaster Over The Cracks**

So how did schooling continue in 2020/21? Many countries' school systems switched to what has commonly been referred to as 'remote learning' almost overnight. This terminology has been adopted from the business world of 'remote working', meaning you should be doing the same thing you were in the company office, but now you're in another location, most likely your home. This is where the similarity with the adopted business terminology ends. For many professionals their desk or office job can be done remotely with little or no change to their productivity, communication and output. In fact, in many instances, they end up being more productive due to time gains from reduced travel, reduced meetings and possibly being online and connected for longer. However, for the majority of students, remote learning is nothing like in-person learning. There is little to no friendly chit-chat with friends between classes, there is less physical activity and movement throughout the day, the boundaries and routines imposed by the school environment are not felt at home and lastly, the normal, healthy 'screen time' limit completely disappears.

In my own familiar experience, we have three primary aged children (12, 9 and 5) who were suddenly forced online by school closures. Thankfully, I was not working at the time which, lucky for them, enabled me to be their pseudo personal assistant for the next 4 months. I had to check three different email accounts before breakfast, manage multiple google drive folders, a variety of textbook apps, some that didn't work on a tablet, others that didn't work in a browser, print worksheets (I was forever printing worksheets for the 5 year old) and literally run between different rooms as IT support, to resolve Bluetooth connectivity issues, headphone charging, admin screen time authentication... the list went on. Then somewhere in between this, I also needed to make them all lunch - because the school had decided to keep remote learning as 'normal' as possible by continuing with their regular school timetable. This meant they all had lunch at different times. It was manic, frantic and stressful for all concerned, and it took its toll on us all in different ways. There is no need to detail more here because I know this was a shared experience for families globally, perhaps not identical, possibly worse, but maybe it was better for some of you.

Schools approached remote learning in different ways - and I would argue most schools probably got it wrong. Initially, it wasn't really anybody's fault - governments were telling institutions that the closures were only for a couple of weeks, a month at best. So, educators tried to keep continuity in school programs and timetables by just scheduling zoom lesson after zoom lesson, just like students would move from classroom to classroom. Stories from the media across the globe tried to make light of the situation that some children had more 'zoom' meetings than their parents did for work. But, when the novelty wore off many parents, students and teachers, they realised that the 'zoom' solution was a poor Band-Aid that didn't cover the systemic cracks in our wide and diverse industrialised educational systems.

There was an assumed position from schools that households had enough screens to go around to serve all the children in a family for 'zoom' lessons, let alone serve the parents or extended family working from home. In many families, this was simply not possible, whether that was because parents could not work from home due to their job type, or the fact there was only one computer in the household. This is a fundamental challenge of remote learning. It shines an enormous spotlight on the digital divide, widening and heightening it until it has become a digital chasm. As EdTech companies saw surging demand for access to their platforms, which many provided free due to the pandemic, the 'haves' rarely read about the 'have-nots'. Unfortunately, in our high-tech world, there was still not enough 'tech' for the people who needed it most.

However, simply putting devices in students' hands doesn't solve the problem either - in some cases it just creates another one. When "over half of the world's population still has no access to the internet" (1) there needs to be a lot more thought going into the models of delivering learning. Schools and governments have spent too much time and money doing risk assessments for low-risk incursions and excursions but absolutely nothing to assess the risk on continuity of learning if schools were forced to close due to an external threat.

It wasn't all bad. Though remote learning has brought many challenges, some students seem to have been thriving in the new circumstances.

"Increasingly, teachers in our audience are reporting that a handful of their students—shy kids, hyperactive kids, highly creative kids—are suddenly doing better with remote learning than they were doing in the physical classroom." (Edutopia, April 2020)

Reasons suggested, but untested as yet, as to why some learners have preferred remote learning, range from less distractions, getting more sleep at home, less pressure and the ability to manage their own learning time and schedule. As mentioned previously, most schools were left to their own accord as to how they approached remote learning. In my neighbourhood alone, my children's school was running the same timetable as before from 9-5  - including swimming and tennis lessons (yes, they were as funny to watch as they sound for remote learning!). Yet, the American school around the corner had reduced the school day to 3 or 4 'zoom lessons' only, mostly in the core English, Mathematics and Science areas with independent learning projects for the students to manage in their own time. These two approaches are worlds apart and are highlighted here to demonstrate some of the extreme differences in remote learning that many students and families have experienced during this unprecedented moment in history.

## Long Term Impacts On Schools And How Edtech Can Respond

Before COVID-19, many schools, perhaps even the majority of schools, were ambivalent towards EdTech. Whilst EdTech has been slowly transforming schools since the earlier days of television and the overhead projector, the enormous shifts that our personal and commercial worlds have seen with technology in the last 10 to 15 years have still not truly been felt in schools, until now.

In fact, in the previous 12 months before the COVID-19 crisis, a number of school systems globally, especially private institutions, were rolling out mobile phone bans or restrictions during the school day. France implemented a nationwide ban in 2018, China around a similar time, Australian states started banning and reviewing usage in 2019 and around the same time the UK acted in a similar fashion (Conversation article, source 9). In late 2019, "The social dilemma", a Netflix documentary on the perils of addictive mobile phone apps and the companies that push them, highlighted the insidious side of too much screen time. Our social and emotional relationships with our peers and families were seen to be at stake, and schooling, education and learning were intrinsically connected to relationships. Schools that had once embarked on expensive, ambitious laptop and tablet rollout programs were now educating their parents on how to manage screen time at home. They were reverting to managing the devices at school and restricting them to be used solely for learning. Many of these 'early adopter' schools had witnessed first-hand the benefits of connected classrooms and digital/online learning, as well as the perilous slippery slope of addictive behaviours and loss of social connections and desire.

But what about these previously mentioned ambivalent schools? For the majority of them, they were forced into remote learning by utilising whatever systems they could access within a week or two and cobble something together. For many, it was a combination of Zoom, Google Meet or Google Classroom or some other Learning Management System like Canvas, Microsoft Teams, Schoology, or a myriad of other options. At a basic level, it was emailing worksheets or a weekly lesson schedule to parents and hoping for the best. Teachers who had perhaps never even used a video call before were now forced into recording videos of themselves or the whiteboard, ordialling in to live calls with their classes.

"Responding to the changes that the COVID-19 crisis has wrought on education systems around the world requires building on what we know works, as well as looking ahead to what we know students will need." (McKinsey, Sep 8, 2020)

Many schools would not have an EdTech strategy, let alone a key leader in the school dedicated to ensuring implementation and integration of said strategy and tracking success. It is highly likely that, from 2020/21, there will be a surge in new titles and positions in schools reflecting EdTech integration.

"Remote and online learning are here to stay. The need is to determine what combination of remote and in-person learning delivers the highest educational quality and equity. As institutions refine this hybrid model, they have a once-in-a-generation chance to reconfigure their use of physical and virtual space." (McKinsey, Oct 2020)

As highlighted in the quote above, delivery models and terminology such as remote, hybrid, blended, and physical learning have been thrown around with abandonment. Given the intensity and immediacy of the impact of COVID-19 on education there is still much confusion amongst both educators and parents on what these delivery models are or mean, and whether one is better or preferred than another. Some terminologies are also being used differently in various countries, adding confusion to the global conversation on education.

**For your quick reference here is a summary:**

**Remote learning** - learning via video calls/lessons at home, all lessons in a program are delivered this way.

**Face-to-face/In-person learning** - the traditional model of schooling most of us are used to, where all lessons are conducted at school in a dedicated building

**Hybrid learning** - a combination of in-person learning and remote learning that is happening synchronously, or at the same time, ie. some students are in the class with the teacher and some are at home on camera. It can also mean some face-to-face days at school and some remote (perhaps the most misused or confusing term of them all).

**Online learning** - a completely online course that most likely involves no 'live' teacher running synchronous lessons. Mostly pre-recorded modules delivered through an online platform. Often used in commercial training situations.

**Blended learning** - a mixture of learning mediums, probably first known via 'flipped-learning' a term synonymous with Salman Khan from Khan Academy as students could watch online videos of theory or instruction at home and work on problems and questions in class with a teacher. Blending learning is still mostly face-to-face but involves asynchronous aspects such as online learning and other digital resources. It really has the flexibility to take the best aspects of other models and utilise them as the teacher sees fit.

(Please note: the above terms are not exhaustive and do not claim to be 100% oxford dictionary definitions, they are layperson guides to help us discern the jargon).

School leaders need to be asking their teams - what model do we think is best or what model best fits our school and our learners? Once an answer to that is established, you then need to bring your teachers on the journey with you and let them be part of the team that selects the EdTech platforms you need. It is understandable that during the pandemic, schools rushed to whatever platform contacted them first, sometimes multiple ones with little consultation or review. It is time to realise that, in the long term these will come at both a significant financial cost and more importantly, a learning cost if it doesn't meet the needs of your staff and students.

In my opinion, Blended learning is the most workable and suitable long-term solution. It provides the flexibility that schools need to serve their learners and community. It is how we best work as adults, using the efficiency of online meetings and platforms when we travel or when it suits us, but we also recognise the enormous emotional and relational benefits that come from face-to-face meetings and interactions. It can enable schools to break free from the rigid timetables and structures of the day, whilst also better preparing our students for the world they will be stepping out into.

"If anything, the COVID-19 pandemic affirms our conviction that we must bring about change in education to prepare young people for a fast-changing world. We are helping them to be ready for a world that is anything but "status quo." We knew that globalisation, technology, and climate change were bringing about dramatic changes to the nature of work and how our society operates, but the virus just reinforces the volatile and unpredictable nature of life. We must prepare all young people to be resilient and adaptable—and to be able to learn and master the new at great speed, in any environment." (*Mark Scott, Director of NSW Dept. of Education, Oct 9, 2020*)

**The Next 'New Normal'**

So, what did we learn? Where to from here? What problems did EdTech solve and are there more or others it can solve for teachers and schools?

Here are the takeaways I have seen from 2020:

We learned that a lot of countries or regions still need a massive investment in access to devices in order to access their learning (even in 1st world countries like the USA)

We learned that 'remote learning' was not equivalent to remote work and, whilst it worked for a minority of students, it was seriously lacking for the rest

We learned that those students who typically don't like or do well in face-to-face schooling may actually do better with a 'remote learning' approach

We learned that teachers are 'essential workers' and, if students cannot attend a physical learning environment, other than the home, then parents (aka a large percentage of the workforce) cannot function effectively

We learned that schools can be flexible, timetables can change, exams can be replaced, there are other ways to assess and gather data

We learned that relationships are vital and often the social aspects of face-to-face schooling have been overlooked

Here are the challenges I still see in front of us:

- We need to be careful not to throw out what we already know works in education from decades of research and practice.
- We need more student voice in our learning systems not only so students can reflect on their learning but so school leaders can track what matters to them
- We need intelligent thinking around data gathering from day-to-day learning tasks, to measuring effective feedback, time on and off tasks, and multi-modal assessments
- We need personalised learning pathways and systems for all students that connect with their goals and their learning aspirations.
- We need a complete reset of the rigid school daily timetable that includes building in longer flexible learning periods to enable personalised learning
- We need a focus on personal learning and growth, where individual progress is only measured along your own curriculum.
- If we need ranking and comparison-based assessments (for employers or university entry) then they need to be opt-in, not opt-out

Here is where EdTech can help and should focus their efforts for students, teachers, and schools:

- Teachers need easier data gathering tools to track learning progression, engagement, and feedback
- Schools need integrated reporting systems that connect all areas of a system, from teacher class marks and homework feedback to personal well-being and student motivation
- Governments, systems and nations need connected databases of curriculum standards and desired content pathways, ideally also mapped to international standards
- Universities and other tertiary institutions need learning pathways that demonstrate the desires of employers so they can help inform students
- EdTech companies need to think big and utilise artificial intelligence and machine learning to generate learning pathways, percentage success rates of completion, diagnostic testing, and future employment scenarios
- Students need tools that can help them authenticate information (particularly in today's world of misinformation), in order for them to succeed on a personalised learning pathway

According to the 2020 EDUCAUSE Horizon Report there are six emerging technologies and practices being shaped by influential social, technological, economic, higher education, and political trends. For K-12 schools the most relevant are 'Analytics for Student Success' and 'Adaptive Learning Technologies'. Both of these areas have significant potential for leveraging artificial intelligence and machine learning (Horizon Report, 2020).

**In Summary**

George Couros, author of 'The Innovator's Mindset' published the graphic below (Medium, Mar 2021), which broadly illustrates the shift in thinking that I am promoting here. The COVID-19 pandemic has given us a global chance at a reset, to reflect on what defines schooling and how it relates to learning.

## School vs Learning

| School | Learning |
| --- | --- |
| a Promotes starting by looking for answers | a Promotes starting with questions |
| a Is about consuming | a Is about creating |
| a Is about finding information on something that is prescribed for you | a Is about exploring your passions and interests |
| a Is about teaching compliance | a Is about challenging preceived norms |
| a Is scheduled at certain times | a Can happen anytime, all of the time |
| a Often is dates | a Often is social |
| a Is standardized | a Is personal |
| a Teaches us to obtain information from certain people | a Promotes that everyone is a teacher and everyone is a learner |
| a Is about giving you information | a Is about making your own connections |
| a Is sequential | a Is random and non-linear |
| a Promotes surface-level thinking | a Is about deep exploration |

This is not a right vs wrong list, but a simple emphasis of the key differences in a generalised way. There are numerous schools globally that are already promoting and achieving many of the ideals on the right-hand side, and there are times when items on the left are necessary.

Sir Ken Robinson's last recorded words before he passed away from cancer late in 2020 also echo along a similar vein:

"I believe profoundly that getting back to normal won't work. We've pressed PAUSE on many of our social systems but it's time to press RESET on them as well. There is a chance to do that. Lots of people have been spending time at home learning with their children, children with their peer groups. I believe the most successful (and we've spoken to a lot of parents) examples are where parents haven't felt the need to replicate school.

There's a big difference between learning, education and school. Learning is the most natural process in the world. We love to learn, we're deeply curious creatures, highly creative, deeply compassionate and highly collaborative." (Sir Ken Robinson, Aug 2020, YT)

The EdTech community should always be about the learners and the learning. However, often they get lost in a product or feature and forget that the technology needs to be a tool to aid the natural learning process. If it can enhance this process somehow, make it more efficient or save time then that will be a winning product. If it gets in the way, distracts or delays the learning process it will fail.

Imagine if, through machine learning, we could develop an authentic, verified global curriculum map of information. This information could then inform a map of learning pathways that help learners acquire the knowledge to which they aspire (think of something like the learning programs uploaded into the Matrix movie characters, but just a roadmap for us to follow not a digital implant). Perhaps then those messy and wicked problems that the globe currently faces could be the aspiration for all of us to collaborate and solve them together.

# 3 Universities

# EdTech For Colleges And Universities In A Contactless World

## Alex Bäcker, Ph.D.

Co-founder and CEO, Drisit

### The Nature Of Invention

Some of the world's most impactful inventions have been those that dissociate two events that hitherto required a confluence. The telephone, for example, changed communication from requiring two people that were within earshot of each other to allowing them to be anywhere with a phone line. The mobile phone changed that once again, from requiring both people to be next to a phone line to allowing them to be anywhere cellular airwaves could reach.

Another example is mobile wait management. Prior to its invention, students waiting in line for a service had to wait at the place of service, either standing in line or sitting in a waiting room. Mobile queueing allows students to join a virtual, mobile line or queue from their phone, roam freely while they wait while continuing their activities anywhere, for example studying elsewhere on campus. After the invention of mobile queueing, then, the need for a student to be at the site of service was dissociated from their ability to wait in line for that service.

The Storyline 360 invention described below, ensuring students don't skip ahead in an instructional video, achieves a similar dissociation: gone are the days in which students needed to be present at an in-person class in order to ensure they don't skip a lesson.

### Remote Learning

My experience as an educator datesback to my teaching a course on *why we sleep and dream* with Gabriel Kreiman, now a Professor at Harvard Medical School, at the California Institute of Technology. The key for me at the time was involving students in projects that had them experience the thrill of discovery, and realizing that science remains an active field of study with many fascinating unknowns still.

Yet my most recent, and perhaps my most relevant, experience was not as an educator but as a student. I was certified in neurocoaching theory and skills during the pandemic. All of my learning happened online. In my experience, key tools for successful online learning include:

1. Zoom online meetings, including breakout rooms for smaller group discussions, and
2. Google Drive for document sharing and real-time collaboration.

### Educators Speak

Enough of my own advice. I asked leading educators about EdTech that had made a difference in this new contactless world. Specifically, we asked:

*"Alex Bäcker has been invited to contribute a chapter to The EdTech Book, to be published later this year. This book is meant to become the reference book on EdTech, or educational technology. We would like to invite you to contribute to the chapter, by sharing:*

1. *The most impactful EdTech you have used, what problem it solved, how and what the impact was, and/or*
2. *The technology you have used to deal with the challenges of a contactless world and turn them into opportunities"*

Below is what they wrote:

### Nicholas Kilmer I Texas A&M I Assistant Director Money Education (ME) Center, Division of Enrollment& Academic Services:

*Below are brief statements regarding these two education tools, which have by far been the most impactful technologies we have implemented in my office.*

#### *QLess:*

*Even before COVID-19 dramatically changed how higher education functioned, Texas A&M University's sheer size (roughly 70,000 students) resulted in a demand for student services which required a strategic investment in queueing technology. With this in mind, the Office of Scholarships & Financial Aid, with the support of the Division of Enrollment& Academic Services, purchased and implemented QLess. This queuing technology allows our students to Get in Line for Advising from anywhere and then receive text message updates about their status in line. When it's their turn they receive a call back, are helped via Zoom, or are told where to go for in-person advising. This program has helped Scholarships & Financial Aid to remain fully operational at a time when in-person advising raises serious health concerns for both students and staff alike.*

#### *Storyline 360:*

*One of the most effective and adaptable instruction tools we have used at the Money Education Center at Texas A&M University is Storyline 360. This program enabled us to develop eye catching and interactive modules which could ensure student viewing (no skipping ahead), while maximising engagement and interaction via intermittent quiz questions, embedded videos, and more. In addition, Storyline 360 modules can be shared via a simple weblink, within a secured portal, or even as a SCORM package in a learning management system such as Blackboard. Our Center has used Storyline 360 to develop loan counselling modules for the Department of Education's Loan Counseling Experiment, portal navigation modules for new students, modular staff training for office processes, and more. We even used this program to transform our in-person core elective personal financial planning course (Foundations of Money Education) into an asynchronous modular course in response to COVID-19 social distancing restrictions. In every application of this program, student feedback has been overwhelmingly positive.*

**Erin L. Richman, Ph.D. I Associate Vice President of Student Success**
**Florida State College at Jacksonville I Division of Student Services:**

*Just 3 years ago, Florida State College at Jacksonville's (FSCJ) five campus Advising centers were operating with multi-hour waits, unhappy students, and high employee turnover. No data, plans, nor infrastructures existed to catalyse improvement. In early 2018, FSCJ Advising implemented multiple innovations that resulted in sustained, positive, technologically-advanced 'first encounters' with advisement.*

*Frontend student experiences were dramatically improved, grounded in service excellence and degree planning. Employing the philosophy, "you never get a second chance to make a first impression," our priority was excellence. We evaluated patterns during a 6-month pilot study, then scaled enhanced operational processes, data intelligence, and launched integrated, cloud-based appointments/queueing system (QLess).*
*Simultaneously, we significantly improved employee morale (measured by the Gallup Q12) among student-facing staff.*

*Follow-up measures reveal FSCJ Advising's enhancements resulted in increased retention, increased student satisfaction, significantly reduced waits at one-stops, reduced complaints, and, lastly, improved employee morale. Our values for a culture of excellence, trust, and morale converted into engaging experiences for students.*

*To extend the reach of our enhancements, Advising partnered with FSCJ's Marketing on multiple social media campaigns and live website features to promote the new "ease of access" for advising. The campaigns personalized FSCJ advisors and created remote access to services, further enabling students to optimize their time and schedules.*

*As a testament to FSCJ Advising's success and the robust data that we captured, FSCJ's Student Financial Services/Bursar, Registrar, Admissions, and Financial Aid subsequently adopted the same service model as Advising (QLess). FSCJ's students now enter one system for their on-campus needs, thus transforming the student experience from point of entry through advisement. However, what struck me most is the fact that students notice these changes and give consistent, rave reviews.*

*Post-Advising survey data shows students rate FSCJ Advising an average of 4.57 out of 5 stars (see attached evidence of student satisfaction). These operational improvements mean that FSCJ now systematically uses data to capture student satisfaction, as well as plan interventions more effectively. We have launched and improved this innovation over the past 18 months with sustained results.*

**Additional Commentary from Florida State College English Professor, Rawlslyn Francis:**

*"In my role as a faculty member at Florida State College at Jacksonville for the past 10 years, I can attest that the recent changes to FSCJ's Advising processes have fostered an ability to improve our student retention rates and our students' experience of academic advising.*

*The additional integration of the QLess appointment system was incredibly helpful for our online and hybrid students who could easily make their appointments to work within their busy schedules outside of school. I know firsthand that my students LOVED this convenience – they have told me how much different their experience has been in advising. To sustain the professionalism and quality of the experience for students, leadership within Advising scheduled trainings with employees to ensure they were up to date on changes and enhancements."*

Asked about the impact of mobile wait management in their schools, this is what other EdTech professionals had to say:

**Christiana Ravecchioli, Receptionist, Admissions and Advisement, Mesa Community College:**

*"I love the fact that we can [put] cell phone numbers in and students can go anywhere they want pretty*
*much on campus. They don't have to necessarily wait here...Basically, I really like it."*

Indeed, Mesa Community College listed participation "in the QLess sign-in system which extremely enhanced service to students" as one of its strategic accomplishments for the year they launched it. It has since expanded district wide to the entire Maricopa Community College District.

**Linda Jackson, Manager, Arts Student Centre, University of Melbourne:**
"[Our first day with QLess] went amazingly well...the staff and students absolutely loved it."
"There is so much interest in the system I can't believe it."

**Naydeen Gonzalez, Associate Dean of Academic Advisement, Burlington County College:**
*"It's amazing! We've been using it fully...and students are raving about it."*

**Nancy Martinis, Advisor, Sierra College:**
"Real-time dynamic calculation of unique wait times for each queue...helps me manage staff workloads. It gives students the perception that 'something is happening' because with QLess, they see their wait time shrinking and they see the growth and shrinkage of each queue."

**Jeff Danser, Director of OIT Web& Portal Services and Valencia Community College in Orlando:**
"[QLess] is amazing and about as innovative as it gets. So simple, yet so effective in creating customer satisfaction. Brilliant! I will certainly pass the good word on [to] the people I know."

One concern every time you change a paradigm is resistance to change. In this sense, it is helpful to read about the experience of **Greg Morris, VP for Academic Affairs at Dallas County Community College District:**

"One thing great about QLess: You can train somebody in 3 minutes."

**Kimberly Westby, Dean, Student Support Services, Cerritos Community College District:**

"QLess has eliminated physical lines and our busy lobby by allowing students to get in line from their mobile device. This has empowered students to take control of their time and get things done without losing their place in line. Students are no longer frustrated and the number of complaints has been significantly reduced while our department has gained significant insights into our productivity and improved efficiency through the data and analytics collected."

**Curt Eley, Vice President for Enrollment Management, The University of Texas at Dallas:**

"My boss is used to hearing 'we're understaffed' from his departments. I'm the only one who can go to my boss and say 'we served 732 students last week in person'. Nobody else has the ability to give those numbers when requesting more resources."

"This year, we had the smoothest fall semester ever, by a quantum leap, over previous semesters.... QLess was clearly a big part of this smoothness."

"When they met with staff, the students were calm, cool, and collected, rather than angry, bitter, and mad. This is a huge transformation."

"QLess was a key part of us having a great [year]!"

**Amber Kelley, Dean Student Services Austin Community College:**

"We were in the middle of registration, and by the end of the week, my assistant turned and remarked, 'do you know that we have not had a single complaint'...it just turned everything around"

**Impact of Digitization case study: Colin College increases student engagement by 1500%**

Digitising the student wait-time experience has an impact well beyond student and staff satisfaction, impacting not only on public health in a post-pandemic world --who wants to stand in line or wait in a waiting room when your life could be at risk?--, but also on student communication and engagement.

**Business Challenge**

Mobile wait-time management was part of Collin College's strategic plan **to improve student satisfaction, increase staff effectiveness, and optimise workflow in administration.** A key component of the plan was to eliminate the long lines and wait times for students to access services, particularly during peak registration periods.

"The administrative challenges of quickly and efficiently serving more than 50,000 students across seven locations are significant," said Doug Willis, Dean of Student Development. "We researched solutions that could help us better deliver services and reduce wait times benefitting both the students and the college."

In addition to reducing wait times for services, administrators wanted to better gauge student sentiment on a range of activities and experiences by boosting participation in campus surveys. Previously, despite a marketing push on campus, the response to a 10-question online Snap Survey had been poor, and the few responses obtained were largely negative.

## Solution

After visiting The University of Texas in Dallas to observe its successful implementation of a mobile wait management platform, Collin College administrators began rolling it out across the college's campuses. **The results were immediate – wait times were reduced and students were happier,** using the time saved to eat, study, attend class, and participate in extracurricular activities.

"We saw the difference right away – no more long lines stretching out of our offices, **no more unhappy students waiting a long time for services**," said Mr. Willis. "In addition, our employees are able to spend more of their time serving our students and less time managing student traffic in and out of administrative offices."

In addition, the solution automatically prompts students to respond to the Snap Survey as soon as they've completed their scheduled campus business. This has **increased both the volume and favourability of responses, providing real-time information to notify the staff and procedural recommendations**, as well as driving improvements to campus operations and services.

The solution allows students to enter a service queue prior to arrival via smartphone, website, or on-site kiosks. Students are free to attend class or engage in campus activities until their turn arrives.

"Students receive regular updates via text or voice message, keeping them aware of delays or schedule changes," said Mr. Willis. "The solution also gives them **the option of changing their appointment time without losing their spot in the queue.**"

## Results

The average wait time at Collin College **decreased from a staggering 3 hours down to less than 20 minutes.**

Students and staff alike appreciate the more relaxed and positive environment resulting on the elimination of lines and freeing the lobbies. This has **improved relations between students and administration**, which is a big step towards achieving the strategic goals of delivering better service and demonstrating mutual respect.

In addition, the Public Relations department implemented a comprehensive marketing campaign alerting students about the new service, its benefits, and how to access it. The campaign included renaming and branding the service as CougarQ to be consistent with other college tools available to students, including CougarMail, Cougar Web and Cougar News. Marketing tactics ranged from posters, flyers, and other on-campus print signage to digital signage, emails to students, and internal news stories. External promotion included social media and news releases.

After re-launching the student survey using QLess' SMS messaging, **over 1,500 survey responses have been received, representing more than a 1,500% increase over prior response rates** and providing significant data to administration. Collin College uses the data results to determine which campuses, offices, and staff members interacted with each of the survey respondents.

"The survey responses from our students are providing keen insights we were unable to capture before," said Mr. Willis. "While some of our employees were a little concerned about the granularity of the responses, they quickly saw **the value of this feedback in making our operations more efficient and effective."**

### Real-Time Workforce Management

Finally, another benefit of digitizing the student wait experience is the ensuing data on staff activity. A complete digital wait management platform will provide a dashboard for university and college management to be aware of wait times and staff activity in real-time, sending alerts to management mobile phones when warranted. Data includes the percentage of idle staff, the number of students served per staff member, the average transaction duration per employee, the forecast of wait times, the number of students served, trends, and much more.

### Drones And Virtual Presence: The Future Of Edtech

Having devoted a decade of my life to solving the problem of waiting in line, I have recently turned my attention to another problem. What do you do when a pandemic shuts off all field trips and all classrooms? And more importantly, how do you give students the excitement of seeing the world from the confines of the four walls of their classroom even when they return to school?

My answer: Drisit. Drisit stands for drone visit. Or for directed remote visit. Or for distant real-time visit. It's a form of virtual presence, not unlike the way that James Cameron's Avatar showcased a man living vicariously through a robot. The next best thing to teleportation. Drisit will allow educators anywhere to tap onto a drone or camera anywhere in the world and take their students for a virtual tour. Studying ancient Egypt? Let's drisit the pyramids. Studying World War 2? Let's hop virtually from Warsaw to Normandy to understand the scenarios in which the action unfolded. Studying zoology? How about following animals around in the wild?

Like the other inventions I wrote about above, Drisit dissociates phenomena hitherto required together. Before it, people needed to be in a place to direct a camera around to experience the freedom to move around in an area. Before it, people needed to be close to their drone to fly it. With Drisit, educators and their students can "be" anywhere anytime. Perhaps bringing together the people and places of the world can make for a more understanding, more peaceful world.

In conclusion, technology provides incredible opportunities to transform the student experience. Cloud-based software as a service makes these opportunities more affordable than ever before, sometimes requiring no upfront investment. The secret is to find solutions that:
a)    Have demonstrated results, and
b)    Provide superior customer service

There's never been a more exciting time to be an educator.

# Fall Off The Turnip Truck: Online Linguistic Acquisition In Higher Education

## Sarah Langridge Bitar

Educational Technology Development Coordinator at Carleton University

With the movements of our educational system shifting from education being delivered in small rooms to a handful of students, to the current standard of online learning, much about content delivery has also changed. However, one thing that has remained consistent are the instructors who do it for the money and have little motivation to make their classes memorable and engaging. As the world has shifted to a primarily online learning environment, some instructors without digital literacy may also fall back on delivery modes like lectures with a 'talking head'. What should be expected from content delivery in the new learning landscape?

With online learning, creating an engaging classroom is hard for everyone, but language teachers are particularly challenged by the new screen between them and their learners. Second Language Acquisition (SLA) is traditionally best done while interacting face-to-face and having live encounters with those who speak the language. Arguably this is good, but there are still ways that instructors can engage their class and deliver content, whether it be a language or something else, in meaningful ways. This chapter will discuss the movements North American education has gone through over the past century, the importance of learning by doing, a discussion of what makes teaching a language so hard and how to draw in learners in an online environment.

### Teaching And Learning Movements

Schools were first developed not as a pastime, but as a way to elevate the rich and then to educate the masses before they entered the workforce. One of the most basic reasons for this was the need for a literate workforce. Literacy and mathematics have been at the core of the global educational systems for hundreds of years, and maybe, not surprisingly, they are still there. Something educators have turned their attention to recently is called, 'critical literacies'. Critical literacies involve more than just reading and understanding a text, they include interaction with materials, in print and online. Critical literacies also involve looking at topics from different lenses and analysing how people use language to exercise power (Morgan & Ramanathan, 2005). These skills can be applied to social media posts, photographs, graphic novels, ad campaigns and more. Being able to navigate all of these spaces requires enhancing literacy skills beyond the basic 'read and comprehend'. Whether being developed in school-aged children in Norway or immigrants in North America, native and non-native speakers alike need these skills to live in and navigate 21st century society.

There have been four major movements in North American education, each of which represented a different way of viewing teaching and learning according to the prevalent cultural beliefs at that time. The first movement is identified as Standard Education, which took place during the Age of Reason, the Industrial Revolution and the Scientific Revolution. Knowledge and learning were considered through the acquisition model, behaviourism and cognitivism. Standardised Education tells us that, "The teacher was understood to be the expert in a domain, one who selected and preserved what was important to know," (Davis et al., 2015, p. 44). Standardised education is the epitome of what structured and controlled education is like.

The next movement is identified as Authentic Education. Authentic Education uses different approaches rooted in human sciences and emphasises personal engagement, developmental stages, and personalised learning. The classroom became a place where people were encouraged to ask questions and focus on reality (Davis et al., 2015). This movement became strong in the early 1900s with the shift in research to human behaviours and the emergence of a middle class (Davis et al., 2015). Authentic Education also adopted the idea of surface versus deep learning. In this approach, the autonomy of the learner in this approach and that the integration of their knowledge with additional resources can lead to deeper meaning and understanding of the course material. There is also a recognition that deliberate practice can, "enhance awareness and improve performance," (Davis et al., 2015, p. 102).

One of the main things to come out of the Authentic Education movement was a more personalised learning pathway and finding ways to incorporate and draw on students' own experiences to enhance their learning and the classroom environment as a whole. Christian Chun introduces educators to an alternative way of teaching critical literacies. From their own classroom to the trial grounds of others, Chun writes about the benefits of using graphic novels in English Second Language classrooms to teach students critical literacies. With the recognition that critical literacies no longer just apply to text-based items, Chun examines how using texts can develop skills that can be extrapolated to the other areas of literacy, now needed by students. Chun (2009) points out how using graphic novels in the classroom helps students grow by bringing their own prejudices into question and examining, through engagement, "otherness along with the consequences of our own complicity in reinforcing them," (p. 149). He also mentions that using multimodal texts will draw on more student resources and allow for them to engage more deeply with the material. These principles draw on a lot of the educational reform that came out of the Authentic Education movement when students were also keepers of knowledge and able to take responsibility for their own learning.

The third major movement in education is identified as Democratic Citizenship Education (DCE). This movement focused on collective process and cultural inequities, and aimed to promote social justice, in part by recognizing hegemonic structures (Davis et al., 2015). This movement became prominent in the mid-1900s and schools were hugely targeted as they perpetuated social conditions rather than challenging them. Democratic Citizenship Education examines what is explicitly and implicitly taught and recognises that there is a 'hidden curriculum' at work in every educational organisation (Davis et al., 2015). The job of the teacher should be to help students critically analyse data and understand that *nothing is right or wrong* as the learner themselves are, "incomplete and biased," (Davis et al., 2015, p. 121). DCE is about opening up the classroom to create an, "inclusive education approach based on the inevitable presence of diversities," (Davis et al., 2015, p. 161).

The fourth major movement in education is identified as Systemic Sustainability Education, which became more prevalent in the late 1900s. This movement focused on the evolving technologies and how they can be used in the classroom, environmental concerns, cultural landscapes and the advances in brain research and how to orient education toward the health of people, cultures, species, and the biosphere (Davis et al., 2015). Systemic Sustainability Education also recognises the importance of the language and how it, "frees the knower from the limits of the here-and-now," and that it shapes reality (Davis et al., 2015, p. 205). However, Systemic Sustainability Education believes a core responsibility of the teacher, "is to be attuned to variations in interpretation," (Davis et al., 2015, p. 222), and in this case, the teacher is responsible for exposing students to and helping them understand the multiple modalities they may encounter as ways to present information.

This final movement in Education brings us to our present educational landscape and to how learning can be tailored to each student and to their personal needs as well as how technologies can be capitalised in the classroom.

## Learning By Doing: Language

As the educational movements have brought about new ways of viewing teaching and learning, they have also made room for new forms of content delivery to be developed. One of the more recent developments in content delivery, which is becoming popular in language teaching, is Task Based Language Teaching (TBLT) or, learning by doing. Learning by doing can be defined as performing an action, ie. enactment, as compared to other ways of learning something like learning by viewing or learning by listening (Steffens et al., 2015). There is a general assumption that learning by doing creates better memories of an event or action, and so styles like TBLT are becoming more popular.

The use of TBLT has been found to be positive and significantly impactful in a variety of contexts. González-Lloret and Nielson (2015) implemented TBLT in a border patrol training program which used the grammar-translation method to teach new agents Spanish. The new program included more real-life videos, tasks to complete alone or in groups, oral production activities, role-plays with native speakers and computer lab practice. Formative and summative assessment was performance-based and criterion-referenced (González-Lloret and Nielson, 2015). Students in the task-based group outperformed students in the grammar-based group on measures of fluency, lexical complexity and syntactic complexity and results from a MANOVA test indicated that there were significant differences between the groups, with stronger performance in the task-based group (González-Lloret and Nielson, 2015). Sarani and FarzanehSahebi (2012) also found that using TBLT to teach vocabulary in English for Special Purposes (ESP) to university students resulted in a significant difference in learnt technical vocabulary and use in-context as compared with a traditional teaching method.

The literature on TBLT demonstrates that it is a worthwhile practice and should be used in language classrooms, but in order to do so, teachers must be motivated to use it as well. While TBLT can simplify the work of the instructor by providing a clear direction for teaching and assessment, instructors still shy away from it and feel uncomfortable making tasks (Vanderveen, 2018). Not only should classroom activities resemble work-related activities as closely as possible, but instructors also need to know what a manageable amount of vocabulary and grammar would be per unit, how to increase student consciousness in their own learning, elicit answers from them and when to step back (Vargas Vasquez et al., 2016).

Little research has been done on factors which interfere with instructors achieving the goals of TBLT and how training interventions may increase TBLT use in language classes. Ogilvie and Dunn (2010) studied student teachers and their training, which did include TBLT instruction in their Curriculum course, however, they found that the application of TBLT did not go much beyond the classroom and was no utilized in real-life. In their study, many students did not like the use of TBLT as compared to PPP because they could not see the value in the more communicative method, but after taking the course, there was a significant difference in their disposition and outlook on TBLT (Ogilvie and Dunn, 2010). When student teachers went into the field, they sparsely used the TBLT methods, namely because of cultural norms and stigmas around teacher-roles and flexibility to adapt to new practices, which were unusual for the practicum teacher, the student-teacher and the students (Ogilvie and Dunn, 2010). They also found that there was a lack of support for this method in the field and new teachers often gave up using it because they were not able to further their training or find resource support (Ogilvie and Dunn, 2010).

Completing a task in the classroom which replicates a real-life situation provides L2 learners with a safe place to practice and what may be classified in Second Language Acquisition (SLA) research as pre-task planning. When students are in the classroom and practising the language, they are receiving feedback from the instructor and input from their environment and the people they are interacting with. When faced with a task which replicates a real-life situation, they are exposed to the social context and linguistic expectations of the interaction and as such, are able to practice before completing the task for real. The other type of planning, and likely the most common in oral production, is termed on-line planning. On-line planning occurs in the moment and people are forced to self-correct and choose words, possibly through translation, and can be defined as, "the process by which speakers attend carefully to the formulation stage during speech planning and engage in pre-production and post-production monitoring of their speech acts," (Yuan & Ellis, 2003, p. 6). It has been shown that oral on-line planning increases accuracy and complexity of spoken language, but that it has little effect on fluency (Yuan & Ellis, 2003). It has also been shown that pre-task planning improves fluency, as mentioned above (Ellis & Yuan, 2004). On-line planning happens as a person speaks and fluency is often sacrificed for form (De Larios et al., 2001; Yuan & Ellis, 2003). In a typical classroom setting there may be a lot of learning by viewing and listening to the instructor but learning by doing has been shown to improve memory for actions and recognition (Steffens et al., 2015; Engelkamp, 1998; Golly-Haring &Engelkamp, 2003).

## Teaching A Culture

It is understood that teaching a language is more than reading and writing, it also involves teaching the culture. One way to immerse learners in a particular culture in the past has been to provide experiential learning opportunities throughout a course. Moreno-Lopez et al. (2017) studied a group of 172 Spanish second-language learners at a university in Maryland, USA and their experiential language programs. Overwhelmingly, Moreno-Lopez et al. (2017) found that students who had interacted with native-speakers on some level felt exponentially more comfortable using Spanish. Bayliss and Vignola (2007) did a similar study of French second language speakers training to become teachers at the University of Ottawa, CA. The group of student-teachers who spent time interacting with the older students felt the most versed in French culture, even though they themselves had not grown up within the culture (Bayliss & Vignola, 2007). It has been found many times that people who interact with native speakers of the target language feel more confident, often learn faster and may show greater improvement in their productive skills.

Contributing to the idea that interaction with natives is valuable, Kanno and Norton (2006) researched imagined communities and their impacts on education. Imagined communities are a group of people, "not immediately tangible and accessible, with whom we connect through the power of imagination," (Kanno& Norton, 2006, p. 241). Imagined communities can be powerful, as they exist outside of territorial context and help people feel connected to people and cultures they have never met. Imagined communities are useful for teachers who are non-native speakers but want to feel connected to the culture of their L2. This tactic may be particularly useful in regard to teaching an L2 where, as mentioned earlier, non-native speakers are commonly seen as outsiders by native speakers. If someone can feel connected to the culture, maybe this helps motivate them to learn more and makes their transition into the field easier, as their colleagues will accept them as "one of their own". If one feels connected to a culture, not only the language, then they may exude its characteristics. Imagined communities could provide powerful ways for people to feel a part of something they don't automatically belong to. Kanno and Norton (2003) did find this with a Japanese teen who, though living in Canada, maintained his 'Japanese-ness' by learning the language. Imagined communities have also been shown to be powerful in imagined potential and imagined cultural-linguistic ties when a person is born outside of their heritage culture (Kanno& Norton, 2003).

Community involvement may also be key in obtaining language mastery and is undoubtedly the best way to improve one's confidence with a language (Hummel, 2013). In one instance, Bashir-Ali (2006) studied a Spanish-speaking student and her journey through English classes in an African American dominated school. They found that this student changed her speech to match that of her peers and refused to acknowledge her Spanish heritage. The student also changed her speech and habits so as to not sound "white" and to fit in with the dominant group (Bashir-Ali, 2006). Feeling a part of the community meant changing her dialect of English. Leaver (2003) studied people who had obtained a level 4 or higher in a foreign language. She found that a great motivator for the participants had been money, the need for a job, or their desire to further their career (Leaver, 2003, pp. 59). She also found that all of the participants had lived abroad at some point and that they had ties to a foreign country. Also, more than two thirds grew up in bilingual neighbourhoods and nearly all of them worked in positions that required the use of their foreign language skills (Leaver, 2003, pp. 64), all displaying their community ties and involvement with the language. Again and again, the literature shows that it is possible, for numerous reasons, for someone to develop native-like mastery of a second or third language through study and interaction with native-speakers.

## Finding Experiential Opportunities

When teaching online, it may feel that many of the previous experiential opportunities are lost

UNIVERSITY

and that it is much harder to make the learners feel connected to the material. In moments where the additional challenge of distance gets between us and our students, it is time to figure out how to use the technology to our advantage and not to our detriment.

Technology has gifted us the unique opportunity to travel across time zones, all while sitting in the comfort of our own home. This leads me to my first suggestion that guest speakers are invaluable in a language classroom, and most certainly you can connect with speakers around the world through video conferencing. On such occasions, students may conduct an interview with the speaker, listen to a presentation done by him and answer questions about this later in a quiz. It is no longer an issue to have several guests attending one class, as students can be separated into different rooms to listen to the guests or "rotate" from one to another, being given the chance to speak with multiple people.

Another way technology can help us teach is through virtual tours. Many places provide virtual tours, such as museums, zoos and historical sites. Without all the permissions and scheduling chaos of organizing these trips anymore, you and your students can experience a museum exhibit, right at home. Students may be tasked with making oral or written presentations about the exhibits afterwards, or even with creating their own virtual tour. Though online students are inside for your class, this does not mean they cannot take a walk through the neighbourhood and create a virtual tour for you and/or the class. As the instructor, you can decide the parameters, or even linguistic markers they have to use while doing so, and this gets them up and moving around as if they were actually with you walking through the park.

While it may be difficult for students studying online to interact with each other and with speakers of the target language, it is not impossible. Other assignments may be a 'How to Do/Build' night where students are assigned to write directions on how to do something and then they must teach their classmates. This could range from a cooking demonstration to origami. Students may be organized into small groups in breakout rooms and given time to demonstrate their activity to the group, rather than the whole class, as this would take up a lot of time. Additionally, the instructor may pair second-language learners with native speakers they know or with previous students and ask them to conduct an interview, have a virtual coffee time and report back about it or use that person as a resource throughout the term to help them edit written assignments. Setting this up only requires knowing enough people to pair with your students. After this, students are responsible to keep up the relationships or complete the assignment as given. Projects like this can not only help improve your students' language abilities, but also help them feel connected to others and practice networking.

If you are looking for ways to motivate students to attend an online class, consider group competitions. Break students up into groups at the beginning of a course and have a variety of small competitions throughout. Competitions may include completion of warm-up activities, completion of homework or volunteering to lead a class discussion. Do not forget that Breakout rooms may also be utilised for activities like gap exercises, riddle or puzzle solving, preparation space for a debate, or a quiet space for homework help and peer work.

Finding experiential opportunities for your students has never been easier, as anything and anyone that can access over the internet can be brought to your classroom as well!

## Fall Off The Turnip Truck

As the world keeps spinning, more educational movements are sure to come with new ways of thinking about teaching and learning and to bring in new ways to deliver content. As educators, we should not be afraid of these new ideas and modalities, as they have often proven to bring about positive changes in society as a whole, and many social movements have been sparked by education.

We are in a unique position to try new ideas in our work every day and to find next-step ways to involve and challenge our students. Linguistic development and transfer of a culture face additional layers of difficulty in their communication when there are computer screens between teacher and student, but it is not impossible. Using methods such as TBLT and looking for those experiential opportunities throughout a course will help breakup the routine for you and your students, and certainly aid their retention of your lessons.

My final word to readers is this, do not be a turnip (turn-up). Do not be the teacher who is there for the money or who is unwilling to change their approach. 'Fall off the turnip truck' so you can be a part of the 21st century with new teaching and learning methodologies. We can gracefully embrace all the changes that await us if we are simply willing to try.

# The Future Of EdTech Learning In Higher Education

## Sarina Ziv

Co-founder of Smartnotes.ai
Illustrations by Morgan Michels
Creative Director of smartnotes.ai

"We need technology in every classroom and in every student and teacher's hand, because it is the pen and paper of our time, and it is the lens through which we experience much of our world" (David Warlick). Whilst 15-20 years ago it may have been imperative to state the importance of technology in education, today the relevance of technology in education is rarely questioned, particularly in higher education.

Yet, despite the heavy and regular use of applications and devices by college students across the world, the nature of education technology within university learning has far reaching consequences which are still being ascertained today. Ironically, the greatest use of education technology may be originating directly from students rather than from the institutions themselves. To be specific, today's university students are able to collaborate in their learning, enhance their autonomy and even obtain equity from their studies. These are far reaching effects which have been borne and continue to mature outside of university institutions – with the ultimate outcome still unknown.

### Outdated Systems

For nearly twenty years universities in the United States have been using the same software called Learning Management Systems, also known as an LMS, which include applications such as Blackboard, Canvas and more. Although updated LMS iterations have been released over time and new LMS competitors have entered the scene, the system itself has remained mostly unchanged. The LMS usually allows an instructor to place reading or video material online with a requirement for students to thoughtfully comment on the content or upload a completed assignment in response to the content. Regardless, the approach is mostly a one way and top-down interaction between professor and student. This means that technology within education has remained mostly unchanged within the 21st century. However, during this time student technology and usage habits have been changing tremendously.

The reality is that within the last twenty years, society has seen a variety of technological marvels enter daily use, from Google Maps and other GPS services, flash drives, smartphones, tablet devices, e-readers, online cable streaming services, bluetooth, social media platforms, editing software, Virtual Reality (VR) devices, smart watches and more (Independence University). Yet, Learning Management Systems do not offer students much more than spell check within response text fields. For this reason, students have been seeking uses of technology outside the LMS environments. For example, in 2015, just 49% of students worldwide reported that they participated in an online course or benefited from online curricula. A year later, 81% of college students believed that digital learning technology helped them boost their grades (Statista). Given that there was not a tremendous difference between the LMS of 2015 vs that of 2016, what exactly was the digital learning technology which helped students boost their grades so significantly? It's also worth noting that this jump in digital learning occurred *before* COVID-19 lockdowns. To help answer this question, a recent 2021 survey which interviewed 1,000 university students worldwide was conducted and the results, which were surprising, will be analysed in this chapter.

Before jumping into the data, a key question to consider is: what is genuinely at stake in correctly discerning the technology habits of college students? Independent research from August 2020 suggested that the global education technology market could reach $404 billion by 2025 (Holon IQ). What's more, the EdTech industry is expected to have a compound annual growth rate (CAGR) of 18.1% year-over-year through 2027 (Grandview). Given the explosive growth opportunities within the education technologies of higher education, the direction of learning material, syllabi, courses offeredand more are all potentially impacted; therefore, the question of what's at stake concerns educators, curricula publishers, VCs and startups alike. All the aforementioned should be seeking to better understand the technology learning habits of students within higher education.

**Student Survey**

In April 2020, 1,000 students around the world, of varying economic and cultural backgrounds, were asked different questions concerning their technology learning habits and preferences. The survey was conducted digitally and in English. Four of those questions will be examined later on in this chapter; however, the first question was thus: **When it comes to learning online, do you: prefer remote, prefer in person or like things about both?**

[Although this initial question is not directly related to technology, question number one was posed to potentially capture the disposition of students towards different learning environments, especially after a year of institutional lockdowns during Covid19.]

Remarkably, only 6.4% of students preferred strictly in person education over the online-only or hybrid online / in-person options. If there is one notion to take away from the entirety of this research, it should be the understanding that university students no longer view the four walls of a classroom as absolutely integral to the learning experience. Because of this, educational technologies should be viewed as an integral trunk of learning rather than as a mere branch of higher education, else institutions may risk becoming irrelevant. If you're curious about the additional questions surveyed concerning the attitudes students hold towards educational technology and the surprising responses collected, then read on.

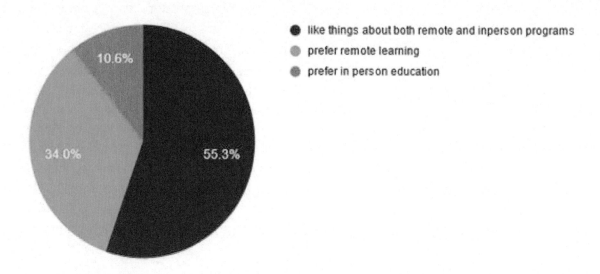

### Learning Collaborations

As Marion Ginapolis said it best, "it is not about the technology; it's about sharing knowledge and information, communicating efficiently, building learning communities and creating a culture of professionalism in schools." Apart from leaving a one-sided comment, many LMS environments deprive the student of a truly collaborative experience. Nevertheless, the last twenty years have provided technology options outside of institutions where learning can and does take place. Whether it's Reddit groups and subreddits, closed and/or public Facebook groups, personalised 'Instachat' Instagram or WhatsApp study groups, or buying and selling study notes – existing applications and platforms outside of universities have become an educational technology tool heavily used by students today.

During a recent 2021 survey students were asked, **"when collaborating online while studying, do you use any of the following applications? Check all that apply."**

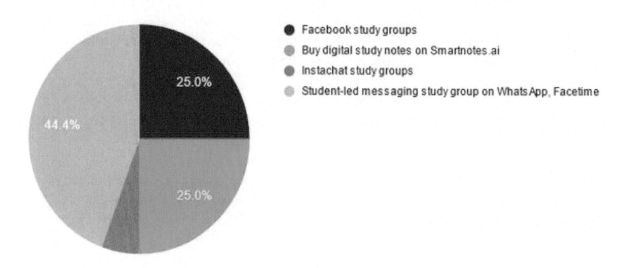

The responses from students revealed that 34% of students create virtual study groups using messaging apps, 19.1% seek out digital notes and study guides created by other students, another 19.1% use Facebook subject study groups and 4.3% learn within 'InstaChat' study groups. The subject of study groups ranges from the expected Physics, Chemistry, and Mathematics to the more obscure 'College Moms Support Group', 'International Students', 'College Homework Help' and beyond. Ironically, the Internet itself was established fifty years ago by researchers at the Massachusetts Institute of Technology, Stanford University, University College London and other institutions as a means of communicating and collaborating over research in real-time. Thus, the clear need for the use of technology within universities, namely virtual collaborating, is not a feature that drives current tools within the LMS experience. Rather than focusing on receiving a one-sided educational content and response format, universities could partake in a universal collaboration platform to discuss research. Until then, social media is happy to do the job and retain that intriguing data regarding the types of topics, questions and content shared.

Furthermore, the survey data offered another intriguing insight into university student technology behaviours. Whilst 19.1% of student collaboration was captured by Facebook, a company that is also nearly 20 years old, there was an equal percentage of 19.1% students who are seeking out digital study notes to buy. Smartnotes.ai is one such platform where users can buy, sell and share study notes (Smartnotes). Some of these notes sold cover specific courses at particular universities and other notes cover broad subjects, such as Calculus, Economics, and Computer Science. The platforms for sharing digital content were heavily used until recently. This is evident in a 2018 study that anticipated CAGR growth of electronic learning materials through 2022 to be at just 1% (Business); yet, that CAGR now stands at 18.1% a year through 2027 (Grandview). A potential factor in this CAGR bump could have been the release of the iPad Pro and Surface tablet which arrived around 2017/2018 and offered a more intuitive smart pen for note taking and study experience. Regardless of the reasons, the data clearly shows that the collaborative trends used by students in university are significant and include the use of discussion groups and purchasing digital notes, student created or otherwise.

**Learning Autonomy**

"Education is evolving due to the impact of the Internet. We cannot teach our students in the same manner in which we were taught. Change is necessary to engage students not in the curriculum we are responsible for teaching, but in school. Period" (April Chamberlain). Whether tools enhance or inhibit learning is a contentious subject, especially when it comes to autonomy.

During a recent 2021 survey students were asked, **"do online study tools, such as iPad Pros and surfaces, enhance your ability to learn/study independently?"**

The results shared by students indicated that 63.8% of students thought that technology tools both enhanced and inhibited their ability to learn independently, 29.8% of students were confident that technology tools only enhanced their ability to learn/study independently and just 6.4% of students surveyed felt that tools do *not* help them learn independently.

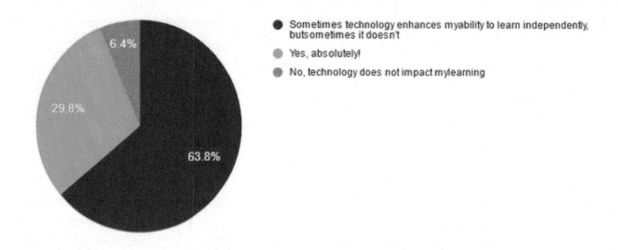

● Sometimes technology enhances my ability to learn independently, but sometimes it doesn't

● Yes, absolutely!

● No, technology does not impact my learning

UNIVERSITY

Unexpectedly, data from this question mirrors the first question asked about remote / in-person learning preferences. Namely, 6.4% of students prefer only in person learning and the exact same percentage of 6.4% of students do not feel that technology enhances independent learning. Because this question was asked of all active university students 18 and older, it is possible that some responses to this survey could have come from students who are older than 30 and were working while studying or who had returned to school for post-graduate studies, and could have been influenced by earlier in-person learning experiences. As a result, additional surveys with age-specific data should be explored. Regardless of the age distribution of respondents, the low numbers related to hesitancy towards technology (6.4%) cannot be denied. Students overwhelmingly see technology tools as enhancing their learning autonomy, and perhaps if learning applications became more intuitive the percentage of students viewing technology as *consistently* enhancing their learning autonomy might also increase over time.

Although not part of the survey, it's reasonable to acknowledge that the aspect which caused students to view technology as inconsistently aiding their learning independence stems again from the outdated LMS environments used by so many institutions. Yes, it's true that a student could potentially learn at a unique, individual pace using a tiered LMS; however, the steps to learning within the virtual environment are predominately scaled from point A to point B without freedom and independence to choose the actual content learned. Furthermore, a choice for the way in which a student could display the knowledge gained is lacking in a one-size-fits all LMS. For example, when iPad Pros allow students to create movies, soundtracks, slide decks, digital notes, and more, why is it that an uploaded, double spaced paper in Times New Roman font is still the expectation? In this light, it's possible that the traditionally tiered learning steps of LMS are becoming obsolete when faced with technology tools which adapt to creativity as well as unique learning styles.

## Learning Equity

Karl Fisch said that, "21st Century Education won't be defined by any new technology. It won't be just defined by 1:1 technology programs or tech-intensive projects. 21st Century Education will, however, be defined by a fundamental shift in what we are teaching - a shift towards learner-centred education and creating creative thinkers." When higher education students become creators, they begin to own a stake in their own learning. This equity in learning is a novel concept since up until now a student needed to become a professional in order to see a clear benefit to the work they put into their studies.

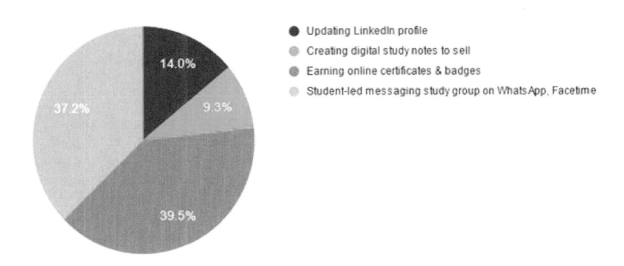

During a recent 2021 survey students were asked, **"do you use any of the following applications to gain equity from your studies? Check all that apply."**

The responses revealed that 36% of students earn online certificates that advertise their achievement, 12.8% of students keep their LinkedIn profile updated such as by taking LinkedIn learning quizzes and 8.5% of students said that they create (rather than just buy) digital study notes to sell to other students. Each of these endeavours are methods that combine technology with growing a personal brand and/or earning money from studies. This is a nascent area and should be further explored. As more students realise that a university education does not necessarily guarantee a career, the choice to grow equity alongside higher education will likely continue to gain popularity. This is especially true as technology tools continue to refine one's ability to become a creator in the learning process. Overall, as the expense, value and pay-off for learning is weighed by students, will it become a requirement for learning that students build their own personal profiles/brands within the university itself?

## Student-Propelled Learning

"The real power of interactive technologies is that they let us learn in ways that aren't otherwise possible or practical" (David Lassner). The data from the recent 2021 survey of university students showed students an overwhelmingly use technology tools to collaborate with one another outside of school in order to discuss school subjects. The survey also showed that a growing majority of students consider technology devices enhancing for their learning autonomy. Finally, and perhaps most nascent in its journey, technology tools and applications may prove most powerful in empowering students to gain equity from their studies by becoming creators within the learning process.

Perhaps the far-reaching impact of education technology can be seen in the recent decisions of universities to do away with the SAT/ACT admission testing requirement. In a time when students can study for this test using the Quizlet application, Facebook test prep groups, and more, rather than buckling down on memorisation test-taking tactics, universities may be doubling down on students as creators of equity in their own right (NY Times). Given that as many as 75% of students ages 7-17 wish to become a YouTuber, with 35% wanting creative and/or self-expressive freedoms, it makes sense that universities might tap into this desire for students to create content while learning rather than memorising facts (Mediakix).

The potential outcomes of this research suggest that applications which help students collaborate and study in real time, technologies that enable students to autonomously learn subjects and independently choose how to show their learning creatively, and applications which then allow students to earn equity from the learning materials created, are all be possible avenues for educational technologies within higher education. As it stands, within just 3 years 19.1% of students are seeking digitally created study notes online to buy, even though only 8.5% of students are currently creating notes. How many more students grow to become creators in the next five years will reveal just how much students and universities have heeded Lassner's advice and allowed themselves to learn in ways that would otherwise be impossible or considered impractical.

## Conclusions

It is evident by the projected market growth, that educational technology was already on an upward trend before Covid19; yet, the introduction to the market of highly intuitive tablets like iPad Pro and Surface may have helped push that growth as much as 1800% annually. Furthermore, the Covid19 lockdowns further propelled a growth trend within digital learning tools and applications. The long-term effects are not yet known, but what seems clear is that technology has proven for all but 6.4% of university students that classroom walls are not a requirement for higher education learning. As such, educational technologies that work outside the traditional box may likewise prove to be game changing.

# 4 Professionals

# Using EdTech To Enhance Teacher Productivity

## Wajeeha Zameer

Middle and High School Teacher

At its very core, every society depends on education as a leading source towards progress and prosperity. Education is the key that helps develop the sense between right and wrong, it has a direct impact on the economic development of the country and the direction in which the country will steer itself. The stronger the education system of any country, the stronger the citizens, and the more economic development opportunities they will have. Education has been instrumental since the beginning of time in honing skills in human beings and helping them evolve. Today, this evolution means being capable of adjusting as a global citizen rather than just contextually. No one plays a more vital role than the teacher in this development. But, if we want to ensure that teachers are able to help students reach their full potential and actualise in all senses, the emphasis on teacher professional development is key. It is the teacher who is involved with the learners during the teaching-learning process, it is also the teacher who deals with all needs, ranging from academic to social-emotional needs; in today's world, skill-building is a huge responsibility that the teacher must shoulder, since they are preparing today's learner for a very uncertain tomorrow and they need to be able to inculcate skills in them which will enable them to cope with the ever-changing world. This, along with the other 50,000 tasks that a teacher has to perform, puts immense pressure on the individual. Ultimately, this causes stress that interferes with the teacher's ability to cater to learners with differing needs, which creates lapses in teaching performance, and an inability to meet curriculum targets.

The rate at which the world is digitising is considered a total social fact as it involves the complete and systemic rethinking of social fabrication. Schools are being handed over the responsibility for preparing the GenZ for practical life, after providing them with formal education. Teachers are expected to cater and develop not just academic skills but also technological literacy; which is defined as how an individual understands and responds to technology at a level that enables them to effectively operate in the modern society. This demand from teachers is profoundly impacting teacher education and over the past few decades, the major focus of educational reforms has been the integration of educational technology in teacher training and continuous professional development practices. However, quite a few studies indicate that the teaching fraternity that integrates technology in the teaching learning process are few in numbers; reasons for this being lack of technology, insufficient CPD (continuous professional development) related to ICT skills being provided to teacher educators and teachers, lack of pedagogical knowledge on integrating technology in the classroom, and the lack of technical support. Nevertheless, despite all these challenges, it is a common expectation from teachers to help students achieve their full potential and help them develop skills that will transform them into lifelong learners. This herculean task now also involves dealing with a generation that is tech-savvy or, can be labelled as the GenZ. Generation Z characteristics involve these learners that are the first digital natives who are being taught by a generation that still is not fully comfortable with technology. This leads to an immense amount of pressure being put on teachers as they navigate through multiple tasks, as well as trying to create non-monotonous classrooms that can challenge a learner who has information at their fingertips. There is more to teaching than simply giving commands or instructions. Teaching needs to challenge, shape, and inspire the learner in more than one way. Undoubtedly, whenever teachers upgrade their skills, it has a profound impact on how their students learn as well, being a clear indicator that teachers' professional development needs to be taken seriously since the teacher is responsible for moulding the learner and ensuring their success in both academic and non-academic terms.

Traditionally, teachers were not even expected to embrace any kind of change or diversity. All they had to do was stand in front of the classroom and give lectures. So, one could say that the entire responsibility that the teacher had was of information dissemination. However, teachers are now encouraged to acquire new practices and understand trends to increase productivity and efficiency which directly impacts a learner's performance. As societal and parental expectations from teachers increase, it automatically results in increased stress levels among teachers, which ripple on to low performance; all in all, resulting in poorer learning among students. Teachers are pressured by the school management, communities, and the entire education system with responsibilities but with the provision of limited resources.

Hans Seyle coined the term "stress". Stress is a Latin word that means "constrict or overexert" (Lazarus, 1976). According to Richard Carlson, today we are living in an era where every other person has a job in which they have to meet unreasonable demands within a given time which leads to stress known as "occupational stress". People experience stress when resources allocated to them are not aligned with their skills and they cannot cope with demands and expectations which they must fulfil. Stress causes a high level of absenteeism and turnover among the employees because they cannot meet the work expectations continuously. Teachers it seems are suffering the most, as they fulfil multiple roles within one job. They are teachers, clerical staff, event planners, disciplinarians, psychologists and the list goeson. Hence, the duress they face is something that even Iron Man would have probably been unable to face.

Workplace stress defines the autonomy of working hours and sitting time on the job, but for teachers, this surpasses beyond and over any normal realm. It is always recommended that the potential stress in a working environment is regarded in terms of the sitting time involved, in case of teachers, we have to take in account the hours they put in well beyond this sitting time. The pressure of performing well under these circumstances, whilst also battling with the constantly changing situation, reflects on the performance and the productivity of every individual. Thus, the pressure that is built up in any working space forms a stressful situation. However, it is noticed that when technology is incorporated into teachers' lives, it automatically decreases their stress level.

Expecting education to remain unmerged with technology is to let it go obsolete. In today's era, education and technology go hand in hand; technology is the propellant that leads educational innovation. With technology within reach, every day in the classroom provides a valuable and learning experience for the teacher. Technology has refined and redefined the teachers' role in society. Today, the teacher can enable her learner to explore new concepts in manners unimagined before. Therefore, the meaning of teaching is no longer restricted to giving instructions and commands - it has a lot more to offer and it has now adopted the ability to provide a distinctive learning experience as well as cater to individual needs.

Education is not just limited to classrooms anymore, it has expanded its horizons and it reaches every home, community, society, and the whole world; today the concept of learning beyond the walls is a common phenomenon although this does create more complexities for the teacher. Now, it is every teacher's job to build and maintain an individual relationship with every learner so that they can comprehend their understanding and cater to their different learning styles, which will result in an increase in recording keeping. Students have become more active as learners where they are responsible to construct and own knowledge by themselves, but this does not mean that the teachers' role has diminished in any manner, on the contrary, the teachers' role has only grown.

It is clear now that every single day in a classroom, a teacher juggles all her tasks all day long. However, if technology is incorporated, a teachers' life can be made easier, then, without a doubt, things become smoother for them. For instance, a teacher is expected to be able to cater to diversity in the classroom, to achieve it whilst preparing and implementing lesson plans. Diversity in teaching is being able to cater to the individual needs of the learners, and it is often called differentiation. Responsible and diverse teaching is crucial for learners because it makes them empathetic, broadens their horizons, and makes them think differently. As every learner is unique, differentiated planning caters to their social, emotional, physical, and academic needs, and, in turn, learners become more confident and vocal. In this situation, technology plays a crucial role, as it backs up the teacher. But the question is, how can a teacher create a diversified and differentiated lesson using technology?

There is no questioning about the fact that differentiation is hard, but technology can help. Blended and digital learning programs become the key to supporting classroom differentiation. However, these programs need to rely on evidence-based maps of how learning takes place within a domain, so that teachers better understand how the current instructional goals are related to prior and future learning, thus, enabling the teacher to effectively design differentiated lessons and provide every learner with an equal opportunity. Moreover, the beauty of digital and blended learning is how it opens the doors of collaboration and communication among peers.

The main agenda of integrating education and technology is how teachers and students gather, construct and transmit their knowledge. There are numerous reasons why technology has become a distinct element of the education sector and fundamental for the learning environment, the most basic of these reasons being that without technology, education will become an obsolete activity with no scope for innovation. With the assistance of technology, teachers can achieve greater productivity and become more efficient, with the technology helping them to remain up to date with new teaching trends and practices. Today, as the class size grows, a teacher is expected to be organised in her day-to-day tasks and provide evidence for every activity that takes place. This daunting task can be made easier using certain technology tools.

Comprehensive, purpose-designed learning management systems, such as those designed using MOODLE (Modular Objective Oriented Dynamic Learning Environment), incorporates elements that make instructional design easy, interesting and innovation but are also able to collect comprehensive data, including the number of times a student clicks on an activity. Such a learning management system can and will be a huge support for teachers.

Again, a crucial question pops up, what will be required from the teachers? Research indicates that even with the provision of such technology at their disposal, teachers are unable to even reach 30% of the teaching-learning excellence that they possess - but this can be rectified with some good planning from school management.

School managements need to realise that for every new technology that can make life easier for teachers, students and schools overall, it will initially make life a little tougher, which means that there will be a need for extensive training sessions for teachers that need to include digital pedagogy. Just acquainting the teachers with the tool is not going to help with how the teacher will execute one tool with differing concepts, nor will it support the process of differentiation. Rather, it might confuse the teacher further and even hinder the process of teaching and learning instead of enhancing it.

All in all, one can say that there are four guiding principles that can help enhance how teachers use technology:
1. The focus should lie in enabling the active use of technology so creation, production, and problem-solving are promoted through learning and teaching.
2. Design sustainable, program-wide systems of professional learning for all teachers, from schools to higher education to strengthen and continually increase their ability to use technological tools; such endeavours will enable transformative learning and teaching.
3. Ensure teachers' experiences with educational technology are measurable both in width and depth for all programs rather than being one-off, isolated courses separate from their actual courses.
4. All technological advancement efforts should be aligned with research-based standards, frameworks, and instructional strategies recognised across the field.

Focusing on the first guiding principle, teachers need to understand the difference between the active and passive use of technology. Teachers must be equipped with the skills and abilities to integrate technology effortlessly into their instruction, in ways that are beyond the conventional use of presentations and communication, and instead towards creation, innovation, and problem-solving. With schools investing more in technology and consequent infrastructure, the implementation of technology can no longer be an afterthought in the teaching-learning process. Teachers' professional development must be focused on in a manner that enables them to ensure that instruction utilises the active use of technology.

The difference between passive and active use of technology in the classroom is a boundary that many teachers are yet to discover. Passive technology use occurs when students undergo activities with little or no interaction. These activities include digitised worksheets or activities that force students to consume content produced by others. On the other hand, the greater the interaction with technology by both teachers and students, the more active the learning process is. Peer–to–peer collaboration, creation, and publication of content by students (including but not restricted to blogging, vlogging, and podcasting), real-time interaction with field experts and other peers across the globe are leading examples of active learning. Seemingly difficult to implement in the classroom, these are not that difficult to design or even manage. My undergraduate philosophy and critical thinking course was a huge success because of how technology played into it. I remember assigning students the topic 'Philosophy and the Many Concepts of God', and allowing them to depict their own concept of God through any preferred media. The results I received were in the form of podcasts, blogs, vlogs and even a studio-recorded song. The students' feedback was that, due to the unrestricted nature of the assignment, they were able to express their learning as uninhibitedly as possible. With the group that had recorded the song, expressing in their feedback that this had allowed them to read the concept, ponder over it, write their lyrics and sing it themselves. Active use of technology in the classroom often results in increased interest and a definite enhancement in creative abilities.

The major divide in education is the teachers' inability to merge technology and pedagogy, creating unintended chaos. Colleges of education should work with an intent to bridge the existing gap between what teachers know and what they should know about technology implementation in modern classrooms. Only this determination can support teachers' professional development around technology and pedagogical integration.

The technology and pedagogy divide broadens due to the rapid manner in which technology evolves, and this becomes the very reason why teacher preparation programs need to be ongoing and continuously designed to increase the teachers' ability to transform learning. To create powerful, expert teachers, the key is to incorporate a combination of skills and knowledge, which is referred to as TPACK (Technological Pedagogical Content Knowledge).

The TPACK framework is by far the most popular and is built on Shulman's Pedagogical Content Knowledge framework, which can be defined as *"knowledge of existence, components, and abilities of technologies and how they are used in teaching, or on the other hand, knowing how teaching might alter as a result of the application of particular technologies."* Though many point out the limitations of TPACK, its use remains widespread for several reasons, including the idea that it prevents teachers from ineffective techno-centric approach, guides their development, provides a shared goal for team implementation, and helps assess teachers' TPACK level and development.

The focus of the second principle is the same, to enable the teacher in both technology and pedagogy. Moreover, to better prepare teachers so they use technology effectively and support transformative learning, a model that is embedded through the learning process needs to be developed. Science teachers need to get experience by creating science investigative learning experiences that enable students to use digital means such as scientific probes, sensors, data collection software, etc. to reach meaningful inferences. Similarly, history teachers can use digital tools to provide students with the opportunity to explore the world virtually, while also providing a perspective of the present thus learners do not just form conceptual understanding but also develop the ability to critique and communicate.

Ultimately, it needs to be realised that teachers are not restricted to one setting. Rather, they work in a variety of settings and have to deal with multicultural classrooms with access to a variety of tools. Every teacher in every country deals with their own set of limitations when it comes to access to technology, but with the way the world is coming together, every student deserves to have a teacher who can articulate the common expectation of effective implementation of technology. This can only be possible if curricular standards, frameworks, and expectations are unified. This unification will allow the teachers to have a common ground to collaborate and prepare learning opportunities in a manner that supports students' learning and the skill development necessary to forge ahead. It also ensures teachers continue to build their skills and move towards research-oriented methods to increase and improve the teaching-learning process.

To continue successful integration of technology, teachers need to be viewed from three perspectives:

1.  Teachers as Learners
2.  Teachers as Designers
3.  Teachers as Researchers

In the Teacher as Learner aspect, learning is not just viewed as transmitted knowledge, but is also understood as a developmental process. Kululska-Hulme approached the idea of training as "training has morphed into development, which can be understood as an ongoing process concerned with changing attitudes and behaviours and preparing for the future". Therefore, we also look at learning as having shifted from being a time-bounded activity to one that lasts a lifetime. The phrase 'lifelong learning' has become a way of life, a common lifestyle, and a fundamental educational skill that teachers especially need to acquire. Teachers need to become self-directed learners, which is a proven distinguishing characteristic of adult learning. Self-directed learning facilitates engagement and commitment towards professional development processes and encourages teachers to seek out opportunities of learning within their professional circles. Thus, as they partake in professional development activities, it is not just a professional decision, it is also a personal one and anything personal, indicates a higher level of involvement and commitment. Moreover, it is often argued that with heutagogy (a type of self–directed learning), since the learners' autonomy is increased, the teachers' withdrawal or lack of interest diminishes from the learning process. Many researches have also indicated that when learners are unencumbered and are given unrestricted access to "play", "explore", and "problem-solve", they ultimately develop critical thinking skills beyond comprehension and this is the same when it comes to allowing teachers to be self-directed learners.

Four characteristics are commonly identified for efficient design tasks, innovativeness, concreteness, complexity, and real-world application. These skills are developed in teachers as part of the developmental process and are ultimately used to generate design-principle-based learning modules. There are two major reasons for adopting the 'Teacher as Designer' approach. First and foremost, learning technology by design is a crucial TPACK development approach and is used consistently in a strategic manner to familiarize teachers with the components of TPACK and its implementation. Another reason is that teachers need to be able to design class activities as second nature, and only by adopting the Teacher as Designer approach and providing rigour in it, can it be expected that teachers become proficient in instructional design using technology.

There can be no doubt about the Teacher as Researcher stance, as it is only through reflective practice that the teacher can understand in-depth what is working out in the classrooms. In this method, teachers are encouraged to take an active role, to engage in research and to also reflect on the practices. It is the centrality of the teachers' Action, Research and Design-centred approach that will help the teacher to involve peers in observing, sharing, and discussing experiences and practices and move towards better teaching-learning practices.

The more autonomy that is given to teachers, and the more support they are given, the easier the professional development and consequent technology integration process will be. Nothing should be rushed, especially when the change is as monumental as integrating not just technology, but also asking teachers to change their entire lifestyle. At the moment, schools are not providing adequate support to teachers when it comes to implementing technology in the classrooms. Schoolsmust become the backbone of the entire process.They need to fully understand the complexity of the procedure and offer their full assistance and support. Schools expecting overnight changes will need to be patient whilst working alongside teachers sotechnology can ultimately become an everyday part of life just as the blackboard, chalk, and duster once were.

# EdTech For Professionals

## Robin Nguyen

CEO& Founder of IBI Global

Education Technology makes it possible for working professionals to upgrade their skills or "upskill" without enrolling in traditional courses and taking too much time away from their job duties. Employers can now see the value of sponsoring the ongoing training of their workforce through eLearning platforms that make upskilling approachable and available to people at just about every level.

Although employers often use EdTech for training their teams, upskilling on an individual level is also on the rise. Professionals who are interested in moving up in their career can build on their knowledge within their field and more.

When people perform the same job day in and day out and stop learning, they stagnate. eLearning is a win-win for companies and employees alike as it promotes innovation and engagement. Employees are happier and more energised when they're learning and experimenting, and companies benefit from increased innovation and thought leadership coming from their own offices. eLearning can spark new ideas and help professionals drive change in industries like marketing or IT where new ideas are crucial.

However, the question is how to make EdTech become a reliable method, as for the past 5 years we have seen a lot of EdTech models that simply don't work. The questions we must ask are: a) did we really understand our target audiences? b) did we really put education as the priority instead of technology? c) did we get involved enough to build an ecosystem that accelerates the work of professional innovation? and, d) did we really take the teacher role into serious consideration and prepare them with proper technological and pedagogical skills?

Blended eLearning conducted by qualified teachers can solve the issues that both traditional learning and eLearning face by combining the best of both approaches. In the case of blended learning in training and development, the "traditional" aspects of instructor-led learning can be delivered online in real-time through live meetings and lectures. Likewise, employees may get a foundation for a topic with an eLearning course and then exercise those skills in a live simulation with an instructor.

Online coaching in the blended eLearning method requires an individual to become proficient enough to achieve the desired result repeatedly. Eventually, the new behaviour becomes a preferred and self-chosen way of behaving.

The best way to develop the required skills is to practice doing the thing you're trying to achieve, under expert guidance of someone who knows how.

Furthermore, a high-quality LMS can track employee progress, both online and at in-person check-ins. Blended learning benefits employees as they can consult with each other during the day and apply what they have learned online.

## EdTech - Reskill And Upskill For Professionals

With the pace of technological developments drastically accelerating in recent years, individuals, especially working professionals, are concerned about their skills remaining relevant in the future. At the same time, learning platforms and training courses for digital skills are becoming more popular as individuals seek to either re skill or upskill themselves outside their day jobs or whilst in-between jobs.

This begs the question: could this become the norm in the future, whereby one has to constantly upskill to keep up with technological developments? The need for lifelong learning is absolutely essential for both now and in the future. You will need to have a degree, but you will also need to develop new skills, reinvent your career and, possibly, even alter your career paths if the current changes across industries continue to increase.

According to the Cambridge dictionary, 'upskilling' is "the process of learning new skills or of teaching workers new skills," while 'reskilling' is "the process of learning new skills so you can do a different job, or of training people to do a different job." While both upskilling and reskilling implies learning new skills, context is everything. Upskilling primarily focuses on helping employees become more skilled and relevant at their current position, while reskilling focuses on enabling employees to be able do other jobs within the organisation.

## Why Upskilling And Reskilling Are Now More Critical Than Ever

Since the industrial revolution in the 18th century, technologies have been changing, growing and adapting at an ever-increasing rate. We currently live in a period that some call the Fourth Industrial Revolution, where advancements in AI and automation are revolutionising and disrupting well-established roles and professions at an unprecedented pace.

The *World Economic Forum's Future of Jobs Report 2018* predicted that by 2022, 75 million jobs across 20 major economies may be displaced by emerging technologies. However, this does not mean that people are being pushed out of the job market. The same report predicts that 133 million new roles are expected to be created by these very same technological advancements. This is good news for people in the workforce, but these new jobs still require relevant training.

In order to stand out from the rest of the competition, both domestically and internationally, companies need to differentiate themselves and make their value proposition shine brighter than others. In order to achieve this, a company has to count on an agile, diverse and creative workforce that is continuously learning and adapting thanks to the essential acquisition of new skills.

Furthermore, we are currently undergoing the greatest financial crisis of our times – a fact which requires companies to think fast, and react even faster in order to survive. This makes upskilling and reskilling indispensable practices in any organisation.

Decision-makers may wonder why they should bother with reskilling their workforce, rather than focus on hiring a new generation of employees that have already invested in acquiring the new skills needed by the organisation. While new recruits have this one advantage going for them, existing employees have many more; enough to make internal talent development a crucial and critical objective.

First, employees that have been working for an organisation for several years have a deep understanding of the company's needs, clients, customers, partners, and the culture. But even if this was not the case, the rapid change of technological advancement means that it takes longer to train new employees than it does for existing employees to keep up with new, paradigm-shifting technologies and the vertical changes. An agile, flexible workforce is crucial for organisations that want to stay ahead of the curve and a culture of upskilling and reskilling is therefore a valuable asset that allows quick adoption of new technological solutions and innovative business practices.

The question is: how do we update the training both pedagogically and technologically? Is it still relevant to document any measurable business results arising from the courses conducted traditionally?

Suppose that you want to become skilled at something: learning a language, telling a business story, negotiating, making presentations or acquiring a technical skill and your primary goal is to be truly proficient in that field or subject, would you:

- Read a book?
- Watch a YouTube video?
- Listen to a motivational speaker?
- Attend a seminar?
- Practise on your own?
- Practise with an expert coach under realistic conditions until you have achieved a level of mastery?

The first option could provide some useful information or conceptual knowledge about the skill, but only the last one will turn potential talent into demonstrable competence. Knowledge is essential but it only becomes powerful when you can practise it multiple times or apply it in your real life under the guidance of an expert. This will push you to perform it to a clearly defined standard, so your mind and body can feel and experience that you are doing it proficiently. If you do not reach that level, you will not have acquired the skill. It is gained only by using the skills to produce a real result.

Coaching the actual exercise shortens the time it takes for an individual to become proficient enough to achieve the desired result again and again. Eventually, the new behaviour becomes a preferred and natural way of operating.

So, the best way to develop and achieve expertise is through hands-on experience, under the expert guidance of someone who knows how, who is experienced. Now, try to guess the real reason behind the endless hand-wringing in the professional training field about how hard it is to get 'learned skills' to transfer from the classroom to the job. Guess why trainers find it so terribly difficult to document any measurable business results arising from the courses conducted in a traditional way.

There is a great deal of difference between training and education - though the vast majority of trainers are not aware of it. Educating is conceptual learning while training is building skills. For most people, there is no causal relation between education and performance. There is indeed a causal relationship between the two. The reason for it is that the concept of knowledge is essential but skills are powerful as they create a desired effect, and creating desired effects is what we mean by performance.

With the help of technology and the support of experts, students can learn and practice anytime and anywhere to build their real competence within a desired time frame. Learners are trained to be proficient at the execution of a given project or task. Only training through technology can help accomplish this. To deliver real training for professionals, we need to start by taking them through the following coaching methods and criteria:

First, the individual must be trained to a degree of being capable of implementing the ideas or the tasks set by the company.

Second, if adopted, the improvement must be measurable as follows:

- Clearly define the level of skill required. What does the performance look like when it is done correctly?
- Clearly define the measurable outcome desired. What is the intended result of the performance?
- Educate quickly and precisely.
- Train, via coached repetitions, until the measurable performance level and the desired result are consistently achieved.

### How EdTech Can Make A Difference

Blended eLearning can solve the issues that both traditional learning and eLearning face as they combine the best of both approaches. Instructor-led learning can be delivered both online and in real-time through live lectures and meetings, and employees can gain knowledge through a course which can then be exercised in a live simulation with an instructor. Therefore, EdTech helps:

- Integrate eLearning into the work environment

Blended eLearning strategy integrates training into the work environment. An online course integrated into a propre LMS would include opportunities for additional practice, ongoing discussion, feedback and coaching to support the effective transfer of new skills.

- Bring single-concept learning into our eLearning method

Taking into consideration that the human attention span has drastically dropped in recent years, eLearning can be designed flexibly by covering only one isolated concept. This is the opposite of the traditional fire hose approach to training, where learners are flooded with more information than they can absorb at one time. Instead, single concept learning focuses on one behaviour change, one specific concept and one realistically achievable goal.

- Focus on master skills and on lots of practice

In online learning this can be done through simulated scenarios or in a synchronous virtual classroom. As an example, you can demonstrate showing someone respect by listening to and acknowledging his or her viewpoint. Once the learner is aware of how this is done, he or she can practice it in a variety of scenarios - under hostile, pleasant or neutral conditions. With this approach, learners can benefit from coaching and feedback with lots of repetitions.

- Cultivate cultural diversity and inclusion on a practical level

As anyone that has travelled extensively or that has worked in different countries will attest, being exposed to different cultures makes you more adaptable and open-minded. It allows you to see how things can be done differently from what you are used to.

The first benefits are the workforce's ability to try different approaches when solving problems as well as its ability to take into consideration the clients' culture, tradition and ethics when delivering a service or a product. An excellent example of the advantages of diversity can be seen when a company's services and products target a specific age group, e.g., young adults.

These two points would also help your company to stand out and attract new clients. If, for instance, you are looking to hire a rebranding consulting firm for the Chinese market, you are more likely to sign a contract with a firm that has, among its employees, either people that have worked in China extensively or that are Chinese, so to make sure that your new brand will be culturally sensitive.

Furthermore, when the members of a team come from different nations and backgrounds, they bring to the business practice a broader set of skills and experiences that enrich the competitiveness of the company and the productivity. This has been proven very useful when competing and scouting for top talents, particularly on the global market.

Studies show that companies that have diversity and inclusion policies are more likely to retain staff and, most importantly, can have a bigger pool from which to choose their candidates. Top candidates prefer to work in an environment that can provide them with and train them on new skills and practices.

The last, but perhaps most valuable, advantage of diversity and inclusivity involves creativity and ideas. Adding different voices brings new ideas, products and services; in other words, innovation.

EdTech, based on its technology, can build the expert eco-system from different cultures and backgrounds to bridge among a diversity of cultures.

**EdTech Helps Professionals Gain Global Competence**

Enforcing global competence is vital for individuals and organisations to thrive in a rapidly changing world and for societies to progress without leaving anyone behind. In a context in which we all have much to gain from growing openness and connectivity, and much to lose from rising inequalities, students need not only the skills to be competitive and ready for a new world of work but, more importantly, also develop the capacity to analyse and understand global and intercultural issues. The development of social and emotional skills as well as values, like respect, self-confidence and a sense of belonging, are of the utmost importance when creating opportunities for all, and advance a shared respect for human dignity.

Despite differences (cultural differences or democratic culture, human rights or environmental sustainability), EdTech can help build educational models that share a goal in promoting students' understanding of the world, and in empowering them to participate and thrive in the professional world.

When we talk about competence, we are not merely referring to a specific skill. It is a combination of knowledge, skills, attitudes and values successfully utilised in face-to-face, virtual or mediated encounters with people who are perceived to be from a different cultural background, and when dealing with individuals' experiences on global issues. Acquiring global competence is a life-long, ongoing process and should be put in a company's key indicators. Below outlines the four target dimensions of global competence that individuals need to apply successfully in their everyday life or work:

- The capacity to examine issues and situations at a local, global and cultural level;
- The capacity to understand and appreciate different perspectives and worldviews;
- The ability to establish positive interactions with people of different national, ethnic, religious, social or cultural backgrounds or gender
- The capacity and disposition to take constructive action towards sustainable development and collective well-being.

Understanding the above will facilitate and improve social and cultural acceptance of scientific knowledge and help establish culturally distinct paths to global sustainability.

Today, any business or professional that wants to be successful on a global scale adopts a policy of diversity and inclusion in their business or development models. We are not talking simply about creating a heterogeneous workforce based on race, gender and disability, but rather adopting a culture of inclusion by understanding first what diversity means in the region in which we operate, and then by integrating it in the daily work dynamic.

EdTech, by applying the proper eLearning framework and methodology, will be the bridge-building best practice for successful business and professional collaborations. EdTech helps encourage intercultural dialogue, negotiation and cooperation between businesses around the world through interactive lessons. The more we interact, the better we understand. By building an appropriate EdTech ecosystem from different cultures (content, experts and tools), EdTech can create bridges amongst a diversity of cultures and also facilitate successful business collaborations.

Our world is no longer just about competitive advantage; it is increasingly about co-operative and collaborative advantage.

**EdTech Ecosystem Is The Background For Building The World Of Professional Innovation**

It has long been known that education technology is a key tool for improving individuals' productivity and the overall learning experience. In today's modern society, technology is a crucial element within the training landscape for professionals. Enabling individuals to have easy access to technology is, of course, the first step in creating a thriving EdTech ecosystem. However, once technology becomes readily available, teachers must create their own landscape in which learners are free to explore, create and grow. Also, companies need to focus on thriving learning systems that enforce the productivity of their workforce. As a consequence, governments will implement the changes and create the regulations that support this system.

Ecosystems, as a rule, are unique and yet susceptible to change. A teacher looking to build an EdTech ecosystem in their classroom has the distinct role of creating a landscape that will nurture each individual learner with maximum success. Companies and organisations have to drive the learning environment where every employee feels empowered to learn and change, and where their learning experience is personalised and decentralised.

An online learning environment is a platform where the sharing of information can take place. Typically, it is the teacher who provides the information which is then passed on to the students. This exchange is still the foundation on which an EdTech ecosystem is built. Teachers and learners looking to work on an EdTech ecosystem from the ground up need a reliable source of sharing information such as Google Drive, iCloud and Dropbox. By choosing and sticking to a sharing service, both teachers and learners can easily share and transfer information and resources. They provide organisational tools that allow the class to categorise, archive and share their work as individuals or as a team. This allows all learners easy access to their work at all times.

Now that teachers and learners have a foundation upon which to build, they need tools that will allow them to create within their EdTech ecosystem.

Content creation tools fall into two categories: single-use tools and open-ended tools. While single-use creation tools are quite time efficient for they often only require students to learn one skill, they are also restrictive in the sense that the creative outcome is already determined by the specificity of the tool. This can be a good thing. When you plant potato seeds, you expect to grow potatoes. And, having a field full of potatoes ensures that no one goes hungry. Yet, variety is the spice of life and to create variety and innovation in your EdTech ecosystem, you need a handful of different seeds that your learners can pick and choose to suit their own preferences. Open-ended creation tools are the key to producing a variety of work within your EdTech environment and allow learners the freedom to curate, create and present ideas in their own way which results in a more vibrant classroom. There are many content creation apps that support a range of multimedia. From writing, editing, creating visual content, such as infographics, data presentation, video and audio; the right tool can open up a student's imagination.

Interconnectivity is the backbone of many thriving ecosystems. Communication in an EdTech ecosystem is also of the utmost importance. EdTech tools are a fantastic way for learners to connect with their teachers and with each other as well as the broader community, both in and out of the classroom. Through services such as Google Apps for Education, both teacher and student can stay connected through Google Classroom. This creates a space where all members of the ecosystem can stay up to date with news, announcements, important information or interesting content. Learners can create a virtual working space for team projects with Google Hangout. Some blended eLearning platforms, such as Adobe Connect and IBI Global, have integrated these brilliant functions professionally to benefit their target customers.

Keeping your EdTech ecosystem connected will mean that all members of the ecosystem are supported and encouraged, no matter where they are. Connecting your EdTech ecosystem with others is also a brilliant way to encourage growth. Learners can generate and publish content into a personal or group blog that then becomes available to a wider audience, meaning that they can work in conjunction with other classes or for other classes. This establishes a larger sense of community and purpose for your students while actively engaging in their studies. Ultimately, teachers must be adaptable and innovative in teaching. Learners have more space to be creative under the support of modern technologies and innovative content. Teaching and learning is more flexible and personalised. The world of innovation is here.

**EdTech For Teachers And Educators**

Over the last several years, many resources, both public and private, have been allocated to provide digital technologies to schools, in order to offer studentsthe opportunity to learn and use technology in their academic pursuits. During this time, the public and educators alike have realised that just having the technology in place does not immediately result in it being used for further education.

Teachers and educators are now at the centre of the discussion - sometimes controversially- and are deeply aected by technology-related standards, requirements, opportunities, and changes.

Technology clearly has the ability to confuse, intimidate, and frustrate learners and users. Learning to cope with these necessary new knowledge bases and skills is a complex process for all. Moreover, educators have additional needs in this learning process as they are urged to immediately and prociently bring the new systems to signicant educational application in their classrooms or lessons. Just as other adults learn new concepts, engage in critical reection, and consider new perspectives, so do educators as they learn new skills and consider how to best apply them to teaching and learning. A critical question for teachers' professional development is how to assist and guide educators and teachers-in-training through these necessary, but complex, steps of growth.

The call to integrate technology into education can be used as a starting point for educators' professional growth. Looking at teacher preparation and professional development not just as technology training but as a bridge between the literature and practice of faculty developments in educational technology with adult education's transformational learning theory.

In considering the educational technology professional development literature, it is evident that the focus has primarily been on technology integration into the curriculum. The thing is, there is no training or book that can fully address the issues of how to best conduct professional development in educational technology, as educators and teachers need a whole system to support them to do the job properly and efficiently.

## Teachers And Educators Can Only Do A Good Job In A Well-Prepared And Properly Developed System

The benefits of online education depend on its successful implementation within an organisation.

Teachers' skills: The main issue for teachers to teach online is the lack of essential skills to optimise the online tools and resources. The level of adaptability and flexibility required from a teacher is quite different from the one needed in a traditional class environment. They also need to learn how to create an attractive presentation and understand how to use online tools in the virtual classroom so that students can work in groups, play games or interact with each other. Teachers also must master how to work with students on projects and how to motivate learners to ensure the efficiency and effectiveness of the courses.

It seems wrong for schools or organisations to expect teachers to do everything by themselves when it comes to their online training. Schools need to build a framework and a proper curriculum for online training, even lesson plans need to be well prepared to assist the teachers. The LMS needs to be very organised and scientific to ensure teachers can access resources, work on the system smoothly and at same time interact effectively with learners.

## Curriculum Model

Within a traditional classroom, it is very common to place the focus of the lesson on the teacher delivering information, while the students are expected to retain what is being presented to them. It is rare that students are expected to engage in problem solving situations that are relevant to their current situations. For online training, project-based learning is taken into serious consideration. Therefore, there is a demand for a redesign of education to meet the demands of a new learning model.

## Strategy From The School Board

With pedagogical shifts in mind, school boards have to alter their previously held ideologies on learning. This change to education is giving teachers the freedom to govern their own lessons and deliver content of their choosing based on the established guidelines and strategy of the school boards.

Schools have to build an online system to deliver training and learning efficiently and effectively. This should form a harmonious synergy of teaching methods, operating systems, curriculum and teachers.

**Student Preparation**

Students are now urged to take on new responsibilities for their learning experience that they have never had before. Students are expected to be responsible for their own learning and employ "reflective, critical thinking skills".

Schools should create solutions that equip students with interactive lessons from self-paced learning courses via mobile/ tablet before the beginning of their live classes. This process helps students write down questions related to their self-paced lessons, to get feedback 24/7 from the teachers in their own time, or at least to be prepared to ask these questions in their live classes.

# EdTech For Professionals

## David Haran

Chief of Staff at HED Unity Ltd and Lecturer in Digital Financial Services

To begin with, it is important to know a little about me. I am the grandson of two teachers from the west of Ireland on my mother's side. My father was the first of his family to go to university. These things matter because, as a result, education was instilled into my parents as a way of combating shortage, as they grew up in times of hardship. Education is at the core of any success that I have achieved. It has shaped my career as an accountant. Over time I have added to my education and obtained a greater understanding of how to learn and how to teach. This occurred on my journey from classroom to EdTech.

These days, I work as a Risk professional with a deep involvement in Finance and FinTech. I specialise in delivering on-time, on-budget model suites for banks, working closely with data analytics professionals and data scientists. This environment has given me an insight into the requirements of major financial institutions in the ever-changing world of Big Data, Artificial Intelligence, Machine Learning, Decentralised Finance, Distributed Computing, Blockchain, Cryptocurrency and other cutting-edge tools and topics. It's a long way from the school teaching that my forbears received and delivered. They would have loved that EdTech has the potential to revolutionise the way we all learn, changing career paths and redistributing wealth as we go.

### Lifelong Learning

My EdTech journey began when I signed up for a post graduate course in Corporate Governance. I had a nagging doubt about how major corporate decisions were made and how things got done. It was clear to me that the only way to progress was to roll up my sleeves and hit the books. As an accountant, I am used to the need for continuing education but, to be honest, at that time, this could be done by attending a seminar or reading some articles. Hardly challenging at all. Since that first course, my record is two more post-graduate diplomas, three fintech courses, the Institute of Directors Chartered Director programme and the Certified Bank Director programme with the Institute of Banking. Additionally (and wonderfully), I now teach a course in Digital Financial Services. It is fair to say that my immersion in learning has been full on, varied and thoroughly enjoyable over the last ten years. There have been many teaching methods, many teachers and many lessons that have guided my journey. My purpose here is to share the benefits of this learning with you and to consequently explain the merits of EdTech for Professionals. These fundamentals are the core of my new EdTech business – the European Institute for Data Analytics (www.EIDA.ie). EIDA delivers practitioner-led training using cutting edge EdTech methods. Let's examine EdTech and EIDA to gain a deeper understanding of the challenges in delivering EdTech for professionals.

## What is EIDA's Approach To EdTech Problem Solving?

Time and place are the first issues that need to be addressed. As a student in New York City back in the 1990s, my method was to obtain recordings of the lectures for the CPA (Certified Public Accountant) exam. Less financially challenged New Yorkers paid for video lectures but we had no machine to play the videos! That's how it started back then. It was a huge struggle. It was unpleasant and often unsuccessful, but it did allow me the means to succeed. The little tape player that I used every day was a wreck by exam time, but from this humble beginning came lessons for EdTech. *Professionals want to control the time and place they learn in so that the environment and their headspace are connected, aligned and primed to succeed.*

The other great lesson from New York was cost. EdTech has the ability to make complex ideas available to learners delivered by **master practitioners** at affordable prices. As a contemporary example of what EIDA can do: for the first-time learners can understand the complexities of building a data model using best industry practice Structured Query Language, visual analytics and predictive analytics methods by interacting with master practitioners using EdTech methodologies. *EIDA's fundamental basis is to allow master practitioners to provide training to those who wish to learn at affordable prices.*

## How Does EIDA Deliver EdTech For Professionals?

EIDA brings together the best in class data analytics practitioners with learners using a learning management platform. EIDA expects teachers to be academically excellent to teach with us. That is the starting point. From there, EIDA's practitioners must expertly do the work of data analytics on a day-to-day basis. This is critical. The theory of mathematics, econometrics, model-building and many other disciplines can be really interesting, but this is EdTech for professionals. *Professionals want to know what they need to know, when they need to know it and in a way in which they can consume it with an economy of effort. Only master practitioners can deliver in that framework.*

Our content is always focussed, specific, time bound and challenging. Lectures are structured into a combination of written slides, video presentations, case studies, short questions and more challenging problems. Professionals will decide for themselves the level of engagement they want to have with their course as EIDA provides a range of engagement models. *Professionals want to be allowed a range of engagement choices to suit their interest in a topic.*

The EIDA learning engagement model is driven by my own experiences as a learner. An example here will help. Given no restrictions on my time, I could probably do case studies for the rest of my days! There is a really brilliant case study that uses the movie "Twelve Angry Men" from 1957 starring, amongst others, Henry Fonda. When it was explained to me that we would be spending a weekend studying and watching this movie, my initial reaction was disbelief. It turned out to be an incredibly instructive learning experience, zeroing in on human nature and negotiation. For those of you who have not seen the movie, it concerns a jury who are asked to come to a verdict in a murder case. Henry Fonda's character engages with the other jurors and we are treated to a master class in negotiation, observation, patience and obdurate human nature. Check it out sometime.

As good as the movie is, how many professionals wish to spend their weekends doing a case study on a movie from the 1950s? EIDA uses the skills captured by me and other colleagues to provide affordable learning for career minded professionals using the core technology of an EdTech platform to locate and deliver crystal clear content. *EdTech and EIDA allow the benefits of technology, learning and delivery to be combined in a best practice solution for time poor executives.*

## Who Are EIDA?

EIDA comprises a group of educators who combine a desire for learning, teaching, knowledge and technology into a cohesive delivery platform that allows time poor professionals to learn from master practitioners. EdTech must be delivered in the manner in which professionals require, at a time of their choosing and within an acceptable cost framework. So, EIDA delivers online courses that help students to excel in the field of data science, opening up a vast range of possibilities for career progression. EIDA is the trusted, premium institute for practitioner-led training. Our courses are designed and delivered by industry leaders, with practical, career-focused learning at the heart of everything we do. The world around us is changing at an increasingly rapid pace, and we firmly believe that data analytics will form the cornerstone to every industry. By equipping our students with the skills set out in our curriculum, they will have the practical know-how to be among the leaders of this technological revolution.

## Platform Economics

EdTech is a wonderful method to reach huge swathes of the learning population that were previously unable to benefit. In FinTech, there is a lot of talk about the unbanked and underbanked. These are folks that do not have access to the services of a bank. It may be inadequate access (underbanked) or no access (unbanked). EdTech contains the potential to provide in precisely the same manner. Take content experts and give them a methodology to deliver to career minded customers, and one has created a value mechanism linking supply and demand.

The EIDA platform does not own the means of production and only cares about the means of connection. It allows for greater information sharing and more flexible real time pricing at times of huge demand. Consumers can provide real time feedback on the service received to enable safety and transparency for other consumers. There is a potential for the redistribution of wealth using a more direct route to market. As time evolves, learning platforms shall become more advanced and data analytics capabilities will increase allowing for a movement away from a one-size-fits-all approach to education.

## EIDA Delivers EdTech To Professionals

While the world of data analytics may be complex, our pillars of learning are straight forward. We seek to educate our students about the underlying theories behind data analytics, teach them how to apply those theories in a practical fashion, and equip them with the project management and communication skills to convey their work in a way that allows colleagues to understand its importance. Data analytics is becoming increasingly relevant in large scale companies, and the ability to properly analyse large swathes of data is vital.

An as an example of what EIDA delivers through EdTech, an excellent data analyst must be able to:

- Ask the right questions
- Interrogate and understand the data
- Develop critical thinking skills
- Theorise based on their findings
- Put forward data-driven ideas
- Provide complete clarity in their communication.

EIDA connects future data analysts with master practitioners. The practitioners teach the skills that different roles require. Students gain immeasurably from practical realities. The hidden learning is that they also learn the practical theoretical necessities in a hands-on, data driven fashion through EdTech engagement tools such as interactive quizzes, Q&A sessions with practitioners and online learning webinars.

## EIDA Educators

EdTech cannot be delivered without a deep and ingrained expertise in your subject matter. Consumers have a huge choice in where they can receive their education. Successful EdTech for professionals must always keep the learner at the heart of everything that is done. EIDA must build trust in the courses that are offered. Learners must benefit from our courses. Their experience must be transformational. Our practitioners must be at the peak of their powers. Allow me to introduce you to some of the EIDA team.

EIDA's most experienced educator received a Ph.D. in Mathematics from the National University of Ireland over thirty years ago. Since then, he has delivered and developed educational programmes across Europe, Asia and USA. He combines this in-depth knowledge of education and training with a professional banking career spanning almost fifteen years. He leads the Analytics function at a large bank and, in this role, has a front seat role observing the latest technologies, techniques and training relevant to analytics professionals in the Financial Services industry. He is particularly focused on ensuring that students receive the education they need to support a career in analytics, regardless of industry. For him, courses must be relevant, contemporary and focused. He personally reviews all course materials for EIDA courses and attends a full delivery in advance of any course being made available to clients.

EIDA's content architect was awarded a PhD in machine learning from the Technological University Dublin, Ireland in 2013 and has published in peer-reviewed journals. In a near twenty-year career spanning quantitative finance and software engineering he has gained in-depth knowledge of financial and computational theory and methodology. He possesses the ability to communicate with both a business and a statistical audience, drawing on his knowledge of economic trends and statistical techniques.

Do these guys seem like master practitioners to you?

## C-Suite Executives And EdTech

Senior executives are often referred to as the C-Suite. The 'C' is of course short for Chief. These folks are at the top of their game. They decide strategies, make decisions and drive companies to succeed. Charles Darwin famously spoke about the survival of the fittest and the strongest surviving in his contributions on the science of evolution. Darwin's famous quote relates to the C-Suite because they are often seen as the strongest of their species. Certainly, they have progressed through the ranks as they are performance led, goal driven and ruthlessly opportunistic.

When Darwin defined the survival of the fittest, many assumed it to be strength of their professional skills or perhaps strength of purpose or the courage of their conviction or perhaps the ability to do things others would not. Let's look at the full Darwin quote here *"It is not the strongest of the species that survives, nor the most intelligent that survives. It is one that is most adaptable to change."*

Darwin realised that the largest dinosaurs became equally as extinct as the smallest mammals, not because of their size or strength, but purely based on their ability to adapt to change. This is a remarkable lesson in the context of the C-Suite. EdTech today is changing the paradigm of education delivery to professionals. Chief executives who champion this change and drive it into their businesses will create a workforce motivated by a desire to learn, grow, succeed and be challenged again at a higher level. EdTech is the change. *EdTech will revolutionise how we learn and it will change forever how careers progress.*

## The New World Of Analytics In Banking

Let us turn our attention to the future and specifically to how machine learning & AI will feature in capital, provisions & stress test models for banks. Here, I would like to draw attention to a couple of realities facing the financial services industry in the short term. I will highlight a key industry issue in relation to analytical techniques available to modellers based on typically available datasets. I will then discuss the key executive issue within organisations – the interaction between executives and analytics. Let me start with the former.

The industry challenge is clear and unequivocal. Regulators and supervisors need to change with the times - consider the typical bank risk infrastructure today. Capital, IFRS 9 and stress testing models are well established. However, they are built using historical data with minimal interaction with recent behaviour. In simple terms, they use logistic regression to rank order good and bad customers based on a historical data set. Models are effectively frozen in time with much internal and regulatory governance to navigate in advance of making changes to models. A typical IRB model development project is likely to take at least three years from inception to final model deployment. These models often focus only on "how much" – how much does the obligor earn, spend, and pay us every month. Machine learning or similar is out of bounds! Try submitting any non-standard approach to a regulator and see what happens. In fact, implicit in the Basel guidelines is the assumption that old style logistic regression (or maybe a decision tree if you are lucky) is the answer to every question. Practitioners know that data used to build the current suites of customer behaviour models is much more interested in how, where, and when you spend your money – and the interactions between these. This has contributed to an ever-widening gap between real-life modelling of customer behaviour and regulatory / accounting. The gap needs to close - and quickly.

The internal challenge is just as great. C-suite executives need to understand that they **cannot rely** on analytics teams to answer their questions. Without data interrogation skills they do not even know what questions to ask. It is akin to driving a car while wearing a blindfold. You cannot see into the data and so your queries are driven by historical experience and hearsay rather than by a clear vision of the complexities and interactions in your data sets. You think you are asking incisive questions but all that is happening is that you are asking questions that have been effective in other studies. Imagine if you could explore and interrogate the data yourself and build a clear vision in your mind of that reality. The insight that knowledge brings is the key to unlocking complex problems and setting a clear path of achievement for an organisation. The ability to analyse data in real time at executive meetings separates the observers from the contributors. EIDA delivers EdTech by practitioners to allow the C-Suite to adapt in Darwinian fashion.

I see junior managers deliberately twisting data or perspectives to answer questions that they want to answer rather than questions their executive posed. Regularly, the executive does not realise that the original question has been changed slightly to a more favourable and/or more easily answerable question. It has led me to the conclusion that one simply cannot function as an executive in the business world of the future without some technical skills, whereas most training today seems to be based on the premise that a broad awareness of data structures and analytical techniques is sufficient for executives. It is not. Let us think of it as a car – you do not need to be able to fix it, but you do need to drive it yourself if you want control over the destination. Thirty years ago, nobody believed that executives would be doing their own typing. They will be doing their own analytics soon – mark my words. Today's middle ranking executive will be a visual analytics capable C-suite member in a decade, or else she will be out of a job.

As practitioners in the data analytics industry, we are familiar with the 2017 Economist article – *"The world's most valuable resource is not oil, but data"* – and events since then simply confirm that statement. The COVID-19 pandemic response is a case in point. The response is as much a process of globally and locally gathering and learning from data as it is a medical emergency. Think of the average recruit to the banking world today. It is highly likely that she will pass her whole career without ever physically touching cash and many will never meet a customer face to face. Instead, she will know customers by their data patterns, recognise their stages in life by their spending patterns, and anticipate their needs using real-time propensity scores that fluctuate like the weather. It will happen in every industry. The core skills are, and will be, analytics skills. And, banking, insurance, entertainment, shopping, and a multitude of other industries will become more and more similar – an analytics function with ancillary services (Finance, HR, Compliance) matching customers with services and products at the right time and the right price. Skilled analytics practitioners will move seamlessly between industries. This has already begun to happen at analyst and junior managerial level. It will happen next at executive level, but only for executives comfortable taking hold of the steering wheel and driving through data to see for themselves what is really going on. It is the equivalent of meeting customers face to face. Early executive adopters of the new analytics skill set will survive and thrive – the laggards will be left behind.

## Are We Ready For An Open Talent Economy?

Deloitte spoke about an Open Talent economy as far back as 2013. They defined it as a "collaborative technology-driven, rapid-cycle way of doing business". It would be characterised by a mixture of employees, contractors and others who would form your workforce to provide agility, scale (up or down) so that the appropriate skills are available in real-time. The World Bank added to this recently when briefing on EdTech. They spoke of the need to empower teachers to deliver focussed learning using innovation to drive multi-stakeholder engagement and to advance the learning ecosystem with data driven focus.

These are the demands that organisations must meet today. Learners will adapt and find a way to change and survive. They will find the best education, provided by the best teachers in affordable and appropriate surroundings. C-Suite executives will be learners and facilitators. If your goal is to be a learner evolving into a C-Suite executive rising to the peak of your industry, then EdTech is your facilitator. Find your tribe.

## Appendix

An Insight topic :Decentralised finance – a practitioner led approach.
Let us now take a look at how EIDA approaches a new and complex topic such as Decentralised Finance. This is a nascent but increasingly important topic for risk management professionals. EIDA shall deliver an EdTech course on DeFi based on the learnings contained below. This is an insight into what a master practitioner considers to be relevant on a burning industry topic. From this, EIDA will use the tools of EdTech to create a compelling product for professionals to advance their knowledge.

Decentralised Finance (DeFi) refers to a financial model/system which integrates distributed ledger technology (DLT) into traditional financial structures. DeFi can be defined as the transformation of traditional financial products into products that operate without an intermediary via smart contracts on a blockchain.

*What is blockchain?*

Blockchain is a particular type or subset of so-called DLT. It is a way of recording and sharing data across multiple data stores (also known as ledgers), which each have the exact same data records and are collectively maintained and controlled by a distributed network of computer servers, which are called nodes. Blockchain is a mechanism that employs an encryption method known as cryptography and uses (a set of) specific mathematical algorithms to create and verify a continuously growing data structure – to which data can only be added and from which existing data cannot be removed – that takes the form of a chain of "transaction blocks" which functions as a distributed ledger. While cryptocurrencies create a decentralised store of value, separate from existing fiat currencies, DeFi offers a decentralised or an 'open alternative' to financial services (e.g.savings, insurance, loans) that are currently provided by traditional financial institutions. In principle, any existing financial service that is centralised could be transferred to a similar decentralised financial service. The DeFi ecosystem includes smart contracts, digital assets, decentralised apps (dApps) and open-source protocols. Using smart contract blockchains, such as Ethereum, dApps can be built to create products to facilitate instantaneous transactions which, in time, will be more efficient than their centralised equivalents.

An open and transparent financial system that is universally accessible is a compelling value proposition. By using immutable public ledgers dApps remove the requirement for a central authority improves accessibility and makes financial services more affordable. The open-source nature of DeFi and the digitisation of assets expedites the development of a wide variety of innovative financial tools and services.

# From Delivery To Impact – EdTech's Next Frontier

## Derek Ariss

Head of Innovation Education at Lightbulb Capital Pte. Ltd.

### Introduction

The other day I met Chris, a young friend, who was telling me about an executive education program they had completed. Surprisingly Chris' tone was deflated. "Derek, I've finished this exec-ed program endorsed by my company," Chris sighed.
"Sounds great," I replied. "Why do you seem down?"
"I don't understand. I spent a lot of time on this course because my boss asked me to. I did the online program, got my certificate but got nothing, - no feedback from management. The company spent a lot of money on this, and it's getting me nowhere."

This conversation made me think about improvements needed in the executive education system. This is what I call the learning dilemma in executive education. Organisations are implementing programs for employees to meet their strategic requirements. Yet, this effort is not translating to tangible, measurable business results. Why and how can we change this?

### Background

The world of business is changing rapidly. For companies to stay relevant, they must continuously upskill their staff on pertinent topics. Application of new knowledge must funnel into the business. Executive education is seen as a critical strategic tool and is a high priority for corporations; it also becomes big business. **(1)(2)** Every university has a separate department, and online learning has made the marketplace even bigger and more accessible to all. Components of success, such as excellent content, online platforms, expertise, and relevant project work, appear to be in place. We know that companies like Coursera, Udemy, Emeritus, and CFTE deliver digitally world-class programs to learners. Information sources are leading academics and experienced practitioners. Courses include practical exercises and project work which contribute to experiential learning. All stakeholders, managers, educators, and learners, are spending resources and effort to make learning work for the organisation. Everything seems to be in place, yet the expected impact of meeting the business's strategic objectives often cannot be observed. The application of the learning for impact fails.

The sequence of events leading from learning to successful application seems logicalenough. First, senior management spend time and resources creating their business strategy, allocating training budget to develop staff to support their strategic objectives. Second, human resources and line management spend time identifying programs and suitable learners. In their minds, the staff is expected to apply the knowledge from these programs. Third, educators are hired to develop and deliver learning programs using the best training methodologies and processes. Fourth, learners allocate time and energy to absorb the new content and look for ways of applying what they have learned at work.

All stakeholders have a role in the process, so it should work. But often, it doesn't.  Program participation does not correlate with participants accomplishing organisational strategic goals. Sometimes the purpose is lost, and employees find the programs irrelevant. A Gallup study indicated that only 4 out of 10 employees feel that formal learning and growth opportunities exist in their companies. **(3)** If the process were better aligned, we would expect that employees would agree that growth and learning opportunities recommended by management aligned with organisational strategy and their personal objectives. Learners would attend programs, apply new insights and deliver a tangible outcome in line with corporate strategy. We want to propose a solution to the dilemma in this chapter. It is a combination of shaping human behaviour and leveraging technology. It will explore the next frontier of professional education and recommend improvements to the existing model. Let's start by introducing the concepts of "delivery" and "impact" and what they specifically mean in the realm of executive education.

### Delivery

We define delivery as the ability to impart new knowledge to the learner. Traditionally, delivery involves how an educator designs and conveys the learning experience to their audience. Delivery methods and technologies must cater to the participants' objectives to create "impact." Typical delivery approaches are; Instructor-led, web-based, and mobile training. Educators have many options to use these various approaches and combine them appropriately when "delivering." A qualitative test for educators will always be to ask themselves: "How will I deliver the information to learners for them to understand, relate to, and empower them to apply it in the workplace immediately?

### Impact

Impact is defined as the ability to absorb the newly acquired knowledge and deliver immediate tangible results at the workplace. Benefits of impact occur in 4 areas: productivity (the application of learning to improve the outputs of the learner), product quality (the application of the learning to create product improvements by the learner), employee retention (the application of the knowledge resulting in improved engagement levels between the learner and the organisation), and performance management (the application of learning resulting in positive contributions by the learner at work which are recognised and recorded).

If delivery is done well, and the knowledge is applied effectively, we would expect positive results in all four areas.

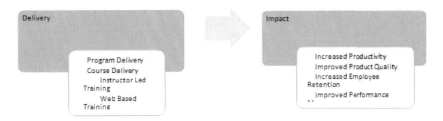

Diagram: Learning and Impact Relationship

## The Actors

Let's look at the three main actors in this delivery-impact relationship; the managers, educators, and learners - and consider adjustments.

## The Managers

The managers (both HR and management) implement the strategic goals from senior management by focusing on questions like: How can the best business value be created from the learner's experience? How can management better support the learner to produce results to create business value? Managers assess their staff's capabilities and existing skills. They identify skill gaps that need filling to meet organisational strategic goals; they enrol staff into the appropriate program to develop the desired skills and record results after program completion. Lastly, they identify if the creation of impact occurs after program attendance.

To support the role of the learner, managers need to link learning to work. To do this, managers must create learning experiences at work to reinforce classroom learning. Management also plays a vital role in shepherding staff attendance to support learning in the job environment. In my experience, this does not occur. Management usually delivers only the process's administrative steps.

To drive impact, managers must become "Catalysts for Change" and go beyond the normal administrative process. A behavioural mindset shift is vital. Managers must change from being passive processing players to owning the staff learning outcomes. An employee study done by Degreed and Harvard Business Publishing, "How the Workforce Learns 2019," concluded that managers have the opportunity to become "Catalysts for Learning." Management involvement is linked to employee performance and staff development. The research highlights the opportunity for managers to "actively" improve employees' learning experiences and professional development by setting learning goals and offering projects to enhance learning skills, and provide regular feedback **(4).** This is recommended.

## Technology And Managers

What is technology's role here? Often, managers have their learning process data in multiple locations and across varying formats. At the best of times, it's challenging to track, manage and analyse effectively.

Imagine if the data was in one place and transparent to all actors. Some technology platforms make this possible. Imagine managers using a system where learning, workforce, human resource management planning, and analytics are integrated. Learning management systems (LMS) have been around for a while, but having seamless cross-functionality is where the future needs to be. Though there are various providers, one player worth noting is **Sum Total Systems**. Sum Total Systems provides software services and systems that include learning management, workforce management, HR, planning, and analytics. The management benefits are tremendous since all critical components of the learning process are managed under one platform.

## The Educators

Educators take the strategic direction from management, develop content, and deliver learning programs. Here, educators must consider the critical factors necessary in accomplishing great results when teaching with technology.

Similar to managers, educators need to apply a behavioural shift involving owning the learning process. But, the type of shift required is different. Educators need to focus on delivering the best learning for participants' needs and ensuring better follow-through of application after class.

Educators must shift from the delivery of programs, where they go through the motions of "educating" participants, to having ownership of the participant program outcomes. Follow-through will assist here. This follow-through concept means that educators are firstly involved in assessing learning results for the participants. Secondly, educators can confirm with management that application and learning in the workplace have occurred. Questions that educators can ask themselves to start the behavioural shift are: what are the learning objectives? How does the program align with the desired business outputs from management? How can I ensure this happens through the activities I create for the participants? By answering these questions, a new mindset in the educator starts to form.

Thankfully, this mindset change is starting to happen. Earlier this year, at an online EdTech Conference, I listened to a talk titled "Trends in Learning and Employee Development". I was surprised that one of the speakers emphasised that L&D's purpose was both to meet employees' goals and needs through learning and to see employees as more human with specific needs.

Earlier, we mentioned follow-through. We know that when constructive feedback is provided, learners improve their performance. Linked to proper feedback is the requirement of follow-through. The concept of follow-through in program delivery is essential; however, it is often ignored. Follow-through ensures that learning is consistent, on track, and the behaviour is transferable to environments outside the class. It makes the application of learning powerful. It is ignored because delivering follow-through is hard to do without management support or guidance. Educators can take on further accountability of program delivery results by committing to follow-through.

## Technology And Educators

From a technology standpoint, educators must feel comfortable with technology. Educators identify how to best use technology in meeting learning requirements. For instance, what is the right combination of virtual instructor, real instructor, and e-learning to develop a great learning experience? Educators can consider the most effective technology tools to provide guidance, present information, design practice, provide feedback, assess performance and current information to learners when it comes to delivery. For example, on delivery, should learning be all online or part face-to-face and part virtual instructor-led? Will content come from websites or the company learning system? On assessments, what is the best assessment format to consider? Is it better to do online testing, simulations, scenarios, or physical project work? Upon course completion, where would the best follow-up exercises occur so that learning and practice are followed-through?

Lastly, when determining the best technology for program delivery, educators should consider how they report back to management on learners' performance. Ideally, assessments would be part of a centralised learning system in the organisation. Information is accessible and visible to all three actors. In such a system, feedback would be tracked, recorded, and reviewed. Data could be collected to identify learners' performance levels relative to their peers'. Systems like, e.g., **Androgogic's Totara Learning Managemen**t system pull together learning, training, and talent development processes and record this data. Tech plays a role in stitching relevant information together and making it accessible to the actors. The result is effective decisions.

## The Learners

The learners are the "doers" of this learning process. They convert the information from programs into desired business outcomes. Conversion to outcomes will only occur if the learner genuinely has a desire to learn. Intention and commitment are the key factors here. Unfortunately, commitment levels by learners are often low both in the physical and digital realm. e.g.40-80% of online courses never get completed. A low learner commitment results in little application in the workplace **(5)**. High commitment levels occur when the learner believes that learning is essential and relevant to their career/personal development. This is a human driver that organisations can and should leverage. **(6)** Hence, the results of applying newly acquired knowledge must link to performance objectives (KPI's). This is the crucial tactical tool for management to utilise.

## Technology And Learners

Concerning technology, learners are subject to various earlier discussed delivery formats. The formats used will, however, allow assessment between the learner and educator to occur. Digital online testing, video presentations, scenario evaluation, and reactions to simulations are all used to provide learning feedback. When a learner completes a program in an integrated learning management system, the educator's score and comments are recorded and available to all three actors. e.g., Own the room: Communication training uses virtual instructors, staged learning, video assessment of learner performance, post-program feedback, and assessment all in one package. Learners and managers get assessment scores as well as follow-up exercises and suggestions.

**A Framework To Get To The Next Frontier**

When moving from delivery to impact, all three actors must change behavioural mindsets and leverage technology. We will discuss the existing process and then the newly suggested approach.

In the existing process, the relationship between actors is one-directional, siloed with limited feedback between the parties.

**Diagram: Existing Process**

What is required is a collaborative and multidirectional relationship between the three actors, with technology as a critical enabler. Technology provides the edge of creating a complete learning ecosystem, where administration, documentation, tracking, and even development plans are accessed.

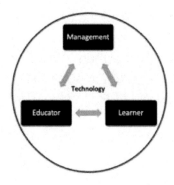

**Diagram: Proposed Process**

All actors can use this one platform which consolidates and connects information. Sumtotal's approach for learning management systems has headed this direction.

Collaboration between the actors ensures that the best results occur. When the management works with the educators and learners, they receive feedback on the education process and track desired outputs. When the educators work with management and the learners, they develop and deliver relevant and engaging content. When the learner works with the managers and educators, they receive content, regular feedback support, and appropriate practice and follow-through work.

As a basis for the framework, we will use Gagne's nine events of learning. This framework is built on knowledge of how humans process information. It specifies the necessary conditions for people to learn **(7)**. We have modified the conditions to take into account all three actors.

The framework suggests nine events of instruction which are:

1. Gaining the attention of the learner
2. Informing the learner the objective of the program
3. Identifying prior learning related to the learner
4. Delivery of the content to learners
5. Guiding the learner on learned content
6. Practising the learning
7. Providing feedback and what was learned
8. Assessing the performance
9. Enhance retention transferring to the job

When we map the actions of each actor in the existing system against Gagne's 9 events, the gaps in performance become apparent (see (?) Table 1). For example, we see an opportunity for educators to be involved with managers and learners at the Gain Attention stage.

| Gagnes 9 Events of Instruction | HR / Manager Actions | Educator Actions | Learner Actions |
|---|---|---|---|
| Gain Attention | X | ? | X |
| Inform Learners of Objectives | ? | X | X |
| Prior Learning | ? | X | X |
| Present content | | X | X |
| Provide Guidance | | X | X |
| Practice | ? | X | X |
| Provide Feedback | ? | X | X |
| Assess Performance | ? | X | X |
| Transfer to Job | ? | ? | ? |

**Table 1 Existing Process Identified Gaps**

Here, we identify that managers gain the learner's attention, but often do not inform them of the learning objectives or look at the prior learning to understand best how previous experience can impact the new learning experience. The communication of learning objectives is often left to the educator to do.

In addition, the managers may fall short in providing feedback, getting involved in the practice, and assessing the learner's performance following the learning event.

The manager's limited interaction hampers the transfer of learning to on the job. The ability to implement learning immediately into the job is vital to developing impact. Research shows that practising knowledge and applying it immediately is essential because" enactment enhances memory by serving as an elaborative encoding strategy" **(8)**. Lastly, the manager does not link the learning to overall performance in the existing structure as part of the learner's development plan.

In the existing process, the educator misses gaining the learner's attention by connecting the content to the learner's job. The purpose of the learning is unclear. In addition, the educator does not do the follow-up with the learner to transfer the learner experience to the job environment.

For the learner, the gap is in transferring knowledge from learning into the job. There is little reinforcement and practice, and after a few days, the knowledge will be lost. Note: Hermann Ebbinghaus developed the theory that humans start losing the memory of learned knowledge over time. We lose most information in a matter of days or weeks unless we consciously review it. **(9)** Hence, frequent regular reinforcement of learning is necessary. In the proposed framework, behavioural shifts and technology solve the dilemma. As the relationship is more like a collaborative network communication between actors, the implementation of technology fills in the gaps (Table 2).

Note that opportunities replace the gaps in the previous framework, and the managers take on the role of "Catalysts for Learning."
Here, managers have ownership of the learning process with the learner. Managers communicate face-to-face or digitally and agree on learner and company objectives. The manager clarifies the program's purpose and the reason for the learners' participation. Lastly, expected impact at work from the program is reviewed and agreed upon. The communication of this information would be recorded in the performance management system.

The manager can review prior learning and design the practice exercises that the learners would experience. These benefit the learner's experience and make the learning relevant. This information can cascade to the educators to apply in the programs. The teaching could be in various forms, e.g., online tests, scenarios, role plays.

The next opportunity is for managers to review the learner's performance of the program and decide how best to enhance learning. For instance, good performers are allocated projects, whereas weaker performers receive additional support in training and testing. Managers can consider how this learning would be practised in the work environment using various projects, assignments, and reports.

Managers can also design learners transfer to job experiences at work. Learners will perform the application of knowledge in the workplace, receive feedback, and have it recorded. In turn, Managers would allocate appropriate rewards and recognition. More importantly, projects that the organisation needs to have delivered can be assigned to proper learners so that on-the-job application serves two purposes.

Lastly, managers would complete a final assessment with the Learners that links into the organisation's performance review process. These outputs would be recorded and used by management to keep track of the results created by the learning programs. This accountability of performance is core to ensuring learners have the drive to apply what they have learned.

Following this new proposed framework, there will be more interaction between managers, educators, and learners. In the active process, the involvement of managers and educators ensures that material taught is delivered, practised, and improved through regular feedback.

| | HR / Manager Actions | Educator Actions | Learner Actions |
|---|---|---|---|
| Gagnes 9 Events of Instruction | | | |
| Gain Attention | Informs Learner of attendance | NA | Learner informed of attendance |
| Inform Learners of Objectives | Opportunity for manager to communicate with learner, agree objectives and outcomes. Information is put into learning system and performance system | Informs Learner of Objective of Class | Understands course but not how it relates to work |
| Prior Learning | Opportunithy to review prior kniowledge with learner to identify further learning opportunities | Presents experiences that stimulate prior learning | Is reminded of prior learning |
| Present content | NA | Delivers content in most appropriate formats. E.g.Online, digital, elearning,video based, performance based, Face-to-Face, Mobile | Receives content and learns |
| Provide Guidance | NA | Gives learner examples, may not be related to work | Accepts and internalises guidance, but examples may apply to work |
| Practice | Opportunity for Manager to design excercises and projects for the learner. The practice will be for the benefit the learner and contribute to the organisations business results | Gives practice activities, may not be related to work | Receives practice e.g. simulations, case studies, tests, project work |
| Provide Feedback | NA | Feedback is immediate specific and corrective | Receives instructor and peer feedback. No feedback from Management |
| Assess Performance | Opportunity for Manger to review the learners performance and design appropriate experiences that improve the learners performance and meet business needs. Information is logged onto the learning system. | Performance is assessed , certificates handed out. Management Informed | Completes assessment receives certificate |
| Transfer to Job | Ideal opportunity to test learner on the field and benefit organisation. Manager can design practice and evaluate learner. Provide regular feedback. Log into LMS and record progress. | Opportunity to contribute | Opportunity to seek out support and work with management and can record progress on LMS. |
| Assessment included in development plan | Ideal opporutunity to leverage performance management and personal development of the learner to create impact. Logged into Performance Management System. Suggest learning resources. (Courses, videos, articles) experiences . | NA | Perfect opportunity for learner to work with management application of learning at workto improve impact in productivity, quality, engagement, and retention |

Also educators would use real work examples for learners to understand.

Once the teaching was complete, the program would continue. The next part of the program would be for the manager to create an opportunity for the learner to practice what they have learned. And the manager would provide the learner with feedback to improve as the learning was done in the work environment. Lastly, the manager assesses the outcomes of the learner in the work environment. They record them in the performance management system.

Technology sits at the core of collaboration between actors. It tracks the communication between manager, educator, and learner. It records the learning objectives in line with the strategic intent. Technology assists in presenting the content, tracking the learners' assessment, providing feedback, and monitoring the progress after the classroom learning. It is also the platform where the transfer from classroom to job results is recorded. Once in the system, results are used to input feedback connection to the organisation's performance management system.

This result will improve productivity, quality, employee retention, and performance management.

Am I the only one suggesting to supercharge executive education with technology? No! The Practices That Set Learning Organisations Apart," feature in MIT Sloan, stated that "Technology also plays an increasingly important role as a platform for enabling Learning and Development to support a company's organisational strategy." **(10)**

I can't help to think that if management had filled in these performance gaps, my conversation with Chris would have been a little more akin to the following dialogue: "Derek, I love my job! I just finished an exec-ed program through our LMS —my boss endorsed the program. We spoke about my career and how this program aligns with my progression plan. I attended the program, learned how to apply my new skills in the workplace, and subsequently, I was challenged to immediately use what I had learned on one of our company projects. I took it pretty seriously because it's all linked to our performance system. My boss liked what I did and suggested a couple of additional online programs to complement what I learned. I'm faster, more productive, and keener than ever to keep contributing. Gottago. I've got some additional practice to do for this upcoming project."

Welcome to the new frontier.

# Infusing EdTech Into University Curriculum To Enhance Career Preparation

## Sunshine Farzan

Group Head of Marketing and Communications at Tricor Group

Technology is a potentially transformational resource for students. But, many higher education institutions around the world are struggling to maximise its benefits in the classroom, during the networking and job search process, and throughout a student's professional development.

Notably, the COVID-19 pandemic has underscored the importance and relevance of EdTech, accelerating digital adoption and forcing most higher learning institutions online to transform how students learn. Outside the classroom, advances in EdTech are also changing how we prepare for careers, search for jobs, train and network.

This chapter explores how career planning, which many would argue forms the very basis for university education, can be greatly enhanced by focused investment in EdTech. EdTech is playing a key role in helping students prepare for the world of work, mastering not only the latest technical skills needed in today's workplace but developing and nurturing the indispensable soft skills they'll need to thrive.

In a fast-paced business environment that demands upskilling and lifelong learning, we explore the ways that EdTech can be leveraged by universities to enhance students' career development.

### Encouraging Collaboration

Teamwork makes the dream work. Group projects do not end with schooling. The word "teamwork" (or similarly "team player") can be found on many job descriptions and key requirements. An extensive range of technology can be implemented in schools to develop the communication, project management and cross-cultural collaboration skills that are essential to being part of, and leading, high-performing teams.

Owing to the mass virtualization triggered by the COVID-19 pandemic, educators worldwide are shifting classroom practices from predominantly individual learning exercises to collaborative learning models. Notably, there are a growing number of ways that technology is boosting collaboration in learning. Here are some of the main applications:

1. **Communication Tools:** Classrooms are using technologies for content development, including document sharing, editing and presentation. Some notable examples include:

   - Microsoft Office 365 and Google's G Suite each provide a collaborative environment for document creation and editing.

- With Blogger, students have a digital space for blogging and working with peers to create content, engage in discussion and provide feedback.
- Padlet creates real-time discussions walls, using audio, video, music, photos and text.
- The multi-purpose tool Wakelet creates a digital space for curating content and sharing ideas on projects.
- Story2 is platform that helps students tell their story for career searching.
- Buncee is another multipurpose tool for digital storytelling and presentations.

2. **Project Management:** Virtual student classrooms can collaborate on project work like never before using some of these platforms:

- For managing project workflow: The leaders in this space are Microsoft Teams and Slack
- Project management (specific for education): Headrush, BeAnything
- For specific assignments and task management: Asana, Zoho, Monday, Trello
- For virtual meetings: Many options but the leaders are likely Google Hangouts, Zoom, GoToMeeting; Microsoft Teams and Tencent Meeting (Tencent releases Zoom-like video conferencing app • TechNode)
- To engage project mentors: Nepris, Educurious
- Discussion platform: Voxer

3. **Game-Based Learning & Training:** This area is increasingly playing an important role in education by encouraging students to collaborate,
   - **Platforms include:** Quizlet Live, Kahoot!, and Gimkit use game-based learning to promote collaborative problem-solving.
- Notably, with game-based learning,educators can immediately act upon data and provide feedback to their students.

## Developing Critical Thinking Skills

In a digital work environment, the focus on critical thinking skills is amplified. In the absence of direct one-on-one training and feedback, the learning models of today must nurture independence and promote problem-solving in all areas of a student's life. The better students develop these skills, the more prepared they are to grow as learners, expanding their acumen for problem-solving and making connections in the world around them.

The problem is that technology is not always taught and used in this way, with some making the argument that technology can reduce critical thinking capacity. The technology itself will not develop critical-thinking skills in students. That is the educator's role, and although today's bourgeoning technologies are powerful tools, the educator's application of these technologies will determine if they help or hinder the development of students' critical thinking skills.

In an Adobe-commissioned global Creative Problem-Solving Study, 85% of educators reported that creative problem-solving skills are in high demand for senior level and higher-paying careers. Meanwhile, 75% of the polled educators agreed that the roles and functions requiring critical reasoning and creative problem-solving skills are less likely to be replaced by digital technologies like AI and robotic process automation.

While we cannot depend solely on innovative technologies as a panacea for our problems, we can leverage them to enhance how we strategically approach and deconstruct everyday challenges. But to realise the full potential of technology in education, we must make some systemic changes to how we teach, integrate and apply technology.

Here are three ways that technology can be leveraged to increase critical thinking:

### 1. Interactive applications can motivate students and improve academic achievements

By engaging students in interactive, multisensory activities, educators can promote elaboration, questioning and explanation. At the same time, multimedia interactive learning can improve student engagement and performance.

In particular, game-based learning and simulations can be particularly powerful tools to help students apply their prior knowledge, acquire new knowledge in new settings, test hypotheses, identify trends, apply evidence and logic to make arguments, solve problems and learn from mistakes. Subsequently, students are able to take ownership of their learning which in turn improves retention of information.

Compared to traditional learning, here are some key stats on game-based learning:

- An increase of up to a 20% in self-confidence of the student.
- An 11% increase in conceptual knowledge.
- A 90% increase in retention when learning.
- A 20% increase in practical knowledge.
- Up to a 300% increase in completed tasks.

### 2. Diverse representations across media clarify complex concepts and procedures

Students are better able to grasp complex concepts when instructions and assignments are explained using a diversity of channels (such as verbal, visual, graphic, symbolic, etc.) and instructional formats in media (infographics, videos, audio, simulations, etc.) Digital learning environments nurture aptitude for critical thinking and increase the accessibility of content by offering students more options for applying their knowledge and skills.

### 3. Technology-driven learning environments help students apply knowledge in real-world environments

Multimedia learning environments that emphasise the student's understanding and practical application of subject matters can increase student achievement and outcomes. Presenting problems in a real-world context makes digital learning more meaningful and accessible to students, helping them to understand the importance of what they are learning. In addition, by encouraging students to connect theoretical ideas to daily experiences, critical thinking is bolstered.

## Building Soft Skills

Many educators make the mistake of using EdTech to only focus on hard skills, namely technical proficiencies, rather than unlocking the power of soft skills. For those not on the bandwagon of soft skills yet, they relate to our personality traits and work style. So, soft skills determine our aptitude for creative thinking, analytical thinking, critical thinking and problem solving.

Soft skills play a key role in our professional lives. Whether we're hoping for a raise or looking to secure a new job, soft skills can be a determining factor. The best part about soft skills is that they're usually transferable across industry sectors, functions, career levels and even cultures.

Upskilling and a desire for continuous lifelong learning is one such soft skill that is needed by companies. A recent IBM report anticipates that in the next three years, more than 120 million people will need upskilling or reskilling. Meanwhile, in just five years' time, the average length of training needed to meet skills needs has increased from three to 36 days. Hiring for traditional skills is simply not enough, as rapid digital transformation is causing some skill sets to become obsolete. Instead, companies need to focus on upskilling and recruiting lifelong learners who have the ability to constantly learn new skills and navigate technology that might not even yet exist.

There are a score of other soft skills that are needed in the post-pandemic workplace, as identified by executives:

- Adaptability and versatility
- Work ethic
- Innovation and digital mindset (not the technical skills per se but rather than mindset)
- Active listening
- Communication
- Collaboration
- Emotional intelligence

## Aligning Personal Brand With Career Aspirations

Personal branding has become a frequently used buzzword. But there's a good reason for that: our personal brand impacts the way we are perceived in the workplace and therefore has a significant impact on our overall career trajectory. Online personal branding as well as social media brand reputation management are critical to communicating the distinctive value a student can offer prospective employers.

Educators must be increasingly aware of how the power of EdTech can be used to build students' personal brands. They must be proactive and create an environment where students feel comfortable using social networks and digital tools to explore what's out there and share their passions with the world.

To begin a personal branding framework, lessons should center around topics like leadership, ethics, digital storytelling and marketing –aimed at showing students how they discover their own unique passions and niches so they can ultimately distinguish themselves in a crowded and competitive marketplace.

Here are the five steps educators must encourage students to take:

1. **Discover your passion and find your niche:** Students must be encouraged to identify what motivates and interests them, from an academic, personal and career (if ready) perspective. But to do this requires self-reflection and goal setting, with an eye on the internship application process and/or post-university plans. Students should start with a simple list of their various interests and build out from there. For each passion, educators should encourage them to come up with ways that they can build upon them digitally. Basically, a digital personal branding strategy should begin using these passions. Furthermore, students can use EdTech tools to take career assessments to help pair their passions with career paths.

2. **Learn from the experiences of others:** Through the digital landscape, students should be encouraged to access video tutorials, blog posts, hashtags and thought leadership experts that align with their passion and niche. Combining these perspectives with their own personal experiences, students will accumulate a wealth of knowledge and lay the building blocks for harnessing their passion and becoming subject matter experts.

3. **Share curated content and join the conversation:** The previous two steps were foundational. This step is where visibility begins. In order to build a reputation and a personal brand, students must develop a platform to showcase their passion. They should be encouraged to use social networks to retweet others in their field of passion and even leave comments on others' content they find interesting. They may also be compelled to join discussion forums so they can become part of the conversation.

4. **Create your own content:** While learning from others and sharing those lessons are critical, true personal branding comes to life when students feel comfortable enough to share their own thoughts, experiences and knowledge on subject matter. Encourage students to create their own original content, such as videos, blogs, podcasts, presentations, online courses, etc. Doing this will help them find their own voice, while encouraging them to use EdTech tools to further explore their passions and build their own brand.

5. **Build your network and make connections:** Students should be taught about proper digital networking, learning basic principles that can empower the way they build relationships online. First and foremost, they must recognise that proper networking in the context of personal branding is never a selfish act. It should always be done in the context of what they can contribute and how they can help others. Secondly, it's never about immediate results either. It takes time to build a network and beginning sooner rather than later is helpful. Over time, students can learn how to build relationships of mutual, synergistic value.

# EdTech For Professionals

## Mridula Pradhan

Consultant - Bid Writing for Learning Solutions and IT Services

### The New Reality

Though a professional degree may assure professional competence and monetary gains to begin with, a degree or even knowledge gained in a conference room does not guarantee sustainable results or professional growth. What is taught in a seminar or a pre-packaged training session may be out of date tomorrow and irrelevant to what professionals are seeking to achieve in their professional life.

EdTech offers a fluid, efficient and convenient way for professionals to tap into a global peer network and benefit from different perspectives, gain insights or even change direction and achieve meaningful professional goals.

### Collaborative Learning In A Real-World Context

EdTech enables professionals (and executives at all hierarchical levels) to meet with each other virtually in a real-world context to exchange knowledge, gain actionable insights and create a powerful professional network. A network of like-minded people who can sympathise with what they're worried or frustrated about. EdTech is informing and enthusing professionals to exchange knowledge and share advice. They're no longer passive consumers of knowledge, but active allies.

### Easy Access, Wider Reach

All organisations and all professions now have easy access to a wide array of digitally robust platforms and rich, valuable content that entices professionals to immerse themselves involuntarily. Video-conferencing platforms such as Zoom, Google Meet, Microsoft Teams and WebEx have made live interaction and real-time collaboration possible from a distance. The digital space is crammed with outreach possibilities and busy, overworked professionals no longer find themselves socially isolated and unable to scale their skills.

### Future-Led Professional Development

Professionals have often failed or faltered because they have had only earnings and profits in mind. Though a professional degree may assure monetary gains to begin with, a degree doesn't guarantee sustainable results or professional growth. Professional situations can no longer be tackled using an outdated approach.

Empowered by EdTech, professionals are re-evaluating their skills and even adapting new, influential personas. By being digitally well-connected, professionals learn by talking to each other, exchanging theoretical and practical knowledge and getting advice on achieving professional goals. At the same time, EdTech is enabling professionals to learn about and adapt to major advances in technology to reduce costs and improve efficiency and to deliver better outcomes and business results.

## Global Trends

Those with legal, medical, engineering or managerial skill sets are also embracing EdTech and acquiring the latest, most-sought after skills, seeking to advance their careers or prepare themselves for the dynamic future.

Seeing the exponential growth in the highly specialised and regulated EdTech sector, law firms were quick to gear up in providing services as legal practitioners specialised in the areas of EdTech lending and finance, funding and investment, mergers and acquisitions, intellectual property and data protection laws.

However, it was only afterwards that law firms caught on to the need to upskill legal professionals by making investments in knowledge management-related resources. It is now becoming increasingly evident to law firms that investing in digital upskilling programmes can pay substantial dividends in terms of lawyer and staff development and as a consequence in client service, client retention, and business development. Though adoption rates among legal professionals were low initially, they're now conscious of the digital divide. To cash-in on the rapidly growing opportunity, a number of platforms are now offering hyper-relevant legal educationacross the globe.

## The Big Picture

### New York

First on the scene was AltaClaro, New York, founded in 2016 by a corporate and banking lawyer with 15 years of experience in large, high-revenue law firms, both in-house and government. AltaClaro is an innovative experiential learning platform providing attorneys with universal access to interactive professional education to bring legal associates to practice-readiness. AltaClaro makes it possible for firms to facilitate fast, meaningful training to their associates: increasing associate effectiveness, drastically reducing training costs, and reducing unconscious bias. Lawyers on AltaClaro's unique platform leverage cutting edge technology for education and learn by engaging in mock transactions, simulations, interactive assessments and virtual feedback sessions with seasoned practitioners that help professionals gain the vital practical skills they need to become "practice-ready".

### Brazil

Civics Educação, a platform created in 2018 by an outstanding young Brazilian professional whilst he was pursuing his Masters at Stanford University, offers practical legal courses on Company Law, Civil Procedure, Digital Law, Law and Start-ups, Arbitration, Contract Law, Real Estate Law, Mergers and Acquisitions, Sports Law, Environmental Law and Constitutional Law (at low cost). The courses are taught by lawyers associated with the most well-known law offices in

Brazil. The free courses on Constitutional Law, Access to Justice and others for preparing young professionals for jobs are also recognised as a legal and valid teaching modality throughout Brazil.

## India

In India, the e-learning platform NotJustLex, intended as a finishing school for law students in India, went live with its first certificate course in August 2020. The platform offers specialised online programmes that are designed and moderated by a dual qualified (England & Wales and India) corporate lawyer with a post-qualification experience of more than 14 years. The platform was sparked by concerns that most young lawyers were ill-equipped to handle dynamic situations because legal education continued to be theoretical; not practical or 'participatory'. The founder's mission is clear:

*"There's a huge gap in what students learn in law colleges and what recruiters at law firms expect. Everyone learns contract law in theory, but no one has seen an actual shareholder agreement. Our legal education system doesn't favour practical applicability. So, commercial knowledge and how the law applies across sectors is very low."*

To bridge the gap between theoretical learning and professional expectation and to provide participants a distinct professional edge in today's highly competitive corporate environment, the focus of NotJustLex is on participatory learning, something that is often not possible in an academic setting. And, it's EdTech that's added this extra dimension to education and the continuing professional development of legal professionals.

Enhelion, another EdTech platform for professional education in India, offers over 400 courses drafted by experienced lawyers and industry experts on various topics in the interdisciplinary areas of law, data science and management to professionals across India. In January 2021, the company announced that it had trained 50,000 professionals and was planning to expand its course offerings by 2022. The courses also cover emerging areas such as AI, Robotics and the Law, machine learning, blockchain, ethical hacking and Drone Law.

Looking at collaborative growth, the company has partnered with 40 of the best law firms, one of the best national law schools in the country and a premier university – one that has the status of Institute of National Importance – to provide university-certified learning. With a theory-based education structure, students and even professionals lack the experience required to excel. The tie-ups with private and government bodies helps ensure credible, practical education in the professional world.

With EdTech being created at scale and being consumed with off-the-scale engagement levels, there are now several players in the market. MyLegalStudio infuses theoretical knowledge with practical knowledge and professional inputs from practitioners, examples and case studies to provide quality content that benefits legal practitioners, CA/CS professionals and entrepreneurs.

And the market is in no danger yet of becoming noisy and overcrowded.

# Wang Li He And Bradley Maclean

## Both Co-Founders Of Daisma/Link Education

Everything old is new again, the Rise of EdTech and the Digital Apprenticeship

The world is changing. Gen Z will change the world, too. Born between 1997 and 2007, Gen Z is the first generation born entirely in the internet age, with high mobile phone penetration. They are the largest generational cohort in history, and the future workforce, business owners and global problem-solvers. It's hard to deny, but their attitudes and expectations are destined to shape the next "new normal."

They are a generation of contradictions, and are unlike the millennials that preceded them, who grew up during an economic boom. Gen Z came of age during the Great Recession amidst unprecedented levels of digital connectivity that have more recently been redefined by the global pandemic.

They are aware of and adept at navigating an increasingly polarised geopolitical landscape, saturated in technology and data streamed from smartphones, social media and 24-hour news cycles. For them, knowledge has been commoditised. Gen Z understands that there is no longer a competitive advantage in simply knowing more than others because "Google knows everything". Instead, they live the mantra that the world cares less about not how much you know but more of what you can do with it. This generation will be defined by their abilities to acquire new skills and mindsets, adapt to new contexts, and nurture their educational experiences.

Unlike their millennial predecessors, who struggled to keep pace with rapid changes, early indicators suggest that Gen Z are optimistic, even hopeful that they will find meaningful work and that society will effectively address the severe global challenges currently shaping their world over the coming decades.

Overall expectations remain high for Gen Zs. Though their attitudes and expectations will shape the next normal, the burden of transition rests with today's business leaders as they lay the groundwork for the future, whilst simultaneously battling the ever-disruptive forces reshaping businesses, breaking up industries and seismically changing the competitive landscape. Today's leaders must lay the foundations to establish broad connections with the next generation to effectively understand who they are and how they intend to shape their world.

### Staying Still Is Not An Option – Work-Based Learning Reimagined

Even now, as we near a return to normal, many companies, educational institutions, and governments worldwide continue to scramble to ensure minimal disruption for workers and learners. In recent years, companies have lurched from crisis to crisis to the point where it could be considered as the new normal. At the same time, remote work and remote education has gone mainstream, though their effectiveness remains the subject of endless debates. Though the pandemic has accelerated many of current trending issues, the rise of intelligent technologies reconfiguring roles and subverting the skills mix has long been on the horizon.

Driven by blurred lines between conventional business roles and technology functions, a new approach was always needed.

As digitalisation and human tasks converge, they will be best tackled by people with a broader, more holistic mindset, backed with specialist knowledge and correlated skill-sets. Interestingly, in the new normal, work will not only be about hard skills; it will be about holistic job skills. Employers will look for something beyond just task-oriented or technical skills. Moreover, companies will seek to hire people with creative problem-solving skills, an eye for details and a collaborative mindset, and the ability to deal with ambiguity and complexity. To succeed, Gen Z will need to be specialists, not generalists, skilled in collaboration, communication and problem-solving and experts at social and emotional learning.

## Enter The Modern Digital-First Apprenticeship

With all of the chaos of the past several years, the global knowledge economy is ending, and the world is quickly moving beyond it. What we have now is an innovation economy, where knowledge is commoditised, and the future of work is more about learning and less about education.

The distinction between the two is subtle but critical. Education is about processes and top-down transmission of knowledge, whereas learning is a much wider concept, most of which occurs in a non-educational context. Today, we know that we have a very large and increasing number of contextual learning opportunities as new occupations and disruptive technologies emerge. Less clear, however, are details about the specific skills tomorrow's workers will require. One thing is for certain is that skills, not degrees – will be the currency of the future workplace.

As a result, we need an improved talent development model to help us meet our dynamic and expanding digital economy's skill demands more effectively. But if formal learning alone won't do the trick, what will? Well, as they say in the digital economy: everything old is new again and accordingly interpreted as "to understand the future, we must look to the past."

As such, we should look to scaling a digital-first iteration of the lost art of one-on-one learning that can make the difference. A "modern technology-driven apprenticeship model" is likely to be the answer. Given the challenges of today, an apprenticeship may feel counterintuitive, even antiquated, in the face of intense workplace time pressures. However, with some modernising and a digital-first approach, it could efficiently unlock rapid capability building.

At its core, an apprenticeship has always been a relationship-driven learning model, established in the realities of day-to-day routines. Providing opportunities for novices to gain hands-on knowledge and insights from expert mentors as they gradually grow skills and act with increasing independence.

The added benefit is that the emphasis on learning via apprenticeship is also likely to provide an overall sense of meaning and purpose through work. Though purpose is personal, companies play a critical role in expressing it. For Gen Z, work-life is likely to be increasingly defined by value, not money. Driven to work for an employer that shares their values, they are likely to prioritise enjoying their work and expect it to make a difference in the world. They are less likely to place importance on making a lot of money in their career, but instead seek employers that demonstrate shared values and purpose.

As such, employers that seek to align personal values with business objectives while building a cohesive culture of continuous development will be the hallmark of leading companies in the innovation economy.

Either way, in the face of the increasing shift towards the innovation economy, business cycles will continue to move faster than the people development cycles. The modern digital-first apprenticeship model will be the change the world needs. It will be focused on fostering capability building and cohesive culture through personalised learning and purposeful work, all underscored by EdTech. This approach will be the driving force in sculpting the next generation of specialised workers who are proficient in collaboration, communication and problem-solving.

As you'd expect, technology will be the backbone of the modern apprenticeship, always omnipresent, fostering personalised learning by adjusting three critical mindsets: learning how to learn, the growth mindset, and feeding curiosity. Before then, though, is one of the most challenging steps: creating clear organisational expectations for both learning and teaching.

## Setting Expectations For Learning & Teaching

As businesses are increasingly distributed across remote and hybrid working models, such structural changes are in part why formal, hierarchical learning programs have continually struggled to deliver real lasting impact. Conversely, a modern apprenticeship can leverage this disconnection. Technology allows for a distributed apprenticeship model, but this must be based on the ideals across the business that everyone will need to share two obligations, 1. the responsibility to learn and 2. the responsibility to teach.

Apprenticeships have always flourished in organisations with strong learning cultures. Partly because a learning culture emphasises the importance of every learner taking ownership and ultimate responsibility for their personal/career development and skill-sets, a culture of personal accountability will be key to fostering mindsets and skills. Allowing them to learn in every context, effectively seeking and acting on feedback, self-reflect on their progress, and deliberate practice. These same principles will be needed to be the building blocks for the modern apprenticeship.

## Learning How To Learn

Too often, training and transformation programs fail because they underestimate the skills needed to learn. If this is correct, then learning itself is a skill. Therefore, it can be assumed that as we unlock these mindsets and skills, it will empower learners to boost their personal and professional lives and deliver a life-long competitive edge against their less-engaged peers.

Most formal learning opportunities account for only a small percentage of the learning a professional needs over a career. Everyday experiences and interactions often impact learning opportunities, but only if intentionally treated as such, with every moment counting as a learning opportunity.

The modern apprenticeship will be centred on intentional learning, forcing the workforce to embrace their need to learn; for Gen Z, there will be no offsites, separate workstreams, or extra effort to learn. Instead, their jobs will be structured to provide an almost unconscious, reflexive form of behaviour.

Continuous learning is the default mode and mindset in which intentional learners continually operate. And even though they are experiencing all the same daily moments and routines as the rest of us, they extract more out of each of these occasions because every experience, conversation, meeting, and deliverable carries an opportunity to develop and grow.

These modern apprenticeships will be built on a solid foundation of self-efficacy, using technology to reinforce the belief that each action is aligned to the desired outcome.
But why?

The purpose is to establish a growth mindset and feed curiosity. These two frames of mind or, more fittingly, "mindsets", serve as especially powerful fuel for learners, and more importantly, neither is fixed or immovable. These mindsets are powerful and often exert tremendous influence on the behaviours of employees. Part of the power of these mindsets is that they can be developed.

## Setting Small, Clear Goals

While goals have long been used to measure employee performance, organisations rarely entrench goal-setting processes into learning. A critical element of modern apprenticeships is to focus on intentional learning by anchoring intangible goals, using curiosity as a source of force rather than a distractor. Game mechanics are the best option to push systematic, clear and bite-sized goals towards learners and will likely result in improved engagement, alignment of expectations, and elevated overall performance.

The challenge is that far too often, the set goals become unmet goals. EdTech will provide effective strategies for achieving and aligning learning goals through three key elements:

1. *Defined, clear and immediate goals:* Learners will be provided with dynamic but stretched goals, visualised roadmaps on the best way to achieve them, real-time coaching and feedback.

2. *Optimally Time-bound:* Deadlines have a way of focusing the mind. These goals will have a defined period in which to meet. While the period of time for meeting a target depends on the nature of the goal itself, the platform should provide a dynamic timeline that accompanies optimal "goldilocks" timing. Demonstrating the timing should be adequate to allow long enough to establish new behaviour, and short enough to produce a sense of urgency and momentum.

3. *Coaches & Mentors:* Learners will be more likely to achieve goals when they enlist others to help and hold them accountable. Feedback needs to be real-time and on-demand. Chatbots and other virtual mentors promise to play a key role in supporting and monitoring progress on achieving goals.

## Removing Distractions

Though Gen Z is the first generation born entirely in the internet age, they face the same distractions and expectations as their millennial colleagues. We need to protect time for learning. Even though the apprenticeship is highly structured, learning needs to be personalised and on-demand. Learners will need a sense of control to balance their time and responsibilities while gaming mechanics will prompt and push reminders throughout the day.

## Actionable Feedback

Feedback is familiar to most professionals; we understand its benefits even when we don't love receiving it. Learners need to be incentivised to seek feedback and actively pursue it within the apprenticeship model. They need to recognise that we all have blind spots that, without intervention, will halt their progress.

Though most likely connected to behavioural triggers, these incentives will include mechanics that incentivise and recognise feedback-seeking behaviours. Like Coaching and Mentoring, Chatbots and other virtual mentors have the potential to play a key role in providing feedback on a real-time and on-demand basis against dynamically updated business and learning objectives.

## Force Deliberate Practice

Practice, especially practice in context, remains critical to learning. The pattern of trying, failing, refining an approach, and trying again is at the very core of building all behavioural skills.

Most of us still believe the adage that "practice makes perfect", but this isn't specific enough. The reality is that doing things repeatedly does little to build a learner's skill-set, whereas "deliberate practice" creates expertise. EdTech promises to provide approaches that will reinforce deliberate practice as an effective practice, targeting skill gaps just beyond the learners' current set of skills.

Furthermore, technology promises to: 1) push learners to shift away from practice that is too expansive but rather focuses on the specific nuances in which are a challenge to the learner, 2) force learners to focus on new areas of expertise and not specific skills that have already been mastered, and finally, 3) enable learners to be opportunistic with no formal opportunities such as formal courses to learn and review new skills; learners can be opportunistic about when and where to practise newly acquired skills.

*Using game mechanics and incentives do drive individuals to both learn and teach.*

Learners should find it easy to identify important skills to the organisation, assess themselves against those skills, express their attitudes and intentions to learn, formulate learning paths, receive support, and be held accountable. Accountability could be as simple as prompts and reminders.

So, as we build the talent structures of the apprenticeship model, everything from initial development plans to real-time, on-demand feedback to the evaluation process itself will help reinforce the strengths of the nascent learning culture. Lasting, sustainable change will always be the issue when it comes to culture change, key stakeholders such as senior leaders will always play a critical role in encouraging apprenticeship: aligning attitudes and highlighting their efforts to develop deeper apprenticeship skills and demonstrating how these capabilities are growing across teams, will be critical.

Providing clear and concise opportunities to align the expectations, areas for growth, and a sense of accountability for learning. Reinforced through communications across multiple channels—for example, in the language and specific channel used to celebrate leaders promoted to new roles or recognition of an individual employee achievement. It's indicated/implied that such approaches will send clear signals that learning is not only valued but expected. Correctly implemented learners are far more likely to buy into the long-term vision. They will wholeheartedly invest their efforts when they see real-world support in everything from people and technology to content and continuing development opportunities.

Simultaneously, the same structures can be leveraged to establish the expectations for teaching. Employees should be aware that their skills and expertise are valuable to the business. However, the seeds of the apprenticeship culture are only firmly planted when the expectation is set that building and developing similar expertise in others is expected, valued, and rewarded.

## Building Personal Reflection As A Business Priority In The Day-To-Day

Metacognition, the process of reflecting on and directing a learner's thinking, is a crucial driver for cognitive tasks, including growing a learner's ability to reflect on and learn from situations. Reflection is needed as a diagnostic skill that allows learners to evaluate themselves and determine their own personalised learning needs relevant to their past performance and with input from recognised experts.
Reflection will be key to empowering learners to unpack their actions and habits, to help them refine the relevant component pieces, and then reframe these pieces back together to improve performance.

Research has shown that reflection promotes learning across three core moments: before, during, and after a task. From a system's perspective forecasting, the cognitive task simply means looking ahead. However, in these moments, learners need to be forced to think ahead about how they might tackle a task, approach the specific problem, or what they will need to say during a difficult conversation. Mostly, we are pushing the learners to reflect on what's coming. Forecasting forces us to learn proactively. It's important to note that, though it's possible to reflect during an event, it's difficult to correct course and make adjustments. Though learners notice what is happening, most will find it difficult to experiment "in the moment." Finally, retrospective reflection provides a unique opportunity for learners to look at a past situation, consider the effectiveness of their actions and then project forward to approach a similar type of event in the future.

Among reflection's many benefits, two stand out: 1) the correlation between reflection and self-efficacy: at its core of learning is a belief that the learner can indeed learn, that as they improve, they are capable of taking the necessary steps and actions to achieve desired outcomes, i.,e levels of performance. So, 2) reflection is a virtuous cycle of confidence, reinforcing a sense of capability, priming learners to become more capable. As confidence builds, resolve is established, and learners become cumulatively confident in their ability to "take on" ever increasingly hard challenges, strengthening their existing skills and building new ones. Further reflection only further adds to their growing confidence—and on and on and on. It's important to note that the cycle can also go in the opposite direction, diminishing confidence.

Equally important, we all work in a fast-paced world, particularly in the face of time pressures, which can be a major obstacle. A learner's brain often simplifies complex decisions into shortcuts or neural pathways. Though it allows those decisions to be made faster and with less effort, reflection allows these old shortcuts to be replaced with newly learnt strategies. Over time, the reflection will continue to diminish a learner's barrier to change.

Reflection builds cognitive familiarity with new processes and approaches because learners have thought deeply about a specific occasion/event in the past and always think about further refinement and improvement. Concerns about making changes become less powerful.

The challenge is that a learner's ability to reflect is threatened on many fronts over time. Being overscheduled, overworked, or mentally overloaded affects a learners' ability to pause and assess circumstances and performance. The noisier the outside world, the greater the need for dedicated reflection time. The modern apprenticeship needs to push learners to engage in reflection and, in many cases, ritualise it - forcing them to create consistent and predictable patterns. Only through establishing strategies for capturing these thoughts and referring back to them will reflection shift from a deliberate complex decision into a shortcut ingrained into their daily routines.

## Bringing It All Together

Finally, even though details about the specific skills that tomorrow's workers will require remain vague, it's expected that game mechanics and feedback loops from dynamic internal and external data sources will help refine and reinforce learning and business objectives, ensuring learning programs remain relevant, timely and contextual.

## Final Thoughts

The next decade will push fundamental changes to the way the world works. As businesses shift towards a new dynamic talent model, the focus is on skills, not degrees or previous job titles. To adapt, Gen Z will need to evolve into specialist workers that are proficient at collaboration, communication and problem-solving, becoming experts at social and emotional learning. They will need to be obsessed with the constant acquisition of new skills; learning won't stop for tomorrow's workforce but will be a life-long journey.

Ultimately, the real test for the modern apprenticeship will be reflected by who gets rewarded, promoted or let go. However, the real winners will be the business leaders and companies that effectively identify, develop, and place the best people into the most important roles. Capable of shaping cultures of high performance and continuous learning while building the infrastructure to harness the humanity, integrity, and creativity of tomorrow's workers — ultimately, those who succeed will be experts in building capabilities and a workforce that is adept at collaboration, communication and problem-solving, all experts at social and emotional learning.

# Purpose & Flow: The Two Most Important Words In The Future Of Technology-Enabled Corporate Learning

## Wang Li He and Yu Zhou

Co-founder of Dasima/Link Education and HR Director of Guandong Rural Credit Union (GDRC)

Even as the world recovers from COVID-19, emerging technologies and increased automation continue to drive the digitalisation of business. Technology is fundamentally changing the way many jobs are carried out. Though the pandemic accelerated technological change, the shift reshaping how we work was already well underway.

Over the next decade, it's likely that turmoil, crisis and disruption will continue to be a likely fixture for most businesses. As a result, business leaders will be forced to grapple with crucial decisions that can upend their business regularly. The winners, the rare few that not only survive but thrive and succeed, will be those that can reinvent themselves to overcome the pressures of today and be flexible enough to respond to the challenges of tomorrow.

The challenge in this new paradigm of work will be that traditionally, talent has followed from strategy development. And though many digitally-savvy executives are already aligning their people, processes, and culture to achieve their organisations' long-term digital success, for the rest of us, business cycles will continue to move faster than the people development cycle. Technology and disruptive business models will continue to break apart industries.
Business is at an inflexion point: as leaders, we have the opportunity to choose how we respond to this moment and reshape our workforce norms and culture, we have a chance to come out stronger than before.

But how?

Many business leaders now realise that to survive and thrive in this new world of work, business and individuals need awareness, understanding and capability to adapt to the changes. They will also need to be driven to think differently about their business models, the skills needed, how employees will couple these skills with new technologies and, most importantly, how to keep up.

Upskilling is nothing new, and in this new normal, the focus for talent is expected to be on skills, rather than job titles or degrees. This doesn't imply that everyone will need to learn to code, but instead a shift towards self-driven learning and development. There will be many different approaches but increasingly, individual employees will need to take ownership for their continuing development and refinement of specific competencies. In return individuals see their return on investment through increasing market demand for their skills by either the current employer or potential employers.

Though, the real shift in talent models will ultimately be reflected by who gets rewarded, promoted or let go. It is expected that business will focus on rewarding and fostering employees who exemplify drive and a passion for self-learning. As a result, it is expected that tomorrow's workers will need to be creative, adaptable, and resilient. So too tomorrow's business leaders will be tasked with putting the best people into the most important roles and shaping a culture that harnesses the humanity, integrity, and creativity of tomorrows workers—aligning them towards a common purpose and empowering them to not only succeed but to the best work of their lives every single day.

Building such a culture and getting the best people into the most important roles does not happen by chance, it requires a disciplined approach to aligning personal values with the underlying business objectives and strategy. The reality is that the future of work is purpose-driven and is deeply personal. Leaders will need to define both how the organisation creates value but how talent contributes to its success. And, as leaders define these values and contributions, existing performance-management and incentive structures will no longer be useful or appropriate.

**Driven By Purpose**

Few would disagree that knowing and living your purpose is key to a full life. However, for most people, they unfortunately wander around for the most part, never understanding their purpose or the impact of their efforts in work or life. For the workforce of the future, defining and aligning purposes rests on the shoulders of business leaders to enable them to grow and be happy at work.

Now more than ever, clarity in purpose is not a choice but a necessity. The increasing shift towards being driven by purpose is not just about creating alignment; it is about creating motivation that matters, by reinforcing a set of core values and actions and purpose that stimulates a continued progress towards these aspirations. This alignment is best when everyone in the business intuitively understands their role in contributing to the businesses success and is engaged enough to take action.

MihályCsíkszentmihályi, a Hungarian physiologist, has studied creativity and productivity, and has conducted research interviews across countless overachievers considered successful in a range of professions, including many Nobel Prize laureates. Csíkszentmihályi's research emphasised that thesecrets of optimal performance is derived from the ability to enter the a state of "Flow" both frequently and deliberately.

Flow, he argued, is an optimal state of being that brings order to consciousness – akin to harnessing an individual's attention, focus and passion. He argued that Flow is so intense that it does not allow us to have cognitive bandwidth left for anything else. It is a state of such profound task absorption and intense concentration that makes a person feel one with the activity.

From a business leader's perspective, building a business where employees are united by a common purpose and empowered to succeed and do the best work every day should be the ultimate goal. Achieving this goal rests on the shoulders of leaders to enable people to grow, be engaged, happy at work and ultimately experience Flow, frequently and deliberately.

The long-term benefits of fostering Flow and engagement at work are numerous, including amplified performance, greater creativity, more access to intuition, and an ever-increasing ability to engage in deep learning. However, identifying and cultivating the conditions that enable Flow is dependent both on an individual's efforts, as well as that of the leadership and the organisational culture of the business.

## How Leaders Cultivate Flow In Work?

The business leader's journey to establish Flow starts with creating the infrastructure that satisfies everyone's basic psychological needs of autonomy, competence, and relatedness.

Autonomy is satisfied by empowerment, enabling employees to decide how, when and where they do their jobs. In contrast, competence is fostered through effective praise, recognition and appropriate on-the-job challenges such as opportunities to learn, mentor or teach. Relatedness on the other hand, is established through high-quality relationships connecting employees as part of a community.

## Cultivating Flow-Through Business Gamification

Though most companies want to engage employees through purposeful work and Flow, it is not always easy. Many focus on external drivers, balancing carrots and sticks. Ultimately these incentives do little to motivate. Failing is largely due to the inability to create the right conditions to help employees develop intrinsic motivation. Businesses need to look inward. This is where gamification can help.

Business gamification is far from a new concept. It's been around for decades.
Though commonly used for knowledge transfer in the workplace —gamification also has the power to reinforce key concepts, behaviours and skills that, when applied, will drive lasting impact. As a result, leaders should be looking to extend business gamification far beyond knowledge transfer.

The key to recent success in business gamification has been the shift from gimmicks such as badges and points to being focused on actual improvements in quality of work. Deployed to drive instant feedback through interactive elements and competition, gamification is proving effective in engaging a wide range of learners at all levels of business.

What does Flow have to do with motivation and gamification? Done correctly, gamification allows leaders to focus on the three elements that sustainably motivates people:

- *Autonomy*, employees are forced to own their performance through the use of dashboards. There's no room for excuses;
- *Mastery* is developed because employees are consistently challenged and given opportunities to receive feedback; and finally
- *Purpose* is clarified because everyone's work is recognised as a part of a whole.

When combined with competency-based learning, assessments, and study recommendations, these three elements become potent drivers of sustainable motivation. Moreover, such business gaming allows leaders to define key performance indicators or KPIs that help structure feedback. Learners will know exactly what is being measured and how everyone is faring, fostering the right conditions to align purpose and ultimately Flow.

Suppose Flow is achieved through effectively balancing "optimal being" and "optimal doing." In that case, it's reasonable to assume that we can't be in a state of Flow all the time. If this is the case, then the cycle of this optimal experience as outlined by Csíkszentmihályi can be deconstructed into four distinct phases, these are akin to other theories of human motivation requiring us to step outside of our comfort zone and challenge our sense of self to move between phases:

- **Struggle Phase**, we experience tension, frustration and even stress and anxiety;
- **Release Phase,** we accept the challenge by stepping away from the problem;
- **Flow Phase**, which comes after release and shifts us from conscious to subconscious processing; and finally
- **Recovery Phase,** our brain rewires and stores the experience of Flow. Recovery, similar to building muscle, is crucial to rebuild and re-balance for learners. Without it, learners won't readily retain the newly acquired skills and knowledge during the consolidation of memories.

Like other approaches to motivations, if an earlier phase is not complete or satisfied; it's difficult to progress to a later one.

This phased approach outlines that Flow can be activated by a set of specific properties being. It must be challenging, it must require skills, it must have unique/clear goals and finally be able provide immediate feedback. So, the key for lasting Flow is that challenges must be neither too demanding nor too simple for an employee's abilities.

**Gamification Is No Game: Applying Game Mechanics**

In effective business gamification, activating Flow will be a critical factor of success for learners to remain energised and focused. From a gaming perspective, there are several elements that can be used to influence and affect the Flows of learners:

- **Mission Driven**: Intrinsic drivers, used to provide instant feedback;

- **Clear goals**: The learners need to have clear goals and objectives. Learners need to be aware and clear of goals to ensure progression through the game;

- **Loss of consciousness**: Flow works best in gamification when learners do not need to concentrate on what they are doing to achieve an action. This is the state where the learner's actions and awareness are merged;

- **Loss of sense of time**: Similar to modern social media and time-wasting platforms, learners need to be hooked by the activities to the point they do not realise that the time has passed while doing it;

- **Direct and immediate feedback**: Like rewards and punishments, learners need to be guided by feedback and know how to succeed.

- **Balance between skills and challenge:** The challenge within the activity can be neither too easy nor too difficult. The challenge must continue to evolve and be adapted to the learner's skill level. An obvious, but a common point of failure for most gamification initiatives. Finally;

- **Sense of control**: The learner must control the situation and the activity, the objectives need to appear reachable. Learners must feel a sense that they can complete the challenge.

## Emotional States, Learner Behaviours

Behind these key elements, and beyond Csíkszentmihályi framework for finding pleasure and lasting satisfaction. There are two distinct types of Flow to be applied in the game design to ensure learners continue to progress; **micro** and **macro flows.**

*Microflows* are focused, emotional and intensely short. While they can be repeated throughout the game, they force users into a fixated state of mind where the learner feels enjoyment and fulfilment, a sense often generated by a series of successful achievements. Without considerations for the microflow element, there's a big chance that your game will fail to engage learners.

Conversely, *Macroflows* last the entire game and indicate learners' progression based on skill level throughout the challenge. Macroflows should be supported throughout the game through rhythm, guidance, positive feedback and rewards.
The rhythm of gameplay and learner inputs are key to switch between micro and macro flows. Suppose there is no real defined pattern in the learner's input experience. In that case, it will be harder to foster microflows for learners.

Unconsciously, as learners naturally progress into a sequence and mood of inputs these patterns will ultimately drive learners to feel good, confident and engaged.

## Visualise Performance

Learners want honest feedback. They are eager to know how they compare with peers and stack up against others doing the same things they do. As learners succeed within the game mechanics, the greater the need for positive feedback to help maintain and reinforce a sense of Flow and engagement.

Beyond the gamified environment, the challenge of learning in the workplace is that feedback is far too subjective. Without adequate measurement of a learner's competencies, experiences, skills and performance, emotions can easily hijack the discussion. Gamification provides leaders with a unique set of tools to define and visualise KPIs that then help to structure the feedback.

## Amp Up Competition Or Drive Collaboration

Gaming is competitive by nature. Running contests within the framework of the game allows learners to tap into their ambitious side. In most cases, it won't be the prize or reward that encourages learners to succeed. Instead, they will be fueled by the competition, an opportune time to see how they compare against their peers in an objective way.

So too, as teams increasingly work remotely, teaming up learners towards a common pursuit or establishing channels for open mentorship can make learners feel more connected, and create lasting relationships. Teaming up within the game will allow learners to feel safer to take risks; allowing them to share vulnerabilities and establish a shared narrative that gives the team a sense of purpose and direction.

## Beware Of The Playtest Effect

More often than not, business game builders do playtests in order to find the right balance between the challenge and the learner's skills, with the goal to find the right balance between encouraging people to join, and stay in the game.

The real dilemma is that in most cases, by listening and relying too much on the feedback from the playtest, the game mechanics will frequently decrease the level of challenge. The rationale is that this will make the game more accessible to more learners. But ultimately, these changes fail to drive macro flows. In decreasing the degree of challenge, the game builders are increasing the potential boredom zone, and minimising Flow - ultimately leading to a boring, stale and unengaged experience.

***

The next decade will see fundamental changes to the way the world works, as businesses shift towards a new dynamic talent model. To adapt, tomorrow's workforce needs to acquire new skills, continuously. Education will never stop but will be a lifelong journey.

Though the real shift in talent models will be reflected by who gets rewarded, promoted or let go, the real winners will be the businesses effective in identifying, developing and placing the best people into the most important roles.

# 5 Frameworks

# The Hybrid Use Of Tools To Create A More Active Online Learning Experience

**Cherry Ma Choi Yi**

Program Manager at CoCoon Foundation

Designing a captivating online experience has never been more crucial. Numerous hours of classes are now delivered online - both by the traditional educational institution and the out-of-school training program and extracurricular activities classes. Students and teachers are demanding new, effective and dynamic ways to deliver content through online tools in hopes to innovate a learning experience that can take place anytime and anywhere. What's more important is that not only knowledge and hard skills in school curriculum like languages or mathematics are now delivered online, but students also have to learn soft skills like physical education, music, or even teamwork.

With the 4th industrial revolution, soft skills like creativity, empathy, and leadership have never been more important. According to the World Economic Forum, there is an urgent need for humans to develop social and emotional capabilities in order toclose the current workforce gap, as automation has the potential to replace jobs that require hard skills and knowledge, while human capabilities are unique and vital for individual and organisational progression. According to the Future of Jobs Report in 2020, the top skills and skill groups which employers see as rising in prominence in the lead up to 2025 include critical thinking and analysis as well as problem-solving, and skills in self-management such as active learning, resilience, stress tolerance and flexibility. A research study conducted by Google showed that social and emotional capabilities like communication, collaboration and empathy are the most important traits of an effective manager, and thus revisited its hiring strategy as well as rolling out more relevant training.

But traditionally, these skills are more effectively learnt in a physical social environment, especially through learning by doing. One of the difficulties in creating effective online learning environments is student isolation, which invokes an individual-centric model of learning that encourages discrete study rather than teamwork (Haythornthwaite, Kazmer, Robins, & Shoemaker, 2000; Morgan & Tam, 1999). To transform education with technology, considering how we can deliver soft skills, especially emotional and social capabilities in an effective and active format online is essential for developing a successful online learning model.

Long prior to COVID-19, many pioneers like Coursera, LinkedIn Learning, and Masterclass have been trying to find the secret recipe for an effective online learning model, yet many still struggle to consistently engage learners through the course, with a general completion rate ranging from 3-6% (Lederman, 2019). This may be largely due to the fact that these courses are designed in the similar format, with a series of pre-recorded videos as a base for the content, with some reading, tasks, and discussions to be completed by the learner. Most of these courses are putting learners in the passive receiver role and are heavily dependent on the learners' motivation to be

FRAMEWORKS

engaged and progress through the course.

While Coursera, LinkedIn Learning and Masterclass focuses more on professionals, under COVID-19, formal education for students also has to be shifted to be conducted online. Teachers now find themselves recording videos in an energetic way - or sitting in front of a computer screen trying to explain their subject like any key opinion leaders in social media. To better engage learners, they might also start blogs or study platforms like Google Classroom to structure student's learning through clearly laying out the learning objectives of each video or providing additional resources to support learners to learn a specific topic.

Regardless of the online learning delivered by the traditional platforms or the adopted online learning delivered by schools, both are heavily dependent on a one-way information delivery, where learners are passively receiving information. Research has found that this format of online learning has not been effective as there are less opportunities for direct, facilitated communication and engagement. Empowering the learners to learn more actively helps to cultivate soft skills and human capabilities. The National Training Laboratory suggests that most students only remember about 5% in a one-way lecture format, and 10% of what they read from textbooks; but retain 75% through learning by doing and 90% of what they learn through teaching others.

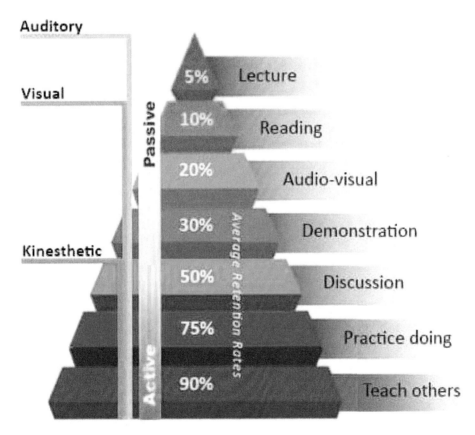

Adapted from the NTL Institute of Applied Behavioral Science Learning Pyramid

So, how are we to design a more effective and active online learning experience, especially towards soft-skills development?

According to research from the Open University of Israel, teaching presence and social presence are two of the most important factors to determine whether online learning is successful (Gorsky&Blau, 2009). Teaching presence is defined as "the design, facilitation and direction of cognitive and social processes for the purpose of realising students personally meaningful and educationally worthwhile outcomes" (Anderson et al., 2001, p.5). The teacher or instructor has to post regularly, responding in a timely manner and modelling good online communication and interaction. Social presence is described as the ability to project one's self and to establish personal and purposeful relationships (Rourke et al., 1999). Richardson and Swan (2003) explored perceptions of social presence in online courses and found that students' perceptions of social presence were highly correlated with perceived learning and satisfaction with their instructors. Thus, an interactive, real-time, and community-driven learning experience is essential for learners to be engaged and effectively learn the subject matter, especially on soft-skills development.

To create a high teaching presence learning experience, it is important to utilise different online tools to create a multidimensional, blended learning experience for the students to learn through different methods. For example, while using Zoom or Google Hangouts as an information delivery platform, adding interactive tools like Slido or Mentimeters can help learners to engage in processing the information by submitting their ideas on a word cloud or quiz, while the instructor can also give real-time feedback, which can not only increase the interactions between teacher and students, but also create a stronger community. Additionally, using interactive whiteboard tools like Miro or Aww App can allow learners to practice by doing and engage in group discussions by sharing their ideas visually, which helps the students to systematically learn sophisticated concepts.

Using a combination of these tools will not only increase engagement from the learners, but also simulate learners with different learning styles, thus enabling them to shift from a passive to a more active role in the learning experience.

Let's explore how to create an active online learning experience with high teaching and social presence through the example of entrepreneurship education. Through learning entrepreneurship, students not only have to be fully engaged in the process to have a successful outcome of building their idea, but also learn some of the most important 21st century skills like creativity, collaboration, and communication. The Innovation Camp in the Jockey Club CoCoon Student Entrepreneurship Training Program (JCCSTEP) uses a variety of tools to engage participants to ensure an active learning experience for each participant. The JCCSTEP Innovation Camp is an intense experience in which students from ages 15 to 17 will be grouped with other 4-5 teens outside of their schools to create innovative solutions in 4 days. In August 2020, the 3rd Innovation Camp was hosted online for 91 participants from 17 different schools in Hong Kong. Throughout the 17.5 hours of online sessions, participants were engaged in a variety of online tools to help them engage with the process of ideation, working effectively as a team and sharing their ideas with the wider group and investors.

FRAMEWORKS

Active learning is all about engagement. Compared with physical learning, where the teacher can only ask for inputs from one or two representatives from the audience, online learning has a huge potential in engaging many learners at the same time. In the Innovation Camp example, one of the common questions asked was "What is Innovation?". Compared to a physical session, where speaking up is normally dominated by only a few "star" students, in the online session, each participant can share his / her ideas and insights with fellow participants on Sli.do in real-time, with all the submitted answers shown on the screen immediately. The host will then be able to quote and discuss each learner's feedback on the question and compare and contrast the opinions of the group. This opens up the discussion from a dominated few to a diversified mass.

Additionally, a gamified, competition element is also added to recognise and reward students who are actively contributing to the discussion and conversations. Whenever the instructor has asked questions, students who responded in the chat box or through Sli.do will gain points for their team - and this showed significant effectiveness in engaging learners. Miro board is another great tool to enable teams to learn sophisticated concepts like design thinking or leadership in a systematic manner. After the host has explained a concept like empathy, the team will come together on their Miro board and practise using the tool (e.g. Empathy Map) together on imagining what pain points their target customers face. Through this co-creation process, not only can students learn through practising, but the group facilitator can also give real-time feedback to students on their work and ideas.

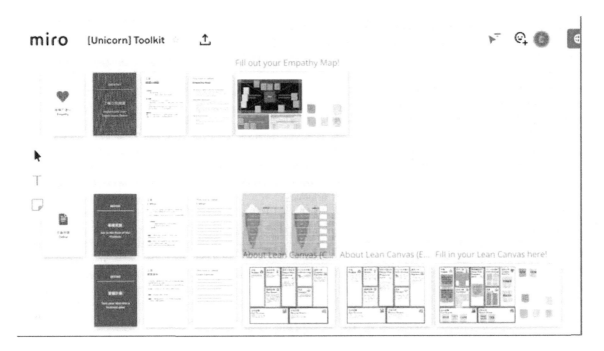

(Photo description: JCCSTEP Innovation Camp Miro board for each team to learn design thinking and ideation)

Another important aspect in active online learning is creating a strong social presence for learners.

Social presence involves a feeling of connection to other classmates, which often functions as a factor for motivating a student's learning (Sweet & Michaelson, 2012). Designing the online learning experience with different social aspects is crucial in keeping students stimulated, especially when students are isolated from learning online. In the Innovation Camp example, as most learners come from different schools and have not met each other prior, creating a social environment where they feel comfortable to share and contribute is crucial for idea generation. Grouping students in teams and intentionally adding in online icebreakers or team building activities like virtual scavenger hunts allow participants to feel trust with their teams and thus be more willing to turn on their cameras and mics - which is crucial for interactive group discussions. Some EdTech tools, such as Miro, are more suitable for smaller group engagement, whereas Slido and Mentimeter are more effective at engaging a large group of students and creating a strong community bond.

Looking at the learning outcomes, 87.9% of participants declared that, through the online innovation camp, they were able to meet like-minded individuals that they would consider as friends. 97.8% of participants indicated that they are aware of the importance of teamwork in an ideation process with 98.9% agreeing that an excellent team requires each team member to proactively take on responsibilities. These results indicate that online learning, facilitated with an active learning design, can equip students with vital social skills such as working with others and creating a social community. With an interactive and engaging learning design, 92.3% of participants stated that they liked the ideation process of coming up with their product idea and 98.9% of participants agreed that they were satisfied with this event. One participant described Innovation Camp as a "very valuable and rewarding experience, the skills learnt are not only useful for entrepreneurship, but also useful in our daily lives and group projects."

With an increasing amount of learning shifting online, creating an active and engaging online learning experience has never been more important. The online experience should promote discussion, learning by doing, and even teaching peers to increase the learning experience's effectiveness. Teachers should create an interactive, real-time community-based environment, adopting a hybrid use of online tools to empower students to take a more active role in their learning.

At the end of the day, an active online learning experience should move beyond simple replication of the physical learning environment. Teachers are invited to challenge the status quo of how we deliver knowledge and skills, reimagining the way we teach by unlocking the power of technology. This will be the future of education.

FRAMEWORKS

# Online Learning Frameworks

## Danish Sayanee

Business Development Manager, PINNACLE Innovation and Education

A discussion on the online learning framework is incomplete without first engaging with learning theories. A large number of theorists and educationists, including philosophers and psychologists, have contributed to the theoretical development of education since the beginning of time. Even today, these theories help us cater to the different factors that influence learning, identify learning types and styles and modify and differentiate our classrooms.

It is only when educators have a better understanding of these various theories that they will be able to choose appropriate teaching alternatives that fit the demographics of their class and the individualised needs of the learners. However, to cater to today's learners' needs, especially the ones who are digitally apt, a teacher needs to apply these theories to the technological age.

In 2003, Van Buren and Sloman proposed that around 62% of learning technology initiatives do not meet expectations. One of the main causes for this major failure (or unpreparedness) was identified by Driscoll and Carline, who stated that the grass root realities of classrooms were not kept in mind while designing e-learning content.

However, more important than designing e-learning content is the actual integration of technology into the curriculum. Driscoll and Carline emphasised the need to monitor the efforts of those who are looking after the e-learning process, to find an easily implemented universal solution for all those struggling. There can be many reasons for these disappointing numbers, including lack of understanding of the project, content, budget, and schedules. Driscoll and Carline suggest that a guide, with the focus on main issues that are solved on a priority basis, should be developed to help educators solve issues one by one.

Today, we have several definitions of learning. Some of these definitions of learning include: learning as an activity of the mind, of behaviour change, how individuals process data and information, how well they memorise and recall information, how individuals negotiate socially, critical skills, construction of knowledge, understanding of concepts and evolving them with time, contextual change, active learning, relating perceptions to surroundings and thinking skills.

Now the question is, what is learning to you?

Learning theories are based on observations and experiences that also take into account the variables which have an impact on learning and how they can be supported. Then, we have models of learning which explain and redefine the role of technology and how it facilitates learning. Learning theories provide the base for the construction of a learning framework, helping the designer to feel content and confident about their design.

A learning theory *is a set of various concepts that perceive, explain, describe and provide guidance to people.* Some theories are relevant to the current world of education. The first theory we have is behaviourism, which, despite being developed in the 1920s, is still used in modern schools in the USA. This theory states that people learn through the behaviour which is present in their surrounding environment. One famous experiment based on the behaviourism theory was conducted by Ivan Pavlov, John Watson, and B.F Skinner. In this experiment, whenever a bell was rung, the dog was given food. So, after many bell-ringing and food-giving, when the dog heard the bell, it would salivate. This is called conditioning; a learned behaviour that is done repeatedly in the same manner until the subject of this treatment gets used to this behaviour. However, humans are more complex than animals. After several experiments, it was concluded that humans require reward or punishment to learn a behaviour. Skinner also performed a similar experiment on pigeons, where he rewarded them with food when they correctly pecked a target. Though in the initial stages their behaviour was quite random, later in the experiment it was shown that they could connect stimuli with the response. According to Skinner, reward and punishment have the capacity to mould behaviour, encouraging people to act in a certain manner.

Next, cognitive theory came as a response to behaviourism. The cognitive theory explains how the mind interprets, processes, and locks up information. In this entire process, individuals are active learners. This theory has been supported by many famous psychologists such as Piaget, John Dewey, and Brunner. The human is understood to be complex, with the mind making its own decision and choices. Humans' emotions and experiences are understood to be a huge part of their learning process.

Cognitive learning helps us comprehend how mental processes influence our learning process or experience. Many cognitivists argue that an individual's cognitive processes impact prior knowledge as new knowledge is acquired. This particular approach focuses on comprehension, generalisation, analysis, synthesis, evaluation, and decision making. The cognitive approach focuses on how students can learn and build a strong mental process so that they can grasp concepts clearly and can apply them in real life.

Next, we have the theory of constructivism, which states that learning cannot be acquired when learners are passive, but can only be achieved when they are active. According to this theory, humans are understood as having free will, which enables them to construct their knowledge. Whilst behaviourism assumes that individuals have no control or choice and cognitivism claims that individuals deliberately make attempts to make sense out of their surroundings, in the constructivism approach, new ideas are tested with experiences.

Ideas are not just tested by teachers; they are also tested by peers. Moreover, it has been observed that knowledge and information are mostly acquired in social settings, including schools, colleges, and universities. In this approach, knowledge is not just content or information, it also consists of the values and norms of our society. One of the core elements of this theory is that each learner is completely different as a result of their highly personalised life experiences, meaning that human behaviour cannot be predicted. Therefore, the most important factor in learning is the social context. Now, let's take a look at various theories within the constructivist approach.

American psychologist David Amusable's theory states that all human beings relate acquired new knowledge with their prior knowledge. The foundation of this theory is based upon achieving quality learning through contrasting concepts and knowledge, as opposed to simply memorising.

Next, we have the theory of Learning by Discovery by the famous American psychologist, Jerome Brunner. This theory relates to the approach of constructivism, where learners construct their knowledge based on experiences and surroundings. This theory observed that students learn best when they face a problem, solve it, and later relay to their peers.

Then, we have the socio-constructivism theory by the famous Russian psychologist, Vygotsky. This theory states that learning is primarily done through social interaction. The way people socialise with each other plays a vital role in learning and building up connections of prior knowledge and experiences.

Then, we have the Information Process theory. This theory concludes that individuals process data and information without having to come in contact with the 'real' environment. In this approach, the individual can acquire knowledge through cognitive processes.

Next, we have the Social Learning theory. This theory was developed by famous Canadian psychologist Albert Bandura. Bandura's theory states that an individual can acquire data and information through cognitive processes and relationships with the environment. Social status and demographics play a vital role in this process.

Last but not least, we have a theory of Multiple Intelligence, presented by Howard Gardner. According to Gardner, each individual has eight pieces of intelligence. These eight pieces depend on the varying and individualised social, cultural, and environmental factors. Gardner states that every individual has a different learning style. Some learn through listening, some through writing, or some by reading.

The consistency of constructivist approaches to learning has led to the integration of technology in education. Today, we have a fusion of the constructivist approach and the technological era, which is now known as Online Collaborative Learning (OCL). The Online Collaborative Learning theory is one where learners are motivated to work together with their peers and construct their own learning paths. A problem is assigned to each learner, for which they have to come up with an innovative solution. As a result, the learner constructs their knowledge by doing, becoming active learners in the process - though this does not negate the role of the instructor. A teacher is a facilitator, showing learners the pathways to achieve their goals and their role in Online Collaborative Learning is to assist students as per their needs. Teachers and learners are expected to maintain norms, values, and discipline to ensure that the learning process is fruitful.

The education sector has also changed dynamically. Initially, classes were teacher-centred, but now students play the main role. In traditional teaching, the instructor would transfer their knowledge to the students while giving the lectures and students were expected to passively memorise. Now, the ball game has completely changed. Students are the ones who construct their knowledge and take ownership of it, and the teacher is a facilitator.

In today's world, no company wants to hire a rote learner - everyone is looking for someone creative, innovative, and who thinks out of the box. Educators are tirelessly attempting to create collaborative learning environments to improve communication and community, to better prepare them for this new working world. And, today's learner has a lot to share.

There has been a complete evolution in communication. Initial communication took place through the telegraph, invented by Samuel Morse between the 1830s and 1840s, which was then replaced by the telephone. Later, the radio both sensationalised entertainment and provided an element of learning, a medium through which news travelled from one place to another. After the radio, television better enabled people to connect with global news, modern entertainment and also encouraged the propagation of educational videos. Then came the era of communication satellites, and the world of the internet was not too far behind. Primarily, the internet was used to communicate through email, but this soon progressed to computer conferencing and search engines. The first online course for adults began in 1981and the first online program for executive education began in 1982. In 1983, networked classrooms appeared for primary and secondary education and in 1984, the first virtual classroom was set up for undergraduates. In 1989, the first large-scale university online courses were set up in the United Kingdom and the rest of the world followed soon after. Today, we can see that online education has influenced all the sectors of learning, from formal to informal education.

Now, there are a variety of approaches to online education, including a completely online system, a hybrid approach, or an enhanced system. As the name suggests, completely online is where learners are registered to courses that are fully operated on learning management systems, from registering to and classes to assignments and exams. In the hybrid approach, though the physical presence of learner and teacher may be mandatory, technology is used to create a collaborative learning environment. In the enhanced mode, the system is run on cloud computing.

Collaborative learning is now the global standard for online learning. It is expected that students will be able to acquire 21st century skills, such as problem-solving, innovation, and teamwork. The idea of collaboration is to give the student opportunities to exchange their ideas, norms, values, and culture. The teacher is a facilitator and the learners are expected to take more responsibility for the construction of knowledge that they seek to acquire.

Over time, researchers have shown some level of satisfaction of learners' achievements with the online learning framework., though there remains a list of things that can be improved, including structure, classroom size, teacher's profile, prompt replies or feedback on discussion various discussion forums, learning activities, and group work strategies to enhance the wholesome of online learning framework. Still, many new models for online learning systems are yet to fill the gaps. Teachers must gain competency over online learning frameworks and instructional design if they are to create metacognitively enhanced learners with the skills to adapt in our rapidly evolving world.

# Creating Active Learners At University

## Gauthier Lebbe

Content Editor at Wooclap

**The Importance Of Combining Edtech Tools With Pedagogical Principles**

In March 2020, the weekly downloads of educational apps saw a 90% surge when compared with the weekly average of the fourth quarter of 2019 (CNBC 2020). This shows that the Covid-19 pandemic has accelerated the speed with which EdTech has been integrated into the way we teach and learn. This swell in EdTech users is, predictably, matched by a swell in the industry's worth, tripling from $107 billion in 2015 to a predicted $350 billion by 2025 (CNBC 2020). As EdTech becomes increasingly central to our university experiences, it is important that we **not lose sight of the pedagogical principles that must continue to serve as the bedrock for all future developments in EdTech**. Indeed, no matter how engaging a lecturer or the latest flashy tool they might use to capture their students' attention, if these are not also helping students to understand and retain the information being taught - a key part of allowing them to think critically - then it is unlikely students will be able to apply essential concepts and skills anywhere beyond the lecture hall.

In this article, we would like to review basic cognitive and pedagogical scientific principles, to then analyse the most effective ways to apply them in a university setting, transforming university students into **active learners enhanced by the latest EdTech.** After detailing some of the key discoveries in educational science, we will discuss how these can best be applied to improve two crucial aspects of university education: professors structuring and teaching lectures, and students most effectively revising for exams.

**3 Key Principles Of Education Science**

Let's start by introducing three core principles of education science: **active learning, retrieval practice**, and **spaced or distributive practice.** We have chosen to focus on these because they are fundamental principles of effective learning, they can be easily implemented into any teaching strategy, and they are the foundation upon which we - Wooclap - build and develop EdTech tools.
As such, these cognitive strategies can be combined with a wide variety of digital tools, depending on individual tutors' preferences and the tools at their disposal.

1. Active learning

Active learning is almost always described as "an approach to instruction in which students are asked to engage in the learning process" and starkly contrasted with traditional - "passive" - learning methods. Examples include problem solving, paired discussions, case studies, role plays, team-based learning, and so on.

Active learning can be summarised as **"learning by doing"** which, while painting an accurate picture of what active learning looks like on the surface, does not mention the underlying processes that make it such an impactful learning method. That is what we'll be focusing on here.

Specifically, we will look at how active learning enables students to create durable, usable, and accessible memories. That is, after all, the objective when learning anything.

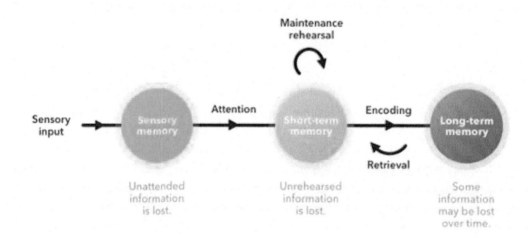

*Image recreated from "The Science of Learning — What Every Teacher Should Know", EdX:*
*https://www.edx.org*

The model above shows that information our senses pick up may or may not be stored in our *long-term* memory, depending on how we process that information in our *short-term* memory. So, **how do our brains select which information to retain?** Does taking notes and paying attention in class - in other words, processing information in short-term memory - guarantee a student will remember that information by the lesson's end? Unfortunately not.

Instead, how much a student learns mostly depends on whether they were able to **link the new information in their short-term memory to what was already in their long-term memory** (their prior knowledge). This linking process between working memory and long-term memory - the core of **active learning** - is what will create and store memories of this new learning.

Therefore, if a student mostly listens to and watches a lesson, without being given the chance to actively process new information, it is unlikely to be stored as new memories. Why? Because most of their thinking and processing takes place solely in short-term memory, which is soon lost.

When teachers **integrate concepts of active learning into their teaching practices,** students are more likely to be able to apply essential concepts and skills beyond the classroom.

2. Retrieval practice

Retrieval practice is a well-known active learning method that involves **trying to recall information that has been previously stored in long-term memory**. It is straightforward, easily implemented, and can greatly improve learning, because:

- Trying to recall a memory can **modify, reorganise, and consolidate** it better in our long-term memory.
- A recall often creates new retrieval pathways to that memory, making it **easier to retrieve later on.**
- By searching for a memory, we tend to activate information connected to that memory, linking it in a **more networked and structured context for easier future access.**

How does it work?

Cognitive scientists have found that, instead of studying by highlighting parts of a text or taking notes, students can improve long-term memory and learning more effectively through retrieval practice (Rowland, 2014). In essence, after reading new material for the first time, students **try to recall the most important information** it contained without looking at either the text or their notes. Once they have completed the retrieval, they **check the material to see how accurate and complete their retrieval was.**

Trying to recall information may sound more difficult than re-reading a text or looking at notes - and it is - but that very struggle to recall is what improves our memory. Here are 4 reasons why:

1. **The act of retrieving a memory modifies it**. Retrieving a memory is not like finding and opening a file on a computer. Instead, we re-construct it from the memory traces that constituted it when it was first made. By struggling to retrieve and reassemble a memory, we strengthen it.

2. By searching for a memory without the help of external triggers like notes or a text, we are **creating a new retrieval pathway** to find that memory. That way, we won't need any external triggers to find this memory the next time.

3. When searching for a memory, we are also likely to retrieve related information.
This can help **organise memories and link them in ways that might make it easier to retrieve them later on.**

4. **Failing to retrieve information can be useful**. It shows which information requires additional studying, to further strengthen the memory and make it more likely to be retrieved in the future.

## Spaced Practice

*"With a considerable number of repetitions, it is much more advantageous to distribute them properly over a period of time than to group them together in a single step."* This is the result of the century-old pioneering studies of psychologist Hermann Ebbinghaus (1850-1909).
*The forgetting curve: spacing out repetitions strengthens memories.*

He based his research on his own experience, and found that, **in the long run, repeated studying of the same information spaced out over time leads to greater retention of that information** than using the same time to memorise the same content in a single session. In other words, attempting to memorise content at the very last moment before a test - also known as "massed practice" or "cramming" - leads to lower performance than spaced practice. The effect is demonstrated by the results of a study by Rawson and Kintsch (2005).

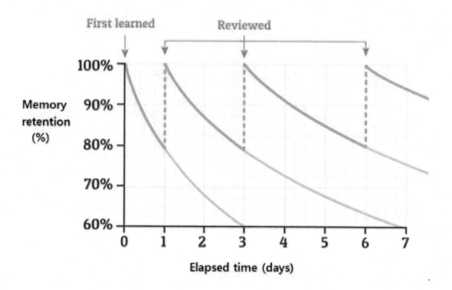

Fig. 1 shows the effect of crammed versus spaced reading on an immediate versus a delayed test. In short, **massed practice is more effective if the test comes immediately after the reading, but this benefit fades out after a mere day or two.**

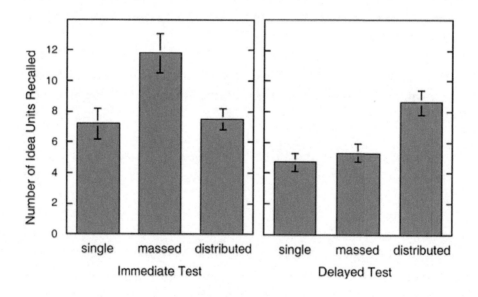

*Fig. 1. Number of idea units recalled as a function of study group (single, massed rereading, or distributed rereading) and time of test (immediately after study or with a 2-day delay between study and test). Results from Rawson and Kintsch (2005).*

Ebbinghaus' remarkable intuition has since been confirmed in a wide variety of areas - including motor learning, recognition memory, associated pair learning, free recall, word processing, statistical learning, and vocabulary acquisition - and in many populations: children, adults, animals, and even patients suffering from amnesia. Despite the increasing number of observations highlighting this effect, **distributed practice is not so common in learning habits.** If you have noticed this before, you are not alone: in 1988, Frank N. Dempster wrote an article in which he called the poor use of spaced repetitions *"a non-application of psychological research results".*

Since then, a meta-analysis of the distributed practice effect (Cepeda et al., 2006), conducted over 184 articles, shows that **spaced learning of items consistently shows benefits, regardless of retention interval** - that is, the separation between the final study and a later test. Moreover, **learning benefits increase with longer time lags between learning sessions. The average observed benefit from distributed practice is 15% more retention, for both children and adults, compared to massed practice.** These effects don't last forever, though: once retention intervals become relatively long, further increases have no effect on - or may even decrease - memory.

As is often the case, there are a few caveats. Despite having investigated the topic for so long, psychologists aren't yet able to determine the optimal interval between rehearsals of the same material. In addition, we know little about the effects of expanding or contracting learning schedules on retention. Future research will therefore need to focus on these aspects.

## 9 Practical Applications In Higher Education Course Design

Because theories and research from the science of education are only ever of real interest in the context of course design and student revision, we will discuss 9 key applications of active learning, retrieval practice, and spaced practice in higher education. These allow for great flexibility in how to teach, depending on professors' preferences and subjects.

1. Engage students early

A great way to engage students in learning at the beginning of class is to present that session's conclusions or objectives. That way, you'll repeat and emphasise the key elements you want to convey.

Other examples to engage students at the start of class include telling a compelling anecdote, asking provocative questions about content or concepts, and conducting a demonstration relevant to the material presented that day.

2. Split your course content into units, or "chunks"

"Chunking" essentially means breaking down information into bite-sized pieces, to allow the brain to process new information more easily. Research has shown that, on average, individuals can store seven items in their short-term memory. In other words, giving students too much material at once is counterproductive, because any excess information will be lost.

This means that if you are explaining something complex, something that requires the learner to hold several factors in mind to understand the concept, the information is best broken into bite-sized pieces.

3.  Switch up the format

According to cognitive psychologist and neuroscientist Professor Stanislas Dehaene, the main contributors to successful learning are **attention, active engagement, feedback**, and **consolidation.** He refers to these four fundamental elements as the "four pillars of learning":

1.  Students can't learn without paying **attention** to what must be learned. In practice, that means a teacher must first draw the students' attention, by quizzing them or adjusting the tone of their voice, for example.
2.  To remember new information, passively listening to the teacher is insufficient. Students should be **actively engaged,** asking themselves questions, speculating about potential hypotheses, performing experiments to fully understand what they are learning.
3.  Dehaene believes making errors can be beneficial - if one understands what caused them. This is why **feedback** is important: it allows the learner to move past the mistake and correct it, provided they feel confident and encouraged, rather than criticised and mocked.
4.  Memorising new information or acquiring new skills is merely the first step: that knowledge must be **consolidated** if it is to be durable and used automatically, almost unconsciously. In traditional teaching methods, these elements are in short supply. If students are to pay attention, be engaged, have the opportunity to receive feedback, and consolidate their learning, teachers must alternate the format of delivery of their course material: presentations, quizzes, debates, videos, peer-to-peer instruction...

4.  Insert interactive quizzes into your lectures

As we've seen, retrieval practice is not only a great way to improve student engagement and attention, or measure their understanding of course material. It also structures their knowledge.

Online quizzes are an easy way to implement retrieval practice in your courses. Some of these quizzes can also be designed to test the deeper understanding of students, making sure they are able to transfer their knowledge to a new context.

5.  Use concepts your students know to explain new material

As we've seen, active learning aims to link new information to students' prior knowledge. By using pre-existing concepts and previous material to explain new concepts, students strengthen their network of knowledge.

To reactivate prior knowledge, you can ask students questions about material seen in previous classes, or simply ask them to summarise what they learned during the previous lesson. In other words, include retrieval practice exercises in your course design!

EdTech can help you implement and scale retrieval practice in your lessons. Student response systems, for example, allow you to perform the exercise with all your students at once, collecting their answers and providing feedback to each individual learner.

6.  Recap subject matter seen in previous classes

Despite being a very effective learning technique, spaced practice is seldom applied. You should not hesitate to review content during the weeks or even months following initial exposure, to improve retention of information and promote long-term learning.

Again, this can be combined with retrieval practice. In an article titled "Teaching the science of learning", Dr Yana Weinstein and her colleagues recommended creating opportunities to revisit concepts throughout the year. It may require some planning, but refreshing old content takes only a few minutes, whether by asking students to write a 1-minute summary of previous classes, or asking them to brainstorm and reconstruct past concepts.

7.  Pair each concept with images and examples

When you provide metaphors and examples, and you combine verbal explanations with graphics and images, students encode the same information multiple times, which greatly facilitates their brain's storage activity!

Students can then use visual and auditory processing capacities of the brain separately, rather than potentially overloading the visual processing capacity by viewing both the images and the written text. To that end, there are myriad online platforms on which you can create engaging, interactive presentations that support and illustrate your course material.

8.  Set aside time for questions

Giving students the chance to ask questions and reformulate the concepts they are learning allows them not only to *know* these things, but to know *how* and *why* they work. Questions raised by students activate their prior knowledge, focus their learning efforts, and help them elaborate on their knowledge (Chin & Osborne, 2008):

*"Put simply, the act of questioning encourages learners to engage in critical reasoning. Given that asking questions is fundamental to science and scientific inquiry, the development of students' abilities to ask questions, reason, problem-solve, and think critically should, likewise, become a central focus of current science education reform."*

"What if there are too many students in my classroom, or if they're scared to ask questions in front of their peers?" In that case, EdTech can help both you and your students: there are student response systems that give all students the opportunity to ask questions - anonymously!

9.  Integrate peer-to-peer discussion

This teaching method, put forth by Harvard University Professor Eric Mazur, has several positive effects on students: they are more committed, they can externalise their answer, they shift from facts to reasoning, and eventually, they get emotionally invested in the learning process. Here's how it works:

- The students are given the course material before class so that they can read it at home. This way, they can prepare for the lectures.
- During class, the professor briefly summarises the topic and provides the students with a conceptual multiple choice question. This sort of question focuses on one key notion at a time and does not require equations or written reasoning.
- Students think on their own and answer the question. The professor faces three potential outcomes:

  1. Less than 30% of students chose the correct answer. Initial understanding is very poor, hence it is necessary for the teacher to review the concept, before asking the question again.
  2. Between 30 and 70% of the students in attendance have answered correctly. In this case, students are invited to spend some time trying to convince each other of the choice they made. After a while, they must answer the same question again.
  3. The rate of success is greater than 70%. This result is satisfying: the professor provides feedback and proceeds to the next concept.

Besides boosting the performance of the students, this method has several other advantages:

- Students have to externalise their answer, turn to their neighbour and convince them of their reasoning;
- By doing this, a student's answer changes from a simple fact to an articulated reasoning;
- Eventually, students get emotionally invested in the learning process: research in cognitive sciences found that the emotional kind of encoding is among the best to store information.

These 9 applications can be implemented in and adapted to a tutor's teaching habits, preferences, and strategies. Of course, as the pandemic has made abundantly clear, lectures are only one part of the equation. Nowadays, the emphasis is on learning continuity. In other words, how do we design courses and curricula in such a way that meaningful learning can be achieved anywhere?

This goes hand in hand with learning autonomy: teaching students how to learn and thereby enabling them to ensure their own learning continuity. As the field of education enters a new stage in which digital tools and distance learning are more present than ever before, students must be taught - ironically - to manage their own learning.

With that in mind, let's conclude with 5 neuroeducational best practices students can use to improve their learning.

### 5 Best Practices To Optimise Revision

If we want students to be able to learn outside the classroom, we must first give them the tools they need to become autonomous learners. These 5 practices are meant to help students turn revisions into effective learning sessions, by understanding what happens in their brain when they revise.

1.  Activate your neurons

When we learn, our brain changes: brain plasticity allows **neural connections** to be created, and our knowledge is encoded in these neural networks. So, we need to create and strengthen - and sometimes undo or weaken - the neural connections related to learning. In any case, we need to adjust them.

2.  Space revisions in time to activate your neurons repeatedly

Activating neural connections once is not enough to learn. These connections are established and strengthened gradually, so they must be **activated repeatedly.**

From a pedagogical point of view, this means planning learning activities several times.

As we've seen, if two learning activities are related to the same subject, it is best not to do them one after the other, but to space them out over time. This will help maintain brain activity throughout the exercises, which would otherwise tend to decrease, and makes it necessary to sleep between activities. When we sleep, our brain reactivates the same neurons as it does during the day. In other words, s**leep contributes to the consolidation of learning!**

3.  Explain

Explaining *why* an assertion is true or *how* a process works requires us to not only retrieve memories, but also make connections between them. In doing so, we create connections between different groups of neurons: we **build a system of knowledge**. This type of exercise therefore helps us to structure our knowledge and increases our ability to retrieve information from memory, and thereby our ability to learn.

4.  Perform memory retrieval practices

When we make an effort to remember information, i.e. to retrieve it from memory, we strengthen the neural connections related to this learning. This activates key regions for the efficient encoding of knowledge in our brain.

There are 3 elements that make up a successful retrieval practice:

1.  It is important for students to **receive feedback** about the **accuracy** and **completeness** of their retrieval. The importance of this feedback will be explained in the final principle.
2.  Retrieval practice **works best when it is not graded**. This encourages students to use the learning method on their own, rather than linking it to stress and performance anxiety. As students become used to and confident in retrieving what they know from their memory, retrieval practice can even *reduce* anxiety.
3.  Effective retrieval practice is difficult and involves struggle. Students need to **know that**

**this struggle is beneficial**, because it means that learning is taking place.
4. Maximise feedback

When we give an answer to a question, just as when we interact with our environment and look at the effect of our actions, we receive feedback. If this feedback indicates that our action was appropriate, we call that **positive feedback**. Conversely, **negative feedback** indicates that we made a mistake. In both cases, feedback is essential for adjusting neural connections.

Positive feedback releases dopamine in the brain, which creates a sense of pleasure: when you complete a task, you usually experience **satisfaction**, which is important for learning because it can increase **motivation**.

Negative feedback is also important because it can trigger **corrective mechanisms** in the brain. This is one of the most important pedagogical factors for learning, because feedback helps **limit the repetition of errors** rather than reinforcing them, as would be the case if you were training memory retrieval without feedback.

That concludes this article on the importance of sound pedagogical principles as the foundation for the development and use of EdTech in higher education. We'll leave you with a little challenge: close your eyes, and see how much you remember about the three fundamental principles we discussed... And don't forget to check how well you did!

# The Rise Of Behavioural Science: A Roadmap For The Future Of Adult Learning

## Ivan Palomino, Elena Agaragimova, and HarukaMarufuj

Founder and Managing Partner, Co-founder and Managing Partner and Director Organizational Leadership & Culture, all Bessern

### Introduction

Globally, organisations have spent more than 370 billion USD to train their workforce (Statista, 2021), with 70% of employees claiming that they are not prepared with the right skills to master their jobs. (Crowley & Overton, 2021)

Despite advances in learning technology, the biggest challenge for corporate training is in the delivery, as 90% of training is designed without a well-defined strategy that facilitates it. (Henry et.al, 2021)

According to KPMG's Global CEO Outlook (2020), during the COVID crisis, CEO's have recognised that the lack of appropriate talent is the biggest risk for the future of their organisation. The immediate response has been a focus on resources (often with less budget) and the reprioritisation of learning content, with emphasis on skills to address the crisis, agility, and employee's motivation.

These types of skills and behaviour building need to have a different learning framework as they are reliant on using human mental power to unlearn previous practices, creating processes for self-management, and reducing the natural resistance of the brain for change.

In this article, we will be discussing the science behind the learning process, a behavioural change framework applied to learning, and how technology can support it.

### The Learning Process

There is no general agreement about the definition of learning. As researchers, such as De Houwer et al. (2013) and others have pointed out, even influential textbooks on learning do not always contain a definition of the subject matter (e.g., Bouton, 2007; Schwartz, Wasserman, & Robbins, 2002). However, most textbook definitions of learning refer to learning as a change in behaviour that is due to experience (Lachman, 1997). This is essentially a very basic functional definition of learning in that it is seen as a function that maps experience onto behaviour (De Houwer et al. 2013).

According to Berkley Center for Teaching and Learning, learning is a process that is active, builds on prior knowledge, occurs in a complex social environment, is situated in an authentic context, and requires learners' motivation and cognitive engagement. Although the inputs to learning are usually clear, what is important in the process is making sense of what outputs constitute the occurrence of learning. Needless to say, understanding what it takes to get the knowledge in and out can help optimise learning.

Learning can happen in a wide variety of ways; therefore, the process of learning is not always the same.

## Rote Learning And Meaningful Learning

Rote learning is the memorization of information based on repetition (Mayer, 2002). A common rote learning technique is cramming – which is preparing quickly for a test.

Rote learning can help develop foundational knowledge and supports the ability to quickly recall basic facts (Mayer &Wittlock, 1996). However, it does not provide depth, such as in the understanding of the information. This is because it does not build on the connection between new and previous knowledge. It also does not encourage the use of social skills and at times, may result in misunderstanding a concept. (Mayer, 2002)

On the other hand, meaningful learning involves understanding of how all the pieces of an entire concept fit together. The knowledge gained through meaningful learning applies to new learning situations. This type of learning stays with students for longer periods of time. According to researchers (Mayer, 2002; Schleisman et al. 2018; Anderson, 2020) meaningful learning is active, constructive, and long lasting, but most importantly, it allows the learner to be fully engaged in the learning process. Meaningful learning often supports the learner's problem-solving skills, which are easily transferable to real-life situations. (Hamdan et al, 2015)

Experts have also emphasised the importance of deep understanding over the recalling of facts. Two important goals of all types of learning include retention and transfer (Mayer, 2002). "Retention" is the ability to remember the material at a later time, while "Transfer" is the ability to use prior knowledge to solve new problems. We achieve meaningful learning when both goals are fulfilled.

As it revolves around focusing on the outcome of the learning process, meaningful learning teaches people important cognitive skills. Cognitive skills are what people use to evaluate, analyse, remember, and make comparisons. (Sander, 2011) This is the reason many in the field argue that in the long run, meaningful learning is the most effective way for people to engage in learning.

It is well documented that understanding the information enables longer retention and facilitates greater future learning than rote memorisation. (National Research Council, 2000) Hamdan et al (2015) concluded that learners when engaging in meaningful learning spend less time learning large bulks of information compared to learners using rote techniques. This is because it is much easier to continuously build on concepts the learner already understands. (Shuell, 1992)

The phenomenon where people remember information better when it is meaningful to them is known to psychologists as "elaborative encoding". (Anderson, 2000) Instructors could take advantage of this by making the learning content meaningful to learners in a variety of ways, but it is tricky when the degree of meaningfulness to one is often different from another.

If meaningful learning is occurring, then the learner is fully engaged, and the brain can then organise the information based on what it relates to; this creates the associations that help us learn more and understand better by making connections (Shimamura, 2011). This also means that these facts will be remembered together, instead of individually. Remembering one of the facts (activation) will prime you to remember the others. This has been termed "spreading activation" and learners who are able to use this method of learning, as opposed to rote learning, are able to solve problems easier due to their capacity to apply their knowledge. (Colins and Loftus, 1975; Anderson, 1983; Patterson et. al, 2007)

Passively reviewing information, such as just reading over a word or phrase does not equate to making that information or learning stick. Cognitive and social psychologists argue that memory and learning is strengthened by practice in generating the new information. (Shimamura, 2011) Simply put, repeating, or telling people what you have learned, helps solidify that learning. Thus, to improve the teaching, many researchers, including Shimamura (2011), point out that educators need to capitalise on the generation effect, by encouraging learners to generate, or recapitulate, information as they process it. Even simple retrieval exercises, such as filling in the blanks, improves our memory.

## Memory

While our brain is capable of impressive feats, the reality is that its capacity to store and recall details is limited. Forgetting is part of life and people forget surprisingly fast. Research has found that approximately 56% of information is forgotten within an hour, 66% after a day, and 75% after six days. (Murre &Dros, 2015)
In business, we tend to put the focus on lost information and thus conclude that it is a very costly shortcoming of the human brain. However, the phenomenon of forgetting is not just normal, but it's actually healthy. As Kohn (2014) explains, most of the things we remember are only of short-term importance, and after a day or so, the brain suppresses such time-limited memories to free space for more information.

Human memory is the process in which information and material is encoded, stored, and retrieved in the brain. (Spear, 2014) It is a continued process of information retention over time, allowing individuals to recall and draw upon past events to frame their understanding of behaviour in the present. (Cowan, 2008)

Memory plays a critical role in learning as well as teaching, as it provides us with a framework through which to make sense of the present and future. One can experience the memories by the process of memory retrieval or recall.

Memory recall and retrieval involves remembering different types of memories stored in the brain. Research suggests the speed of memory retrieval and recall depends on the strength of neural pathways formed in the earlier stages of memory processing. (Ramratan et.al, 2012; Rasch & Born, 2013)

## Techniques For Better Retention & Recall

In providing support to their teaching staff, Harvard University's Derek Bok Center for Teaching and Learning advocates three techniques to promote better retention and recall among students. These are testing effect, spacing, and interleaving.

The Testing Effect

The testing effect refers to the process of actively and frequently testing memory retention when learning new information. Testing is normally considered as a method of periodic assessment. However, modern research in psychology suggests that frequent, small tests are also one of the best ways to learn. By encouraging learners to regularly recall information they have recently learned, they retain that information in long-term memory, which they can draw upon at a later stage of the learning experience. (Brown, Roediger, & McDaniel, 2014)

Spacing

According to Brown, Roediger, & McDaniel (2014), when a student repeatedly learns and recalls information over a prolonged time span, they are more likely to retain that information in comparison to learning and attempting to retain the information in a short time span. This means that rather than introducing a new topic and its related concepts to students in one go, topics should be covered in segments over multiple lessons for it to be retained better.

Interleaving

Interleaving has proven to be more successful than the traditional blocking technique in various fields. (Brown, Roediger, & McDaniel, 2014) Interleaving is when students practice multiple related skills in the same session whereas Blocking, which refers to when a student practices one skill or one topic at a time. Learners can also be aware of techniques they can use to improve their own recall. State-dependent memory (Weissenborn&Duka, 2000), chunking (Gobet et al., 2001), and deliberate practice (Brown et al., 2014) are some techniques people can use on their own.

One way to retrieve and retain knowledge is to apply it constantly. Learning itself is an undertaking that usually requires a sizable commitment of time. But, a slow learner who shows up consistently will always outperform a fast learner who quits early. If learning is about consistency, then the question is: how do we maintain this consistency? The answer is by creating a change via habit creation.

## A Framework To Address The Gap Between How The Brain Functions And Adult Learning

Corporations strive to convert knowledge into sustainable behaviours; knowledge retention is not enough to make people want to use what is stored in our brains. Influencing behaviours has been a major contribution from BJ Fogg - a Stanford University professor and behavioural scientist. The Fogg behaviour model is built on the theory that three elements should converge to either allow the creation of a new behaviour, restrict or simply refine an existing behaviour. These three elements are Motivation, Ability, and Prompt. (Fogg, 2009) In the context of adult learning, these principles can be adapted to nudge people to activate a positive attitude towards change and start producing actions or behaviours towards a specific intention.

## Motivation

Motivation is a volatile element for humans as it is often temporary and present when we have a goal or intention. Once people may realise that these things take effort, the motivation may vanish.

The human brain has three underlying drivers to motivate us: Sensation, Anticipation and Belonging. These drivers can be transformed into principles applicable for adult learning:

**Sensation Principle:** Seek pleasure and avoid pain

- Recognition: We tend to engage in behaviours in which achievements are recognised
- Closure: The anticipation of celebrating the completion of an action is a driver towards completion
- Challenge: Using levels to communicate progress and next expectations is a way to engage learners into the optimum flow where actions are kept into their control: still within their capabilities but challenging enough. Both boredom (because the challenge is too easy) or anxiety (if too difficult) lead to disengagement.

**Anticipation Principle:** Our intrinsic hopes and fears influence our emotions

- Autonomy: When we have the control of our own destiny, it reinforces our engagement – deciding on how to act towards a challenge in a risk-free environment enhances engagement in the learning. This is boosted by letting learners set their own learning goals
- Storytelling: The way a facilitator creates a narrative that is personalised, genuine and relatable helps learners engage in different perspectives than their own
- Curiosity: When the content contains cues or teasers of interesting information, people tend to crave more

**Belonging Principle:** Looking for social acceptance and avoid rejection

- Social proof: when we are in an unfamiliar situation we tend to follow what others do to feel safe
- Liking: the message and the messenger have equal importance for engagement. The messenger needs to be relatable and likeable in all human dimensions
- Reciprocation: we give back when we receive. Importantly, giving feedback (from the facilitator or the cohort) determines the level of participation

## Ability

Learners must be able to execute the desired learning actions or challenges. If the action is too difficult, the brain will activate 'fear of change' signals that will create friction. Learners should be provided knowledge and practice in a way where they are maintained in the Flow Channel as described by Csikszentmihalyi. (1990) The actions should be made simple during the training to help minimise physical and cognitive effort.

There is a significant positive persuasion to learn and practice by simplifying behaviours, such as shorter duration of training (micro-learnings), that will limit the physical and cognitive effort. Learners do not need to maintain attention for an entire day, as our brain bandwidth to focus and process information is limited within a much shorter period of time.

The practice of new knowledge should be chunked into micro-actions that can be formed in a matter of minutes. Embedding new behaviours is often achieved by regularly practised consistent action, rather a big action with high intensity of efforts.

Improvements in ability are observed in designed behaviours that have the following characteristics:

- Relevancy: the behaviour should be done in the context of their work and be tailor-made to the learner's specific aspiration
- Simplification: learners should be able to perform actions that are short and effortless, for example two minutes of planning for the three most important tasks of the day
- Consistency: repetition of micro-habits allows us to create rituals that become automated without cognitive efforts. If doing a target behaviour causes over thinking, then we do not see the behaviour as simple, which harms the brain processing fluency
- Feedback: Prompt feedback for learners make it easier for them to adjust their behaviours and maintain their engagement

## Prompts

Despite the fact that we may want to achieve certain actions, we are still at risk of simply forgetting to do it. A learning program should contain a recognisable context or situation that will remind the learner to trigger the practice of the new action. These triggers will activate the new behaviour in the context of the learners' usual work life. Clues to activate are often situations that will help retrieve the new behaviour; the learner should be equipped to recognise existing rituals or timings for the trigger.

The use of technology for notifications is not always the best way to convert a prompt into behaviour as it becomes distracting and inefficient in a world of high cognitive load.

The concepts behind this behavioural change framework have been enriched by several models of successful adult learning such as the AGES model. Cognitive-Based Instruction (CBI) focuses on the different types of learning involved in cognitive functioning and development. Under the umbrella of CBI is the andragogical learning model, better known as andragogy. Andragogy is the practice of adjusting teaching strategies to suit how adults learn most effectively. Adult learning delivery styles have evolved over the years and are now the staple for the design and delivery of adult training and education.

The AGES model, cemented in research within neuroscience, is believed to serve to enhance Learning and Development. As a structure of andragogical learning, the AGES Model enables people to learn quickly, and retain that information for the long haul. (Davachi et.al, 2010)

AGES stands for Attention, Generation, Emotion, and Spacing. The AGES Model describes a style of learning that helps people focus on the content, engage directly with it, experience positive emotions around it, and take breaks between lessons. When organisations take such an approach, research suggests they will maximise their teams' learning and accelerate breakthroughs. (Meeking, 2018)

**How Technology Can Contribute to Enhance This Framework**

Training in the workplace has usually consisted of technology supporting scale but not efficiency of learning. Often, delivery through technology has been a copy and paste of the physical training. However, advancement in brain science and psychology can help overcome this issue.

Technology, combined with brain science, can add relevancy and personalisation to the learning experience, measure the learning effectiveness at a granular level, improve instant feedback loop on actions performed, track abilities and psychological resources to perform actions, predict learning needs and proactively suggest short knowledge and actions and broaden the access to knowledge. The biggest technology contributors come from two areas:

**Artificial Intelligence**

Both neuroscience and AI have the same focus: the prediction of behaviours.

AI can support learning through:

- Curation of content: personalised and time relevant content based on data of context, behaviours, cognition and engagement
- Recognition of emotional state, stress and attitudes through facial and voice recognition in real time
- Auto-generation of micro-habits based on interaction and behavioural pattern of the learner

**Augmented Reality (AR) And Virtual Reality (VR)**

Simulated environments enhance the learning experience within a safe and risk-free context. The human representation of virtual mentors can reinforce the knowledge transfer and make it sensorial: what we are told stays longer in our brain than what we read.

## Learning In The Flow Of Work

The future of learning will be increasingly impacted by how it is integrated in the flow of work. Technology facilitates this process: connecting strategic imperatives to executional capabilities of the workforce, real time streaming of workforce sentiments, creation of peer-to-peer learning social communities, connecting employees to new tasks during the workday, and unbiased ways to assess performance.

The replacement of Learning Management System is not responding to the need to accelerate the upskill workforce. This will be replaced by more intangible platforms with seamless integration with our work tools – some think that this will be the role of Learning Experience Platforms – designed to drive learning engagement through easy discoverability of relevant content.

Thanks to behavioural science, we now have evidence that the way we learn has changed. Different generations learn differently, and EdTech will facilitate the learning process in the future. It has become essential to create individualised (customised), accessible, self-driven, affordable, and flexible learning experiences. Technology is there to enhance the choice of the right content (right time and right context) and will drive efficiency across the learning framework.

Two trending concepts are part of the paradigm change in learning:

- **Agile Learning:** the main idea behind applying the Agile Learning methodology is about making sure that learners need the learning, they are willing to engage with the training and that you can deploy it quicker in very rapid iterations
- **Modular Learning:** providing access to new knowledge and skills in smaller chunks – regardless of career level, without prerequisite work – making learning accessible and easy to digest and apply. It allows us to focus more on future skills vs outdated subjects, contributing to continuous learning and upskilling

Forgetting is widely accepted as part of the learning journey. This happens mainly due to a lack of immediate application of the learning. (Wixted, 2004)

A modular bite-size approach is an effective way to ensure people are:

- focused on what they need to know for their respective goals at that time
- be able to apply learning immediately in real life
- not overwhelmed by unnecessary extra content

A neuroscience-based learning process is about helping people create a process and a set of triggers that can help them automate the use of new knowledge. Applying a behavioural change and habit creation methodology allows us to empower learners to stay on track with their learning journeys, without them having to rely on motivation to keep them going. Furthermore, it is about combining technology with a human touch, not merely leaving people to go through the journey on their own, because individual support and feedback are an impactful part of the learning.

The application of this learning framework is being used across higher education and corporate learning in think tanks such as the Minerva Project and Bessern; with promising results in terms of engagement, knowledge retention, application and most importantly, new behaviours being created.

**Conclusion**

Catering to today's need for updated knowledge requires a model based on "learning how to learn" rather than the simple transfer of knowledge. Technology makes it scalable and measurable, but learning must also be relatable with a human touch, frictionless in the face of volatile human motivation.

The priorities in corporate learning have shifted: The World Economic Forum reported the top 10 skills required for the future, which included critical thinking, self-management, resilience, creativity, leadership, and emotional intelligence amongst others. (Whiting, 2020) A few of these skills such as self-management and resilience were not on previous lists, giving us a clear picture of what organisations require to maintain their competitive edge.

Learning these new priorities requires a shift in learning methodology, where the crafting of new behaviours is the only proof of success.

People can only acquire these behaviours by consistent practice, personalisation, continuous feedback, and measurement of progress. This is where the behavioural model framework has its biggest impact and potential, not only to change individual learning but also corporate cultures.

The biggest disruption in adult learning is in the methodology. Technology is just a vehicle to efficiently scale. We must be conscious of the human psychology of learning before we can apply it with the aid of the increasingly advanced tools we now have.

# Online Learning: Process, Tools, Challenges And Success Strategies

## Puneet Sharma, PHD

Professor | Researcher | Mathematician | Physicist | Mentor | Author

In today's digital age, online mode of course delivery for teaching and learning is gaining ground. Based on my exemplary experience, I will outline some interesting insight on this captivating topic and share tips on student success in remote course delivery. For a pleasant learning experience, the **WHICEP framework** is being introduced to discuss effective strategies for mastering new domains. Making the transition from in-class to online learning a seamless process is challenging. There is a colossal potential of online learning in the coming time and a continuous need for exploring, experimenting, and researching the interactive and collaborative features of online learning tools and applications. In this article, I will discuss feedforward and blended mode of learning in detail for effective teaching and learning.

We've all witnessed a huge transformation from fully in-class to online mode of delivery with the start of COVID–19 pandemic in March 2020. Online learning is an evolving process. It demands a high level of commitment, engagement, focus and adaptation to succeed. This journey starts with lots of new unforeseen challenges and problems including computer literacy, non-familiarity with technology, and other prerequisites (depending upon the subjects), making online learning an unpleasant experience. It is your responsibility to meet prerequisites to be successful in this undertaking. Other issues that may face include distraction, isolation, restless eyes, fatigue, lack of concentration and motivation, time mismanagement, mental health issues, boring content, increased screen time, and feeling lazy, stressful, and anxious.

Thinking of solutions, learning the art of time management is key. It is the most challenging task for many people - but it can be improved. Some tips to improve your time management skills include:

- Breaking your work into manageable pieces
- Taking regular breaks
- Avoiding monotonous tasks
- Monitoring your progress regularly
- Ticking off a task when completed

When watching videos or live lectures, surround yourself with friends that help you stay motivated when learning new concepts. When making notes, try to write down the key words/ideas when skimming the video for the first time. After watching, check your knowledge and understanding of the topic to see if you need to fill any gaps.

Additionally, you should work in the direction of improving your physical, mental, and spiritual health. Spend some quality time with yourself and your family and do some yoga, walking, jogging, meditation, and breathing exercises to improve your overall health. Remember to rest your eyes after focusing on a screen and read outside your curriculum.

Recently, I received an overwhelming response for my tips on student success in remote course delivery [Fig 1]. It highlights guidelines such as instructional plan, office hours, marking important dates, learning management system, discussion groups, self-discipline, staying positive and focused, and evaluations.

# Tips for Student Success in Remote Course Delivery

Written by: Puneet Sharma, PhD
puneetsharma.ca
twitter.com/ProfMathUWC

| Importance of the Instructional Plan | • Course Outline<br>• Expectations<br>• Assessments | • Objectives<br>• Skills gained<br>• Weekly activities |
|---|---|---|
| Mark Important Dates and add reminders | • Google Calendar<br>• Pulse<br>• Apple Calendar | • Outlook Calendar<br>• Add reminders using Apps |
| Learning Management System (LMS) | • eConestoga<br>• Course Shell<br>• Content<br>• Course tools | • Assignments/Quizzes<br>• Class list<br>• Grades<br>• Course Mail |
| Instructor's Office Hours | • Additional help<br>• Ask questions | • Individual appointments |
| Discussion Groups | • To make subject interesting<br>• What is next to learn? | • Networking opportunity with your peers |
| Guiding Principles | • Planning<br>• Self-discipline<br>• Passion for learning | • Integrity<br>• Focus<br>• Persistence |
| Preparation for Evaluations | • Watch/attend lectures<br>• Keep summary sheet | • Practice<br>• Solve sample exams<br>• Make handy notes |

Embarking on a positive experiential learning journey. A key tip for success is understanding the course outline, overview, expectations, assessments, objectives, and skills gained after completing the course. Many students underestimate the importance of instructional plan (IP) that all essential elements mentioned above. IP is being posted for students before the start of classes. In addition, it provides details about instructor's contact information, course objectives, additional resources, grade breakdown, weekly scheduled activities, evaluations and assessments dates and timings throughout the span of course.

To remember important dates for the evaluation part, students are urged to use any of the available app as per their choice, including Google Calendar, Pulse, Microsoft Outlook Calendar, and Apple Calendar. In addition, whilst using a Learning Management System (LMS), you can explore the settings to add reminders for announcements, exams, assignments, and important tasks to complete your course.

Furthermore, ensure that you make yourself aware of your instructor's office hours, and get yourself involved in discussion groups to know what is going on in the subject. Online delivery demands a high level of self-discipline and passion, planning, and motivation for learning. The discussion would be incomplete if we did not share the most important part of being successful in the course – the assessment. Assessment tasks and questions are mostly algorithmic, so keep practising sample tests to build your confidence and keep on top of note-making.

For my own online teaching, I use many platforms, including Zoom, Microsoft Teams, and Bongo. Google Classroom is another popular addition to the above-mentioned list. I appreciate the effort by different companies to make online learning feasible and love the variety of interactive and collaborative features of these platforms during live teaching sessions such as discussion, breakout rooms, screen and document sharing, calling, annotation tools, polling feature, and high-quality video recording of sessions. Microsoft Forms can be used to create surveys, questionnaires, and polls for taking student feedback. As a result, the instructor comprehends the attendee/users need, and this information can be utilised to incorporate and promote diversity, social justice, equity, and inclusion in online education. Educator focus is to empower online learners so that they gain confidence and be successful in their personal and professional lives.

By using technology such as Google Forms, SurveyMonkey, Powtoons and other online platforms, students are able to have an active role in assessment and learning. Instructors and students can be given immediate feedback and use this to help shape learning goals. Technology creates motivation and engagement in many ways and can build on the strengths and knowledge of students.

I also use Piazza (a rich learning platform, free for students and instructors) as a collaboration tool for promoting and creating a forum for active learning. Instructors encourage students to ask questions on Piazza instead of sending emails, and a conducive classroom environment is developed through teamwork and collaboration between students, teaching assistants, and instructors. As a result, students clarify their doubts without delay.

There are numerous EdTech tools available in the market for making online learning and teaching an engaging and a mesmerising experience, including Kahoot, Flipgrid, Nearpod, Pear Deck, Canva, Prezi, Mentimeter, Edmodo, Padlet, Socrative, eduClipper, Projeqt, Thinglink, TED-Ed, ClassDojo, and Animoto. The learners are welcomed to share their experiences of learning. It is always interesting and inspiring to know other learners' success stories. Everyone feels connected, and this amazing environment proves beneficial for all learners.

Additionally, there are tons of digital resources available for online learning - called Open Educational Resources (OER). These are freely available and openly licensed study materials (e.g. video, text, media, Massive Open Online Courses, activities, tools, etc.) that can be used for teaching, learning, and research purposes. Countries across the world are actively creating these resources for promoting online education. A learner can reuse, re-mix, improve, and redistribute these resources under some licences. I enjoy *graphics pen tablets* for online class as it reminds me of using whiteboard for in-class delivery. It makes the presentation more professional, lively, and eye-catching through available annotation tools. For example, Microsoft OneNote digital note taking app offers invaluable features such as converting handwritten notes to typed one. This amazing feature is very useful for diverse learners that require special accommodations. There are many options available for graphics pen tablets in the market these days. Hats off to companies for making digital learning a pleasant experience for learners and instructors!

## Effective Strategies for Mastering New Domains

Written by: **Puneet Sharma, PhD**
*puneetsharma.ca*
*twitter.com/ProfMathUWC*

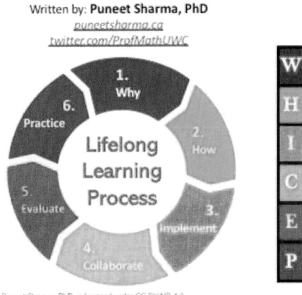

As a part of *lifelong learning process*, I now introduce *WHICEP framework* [Fig 2] to master new domains to my students during the first class. This model may be adapted to different levels and subjects. The pivotal concept here is to notice, understand, appreciate, and apply the important strategies, namely, Why, How, Implement, Collaborate, Evaluate, and Practice. The first technique, Why, refers to asking yourself questions about the importance of pioneering domains. Value your time, energy, and resources to find reasons to be fully convinced to proceed. Spend time to research about the new undertaking regarding cost, usefulness, and necessity. Consult online and find some mentor to understand the key motivation to accomplish the project. Feel inspired, think multi-dimensionally, and explore the relevant real-life applications.

After completing step 1, the next strategy, How, is the keystone in the learning process. There are multiple ways to approach any problem, so investigate the bigger picture of the problem and break it down into pieces. In addition, discuss your study material with an experienced person (senior, educator, professional, mentor). Active listening and discussion make a huge difference and staying positive and patient during your strategy development makes this process enjoyable and fruitful. You can also find relevance and/or connection and importance of the smaller pieces to visualise the bigger picture. Success is directly linked to the thorough understanding of concepts, so it is no doubt that the planning part is crucial to solve any problem.

Implement is the backbone of the learning process - no one can learn to swim without going into the water. Theoretical knowledge alone will never lead to success. Through implementation, we learn right away. Moreover, self-reflection enables learners to develop a deeper understanding of this process and teaches them about the importance of practice.

Collaborate is the building foundation to success. Share your knowledge, skills, and experience with your peers or anyone interested in finding out what you have learned. Teamwork facilitates rapport and trust, and brings forward the best talent among diverse members for outstanding results. It boosts inclusiveness, honesty, patience, novel ideas, morale, and interpersonal and problem-solving skills among co-workers that are pillars for prosperous personal and professional lives. Group work is also an opportunity to grow your professional network and promotes skills like communication, responsibility, active listening, and empathy.

The next step is Evaluate. Assess yourself through available resources, discuss and ask for observation from any experienced person in the field and do your best to incorporate the feedback. Identifying your weaknesses is the first step towards improvement. Monitor your progress continuously, be confident about your achievements and never feel disheartened with failures – these are only stepping stones to success.

This learning journey would be incomplete without mentioning Practice. During regular practice sessions, leave no stone unturned. Research has proven that continuous practice of any activity keeps your mind active and helps to achieve key milestones. Practising a task helps you get closer to perfection. These all steps mentioned in **WHICEP** are correlated to one another in a life-long learning process.

Based on experiential learning and teaching, I now bring forward a few suggestions to help minimise the gap between the online and in-class environment:

- Teachers and students should do their best to virtually interact and socialise
- Teachers should make short videos about the important concepts and examples
- Students should attend live office hours
- Turn the camera on when possible
- Create break out rooms for smaller groups
- Do live video announcements

To make online learning even further effective, there are a few asynchronous/synchronous strategies/activities that can be implemented. These include brainstorming, live Q&A sessions and debates, group discussion, storytelling, and problem-based learning. These activities make learning active, interesting, and result oriented. This way, learners feel connected, engaged, and motivated. Including self-reflection furthers critical thinking, understanding and implementation of the key concepts to real-world examples.

Feedforward is another trending and interesting strategy for effective teaching and learning. Giving feedforward means that we do not judge or rate anyone's performance in the past, but instead concentrate on their development in the future. For ultimate implementation, discuss with students about learning outcomes and expectations at the start of the term, inquire subject interest, follow up continuously throughout the duration of the course, and alter strategies accordingly, for the best interest of students. For example, while learning essay writing or maths concepts, students need to actively collaborate with teachers for continuous feedback before the final evaluation for filling the gaps in understanding and better grades. This way, the teacher can make sure that the student is liking the continuous feedback. Feedforward is constructive, timely, developmental, and a win-win situation for students and instructors. Moreover, this process has emphasis on the task instead of the person. Feedforward technique would be an asset for promoting diversity, inclusiveness, and equity.

In a nutshell, I predict that online education with blended learning and teaching, will be the most popular way of educating going forward. The only element our future generation needs to take care of is the utilisation of EdTech for the betterment of society. *Let us connect, collaborate, cooperate, communicate, interact, support, and share our knowledge to learn together.*

# Education's Trends Explained In Four Dimensions

## Nathalia Kelday
CEO of Edstation

With a deluge of articles, reports, podcasts, and documentaries on innovation in education, following current trends can be challenging and time-consuming. The intent is for readers to contextualise and summarise how education developed through to 2021, and the direction in which it is headed. Four current areas in education and trends will be defined, although, admittedly, grey zones exist among the four dimensions: (i) *Active Learning*; (ii) *21st Century Skills*; (iii) *Technologies;* and (iv) *Time and Space.*

- *Active Learning* accounts for changes in pedagogical methods. The Digital Age caused a huge shift towards a more student-centred approach, overcoming the paradigms inherited from the First Industrial Revolution, in a strong resistance from educators and the institutionalised format of national exams.

- *21st Century Skills* refers to core competencies that students should learn to strive for in today's fast-paced world. To deal with exponential changes in life and work, students have to be intentionally stimulated to develop their abilities to communicate, to collaborate, and to think critically, creatively and flexibly.

- *Technology* signifies the means used to optimise education processes. The pandemic energetically fostered not only the EdTech market, but also helped propagate technological accessibility and connectivity and improved educators' digital literacy skills. The rise of emerging technologies, such as artificial intelligence, expanded reality, and robotics has accelerated considerably.

- *Time and Space* relates to transformations in educational arrangements. Addressing personalised learning needs, students' natural pace in learning is becoming increasingly respected, breaking standardised learning cycles. In addition, to ensure *Active Learning* and *21st Century Skills* are implemented properly, stakeholders in education ought to create classrooms with flexible spatial dispositions and even provide architectural renovations. Distance learning is also dramatically changing where and how students engage with their education.

The framework presented in this article will enable readers to decodify the concepts they find in publications about innovative education when they are exposed to such diverse concepts. Furthermore, it may enlighten educators to adopt and maintain innovations and trends at the forefront of education.

## Introduction

There are innumerable, reputable think-tanks publishing their visions of trends in education, and to such an extent that it is difficult for educators to ascertain which pedagogical tools are best to implement for effective learning and instruction. Indeed, the educational landscape that evolved alongside the Information Revolution is as intricate as imaginable. New concepts and terminologies continue to arise in profusion, and understanding their meaning is often a laborious task. The intent is to offer an overview of the trending dimensions in education and to organise the main ideas related to its vanguard.

Education is now present in every stage of human life, either public or private; either with regulated curricula or as non-regulated courses. Education consists of a series of agents, such as stakeholders, managers, coordinators, teachers, students and families, and community members, to name a few. Furthermore, for each existing program there is a unique pedagogical approach, which presents infinite combinations of learning, instructional tools, and technologies. Considering the complexity that the field of education and technology can reach, summarising ongoing trends in education can be a risky didactic approximation, which could put aside some integral concepts and shorten others. Nevertheless, it can be a powerful framework to understand what the industry is facing.

The framework of this article encompasses solely the transformations happening inside schools and other education institutions. Structural changes in the educational market, such as public policies, mergers and acquisitions, home-schooling, tuition fees and financing, and reconfiguration of higher education will not be addressed. A focus on institutional and class management under four groupings were devised to outline central trends and how they are interrelated. The four dimensions are (i)*Active Learning;* (ii) *21st Century Skills*; (iii) *Technologies;* and (iv) *Time and Space*.

FRAMEWORKS

Learning about these four areas of education will leverage comprehension of what educators and stakeholders of innovative schools worldwide are doing to prepare students, and the strategies implemented by the countries who participate and receive high marks in the Program for International Student Assessments (PISA). Further, it will help understand what UNESCO stakeholders are recommending so that education leads to a more "just, peaceful, tolerant, inclusive, secure and sustainable world". The same patterns can be identified in reports from Pearson, Holon IQ, the World Economic Forum, the World Bank, and the Organisation for Economic Co-operation and Development (OECD), taking into account the aforementioned margin for approximation.

The meaning of the four dimensions will be contextualised to increase understanding of innovative educational concepts. Additionally, the article will present strategies, implementation, and the most common hindrances to these strategies. The diffusion of such tendencies is imperative to ensure continued motion forward for accomplishing education's main goal – to prepare individuals for life and work in the third millennium and empower them to reach their maximum potential.

## Active Learning

Those who have worked with education for more than a decade have probably noticed a recent increase of information for promoting active student engagement in the learning process. Although the Information Age has further boosted discussions related to *Active Learning*, the pressure for reform dates back to 120 years ago, shortly after the international spread of educational systems as they are known today: universal, compulsory and free of charge.

The First Industrial Revolution played a major role in shaping education. In the early days, information was extremely rare and valuable. Considering the pace of innovation at that time, information changed more slowly with academic content remaining current for decades. Therefore, schools and universities served as knowledge sanctuaries, accumulating all of the books they could afford. Few teachers were available to educate all citizens under mandatory school law and, under the pressure of political and warlike motivations, educational systems were forced to reproduce the idea of productivity: a rigid, standardised assembly line.

The outcome of such conditions was a teacher-centred pedagogical approach, which would encourage teachers to treat all students the same, sealed by an abstract idea of the average. Universal education was made possible in the 19th century, with scarce technologies available at the time, because hundreds of thousands of students sacrificed their talents and potential to fit the ideal of sameness in education. Since then, the world has crossed three other industrial revolutions and such patterns are still replicated in the 21st century.

The first person to devise a line between passive and *Active Learning* was American philosopher and educational reformer John Dewey in 1903. According to Dewey, a democratic society stems from children's experiences whilst at school. Thus, the learning process should be participative rather than passive. He declared that teachers' roles should stimulate students' curiosities to motivate learning, rather than focus primarily on conveying content. These statements were made in the context of the Second Industrial Revolution, wherein Dewey had already asserted that education failed to keep pace with the undergoing transformations in society.

After Dewey's assertions, numerous other educators agreed that students should have more space in the teaching and learning process, and that the active learning approach was more effective for cognitive development and for forming well-prepared citizens. The pantheon encompasses pedagogues from various regions and times, such as Maria Montessori (Italy, 1907), Rudolf Steiner (Austria, 1919), Lev Vygotsky (USSR, 1934), Loris Malaguzzi (Italy, 1945), Edgar Dale (United States, 1946), Paulo Freire (Brazil, 1974), and José Pacheco (Portugal, 1976). During the last century, this paradigmatic change often sounded eccentric and idealistic. Unattended voices tried to warn society about the waste of intellectual efforts in schools and the oppression towards students. Regardless of such warnings, the transition would have had prohibitive costs, even for the wealthiest societies. Passive learning seemed to be the only affordable way for education to reach the masses up until the Information Age.

By the time information was released from its confinement of expensive and static physical books, students were offered online classes from the best specialists available and educational documentaries were produced from deep-pocketed budgets. The Information Revolution gave rise to the first generation of students growing up with the internet, enabling students to take ownership of learning and leaving some teachers on the periphery.

If the implementation of passive or *Active Learning* paradigms were a matter of dispute until the beginning of the Third Millennium, today, passive learning scarcely suits students or educators in a world deluged by technology.1The isolated voices in education from past enthusiasts are gaining respect, as evidence flourishes that *Active Learning* is more intellectually and emotionally rewarding for students.

*Active Learning* is defined as an approach to instruction that actively engages students with school subjects through discussion, problem solving, case studies, role playing activities, and other methods. A student-first perspective is employed, in which teachers are not content providers, but advisors who stimulate curiosity and encourage mentorship. Flipped classroom, project-based learning, learn-by-doing and STEAM (acronym for Science, Technology, Engineering, Arts and Maths) are some of the terms that designate forms of application of Active Learning.

The Active Learning approach is associated with working on real world problems and developing students' abilities to become self-sufficient in how they learn, or engaging metacognition, in "learning how to learn." Thus, preparation to learn for a lifetime, also known as "lifelong learning." With the aim of respecting students' interests and enhancing learning efficacy, students may be encouraged to follow "personalised paths," and, similar to games, interaction with content can be adapted to offer objectives, challenges, levels, rewards and feedback, which is called "gamification." Oftentimes, through *Active Learning*, divisions among school subjects disappear, promoting interdisciplinary, multidisciplinary, and even transdisciplinary approaches.

## LEARNING PARADIGMS

### PASSIVE LEARNING

Teacher-centered.
Students are treated as
content depositories. Also
known as Instructionist and
Transmissive learning.

### ACTIVE LEARNING

Student-centered.
Students are self-directed
learners, guided by the teacher.
Also known as Communication
and Constructivism learning.

*1 There are some Asian countries, such as China and South Korea, which still play for high stakes with transmissive approaches for learning. Although they rank in the top positions of PISA tests, when the correlation between performance and hours of study is considered, they show substantial inefficiency.*

Some research centres in education are pushing *Active Learning* to the extreme. Stanford Transformative Learning Technologies Lab, combines multimodal computational tools, such as advanced sensing and artificial intelligence, to investigate new ways to assess project-based activities. Students' speech, gestures, sketches and artefacts may be monitored through the use of these multimodal tools, to better characterise students' learning over extended periods of time. Neurofeedback technology accounts for another technique used by scientists to investigate brain behaviour during intellectual activities, which consists of using a headset with sensors to monitor brainwave signals.

Although Active Learning enthusiasts have gained theoretical and technological support, the paradigmatic shift in learning does not flow naturally in the wake of constant information access; on the contrary, considerable effort is required for student-centred active learning environments. The first challenge regards the upskilling of teachers and pedagogical coordinators to overcome resistance to a new paradigm. In effect, the passive learning approach has been the *status quo* for roughly two centuries, and most of the education professionals learned as passive recipients of knowledge. These educators have been teaching the way they were taught for years, if not for decades. Disarming the resistance to change is a delicate part of the evolving process to improve instruction.

The subsequent challenge is designing a comprehensive pedagogical proposal that encompasses the whole institution. When solitary teachers try to shift their methods without the support of their organisation, they often face serious difficulties: a disproportionate balance of evaluation methods; cultural barriers among students; a lack of assistance from teachers' peers; and teacher training shortages. If the whole environment is not immersed in the same purpose, these teachers' efforts will yield weaker results, which is why a top-down strategy is needed.

In truth, institutions with an absence of a profound and coordinated effort frequently misuse claims of supporting *Active Learning* in the classroom. The employment of a handful of projects and gamifications are commonly taken for active pedagogy, when they are merely punctual participative activities. These institutions may promote training through workshops and lectures regarding *Active Learning* for their teachers at the beginning of the school year calendar. However, should they remain attached to a linear courseware, they will not be able to take the leap. In many cases, an external consultant may be needed to ensure an Active Learning curriculum is taught.

CENTRALIZED      DECENTRALIZED      DISTRIBUTED

*In these three networks designed by Paul Baran (1964), the points are located in the same position. The more distributed the connections, the less vulnerable the model, wherein one point would be damaged. Active Learning pedagogy aims at shifting the teacher's role to the third network, while strengthening the students' shared knowledge.*

Yet the greatest enemy of *Active Learning* may be national exams. When students are about to access higher education, they are subjected to tests that define what type of university they are entitled to enter, in addition to their high school grade point average (GPA), volunteer work, and letter of recommendations. These tests mostly assess heavy loads of informative content, which subsequently forces high schools to adjust their methods to enable students to excel on the exams and prepare for entry. Since student-centred approaches take longer to move through the curriculum, compared to a teacher-led, more passive instructional approach, Active Learning can become prohibitive at this stage in education. This is why more elementary school stakeholders adhere to *Active Learning* whilst finding a high school where this model is central to the curriculum is less common. Promoting deeper learning from elementary school until the completion of high school appears unfeasible, at least until the testing format changes for national exams held for students' entry into a university. The national exams are what mostly drive the school curriculum and choice of instruction.

The *Active Learning* paradigm is almost as old as educational systems, but only in the third millennium has it found the structural changes in communication to become massively feasible. Even with the impulse of the internet and, more recently, the COVID-19 pandemic, this trend struggles to propagate, due to a strong resistance from educators and the constraint of many national exams. *Active Learning* is one of the three great tendencies mapped in this article's framework, and, once established, it gives rise to the second trend, *21st Century Skills*.

## 21st Century Skills

In a world deluged by information technologies, knowledge is growing at an exponential rate. It is evolving at such a rapid pace that science is constantly updated and becoming obsolete in shrinking temporal spaces, causing life and work to change incessantly. In education, exercises, repetition, and exams may result in higher grades, but they will not prepare students in a comprehensive way, nor develop the abilities they need to tackle the third millennium challenges. In stressful, unpredictable and often adverse scenarios, the foundation for sustaining human beings is emulating the *21st Century Skills.*

Although there is an agreement among educators that these abilities are imperative, there is no unique approach to the definition of *21st Century Skills.* In general terms, they relate to individual capacities that are manifested in the ways of thinking, feeling, and in the behaviours or attitudes related toward others. These competencies are necessary to be competitive in the workforce, to participate appropriately in an increasingly diverse society, to use new technologies, and to cope with rapidly changing workplaces.

The notion of *21st Century Skills* is also expressed with terms such as *People Skills, Life Skills, Social* and *Emotional Skills,* and *Soft Skills.* The latter term is frequently used in contrast to *Hard Skills* and outlines how they are differentiated. While Soft Skills refer to those that fundamentally help one maintain balance, live in society and think critically, Hard Skills are technical skills and refer to abilities that are developed through exercises, repetition and memorisation. Unlike Soft Skills, Hard Skills can be demonstrated with degrees, certificates, or other tangible measurements.

*Twenty First Century Skills* may be explained through several frameworks, such as the 4Cs, the Big Five, and the Other 3Rs. According to a report commissioned by the UK Government, the essence of those frameworks combined can be arranged into 5 categories of Soft Skills:

* *Communication skills*, including language and presentation of ideas;
* *Collaborative skills,* including management of group activities and social interaction;
* *Individual learning approaches, including critical thinking, metacognition, and new skills acquisition;*
* *Individual autonomy*, including flexibility, adaptability, and entrepreneurship;
* *ICT and digital literacy*, including use of technology as tools for learning, communication and collaboration.

**POPULAR 21ST CENTURY SKILLS FRAMEWORKS**

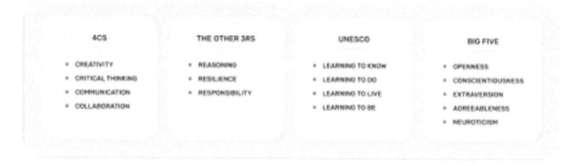

| 4CS | THE OTHER 3RS | UNESCO | BIG FIVE |
|---|---|---|---|
| • CREATIVITY | • REASONING | • LEARNING TO KNOW | • OPENNESS |
| • CRITICAL THINKING | • RESILIENCE | • LEARNING TO DO | • CONSCIENTIOUSNESS |
| • COMMUNICATION | • RESPONSIBILITY | • LEARNING TO LIVE | • EXTRAVERSION |
| • COLLABORATION | | • LEARNING TO BE | • AGREEABLENESS |
| | | | • NEUROTICISM |

An interesting fact about 21st Century Skills is that valued skills change over time. For example, although the need for empathy may sound universal and timeless, during the Cold War, Americans and Soviets were conditioned to have no mercy for one another through newspapers, radioand TV. Pop culture, expressed in movies such as Wall Street (1987), illustrated how success was commonly put above other people. Conversely, Mark Zuckerberg was characterised as an anti-hero for his lack of empathy when bypassing his friends in the movie, The Social Network (2010).

Next, the use of vulnerability as a strength is a recent trend regarding behaviour. In the early 2000s, as Britney Spears became more vulnerable as a person, the public's interest increased while they watched her disintegrate. In contrast, when Selena Gomez talked openly about her depression, and the prejudices her Latina family suffered, she spoke with pride. This illustrates how skills that are valued today may not be upheld in 10 years, while other unpredictable skills may gain importance.

By now, some of the primary abilities that stakeholders demand from graduates cannot be replaced by machines. The more that automation takes over the world and displaces jobs, the more individuals have to restore their human essence and diverge from robotic skills. Moreover, recognising that 'people are hired for their curriculum and fired for their behaviour', several think tanks such as LinkedIn, World Economic Forum and UNESCO are alerting the public to the importance of these new competencies, which society is increasingly demanding of the current workforce. Degrees and certificates are no longer enough to secure financial stability.

Beyond increasing the chances of a satisfying job, *Twenty First Century Skills* also empowers individuals to tackle social and environmental challenges and bring about positive changes. In addition to preparing for exams, educational systems should be modified to carry out new forms of learning, to empower students to positively impact the world when they enter the job market. This is not only a pressing need for humanity, but also a distinct and growing trait of Generation Y and Generation Z, committed to a higher purpose compared to previous generations.

One of the most distinguished futurists of our time, Peter Diamandis, co-author of the bestseller *Abundance* and founder of Singularity University, an institution where student selection is based on potential to positively impact one billion people in 10 years, has designed an uncharacteristic curriculum for elementary school students, almost completely dedicated to Soft Skills. The curriculum is presented below.

| STORYTELLING / COMMUNICATIONS | PASSIONS | CURIOSITY & EXPERIMENTATION |
|---|---|---|
| PERSISTENCE / GRIT | TECHNOLOGY EXPOSURE | EMPATHY |
| ETHICS / MORAL DILEMMAS | 3R: READING, WRITING & ARITHMETIC | CREATIVE EXPRESSION & IMPROVISATION |
| CODING | ENTREPRENEURSHIP & SALES | LANGUAGE |

Twenty First Century skills extend beyond Soft Skills to students' performance in Hard Skills. Researchers from the OECD have found social, emotional and cognitive development are interrelated. Students who are focused, organised and responsible learn approximately a third more in mathematics during an academic year than their peers who are less focused. Therefore, to enhance students' grades, stakeholders in education should invest in implementing Soft Skills' development into the curriculum. Such awareness is propelling governments to include *21st Century Skills* into national documents. Several countries have already reformed their vision and mission statements, their curriculum, and skills progression to include Soft Skills.

These amendments do not mean that Soft Skills were not an object of attention before, but what has changed is its inclusion in education with intentionality. Soft Skills can be learned, practised and taught; though, not through traditional class structure. The best way to develop Soft Skills is through exposure to situations in which students experience real-world problems. The changes in pedagogical approaches to encompass their learning is the second greatest trend in education with a direct correlation to *Active Learning*.

As previously mentioned, teachers must leave behind their role of the sole holder of knowledge and act like mediators. Encouraging pupils to guide their own learning is more effective than keeping attention centralised. Experts recommend that students perform activities with objectives defined jointly by students. Additionally, the more education is conducted as a social process, enabling students to interact with their peers while carrying out projects, the better. Working in pairs or small groups stimulates cooperation, creativity and innovation.

Another considerably beneficial way to enhance the absorption of Soft Skills is by stimulating discussions that encroach the limits of factual contents. For example, to explain the United Kingdom's part in the Second World War, the teacher could focus less on facts and dates and more on how British leaders demonstrated resilience during that period. Teachers could also encourage students to talk explicitly about social and emotional abilities of characters from a book they have read and compare to others, enabling students to better comprehend soft skills.

School leaders can find support in technology to aid the development of *21st Century Skills.* There are many EdTech startups working on ways to help students practice and assess these skills. Furthermore, with chat and video conference systems burgeoning worldwide, students can enhance capacities for distance communication and collaboration with geographically dispersed teams. With access to the internet, students can develop abilities to critically analyse digital information and discern between fake and real news. It also enables the development of digital skills and the ability to create technologies, including programming. With autonomy in connectivity, individuals obtain skills to continue learning for a lifetime.

Before the Information Revolution, knowledge acquired through exercises, repetition and memorisation was customarily sufficient to live in society and to guarantee a steady position in the job market. But in a connected, multidisciplinary and, most of all, unpredictable world, Soft Skills are imperative for career success and advancement. Ensuing the *Active Learning* approach, stakeholders in governments and schools are striving to intentionally develop their students' *21st Century Skills.*

## Technology

The main trigger for change in both Active Learning and in 21st Century Skills were the transformations the Information Revolution brought to the current age. Although the use of technology in education is becoming more widely accessible, it is noteworthy that education is generally on the trail of other industries. As much as school is about preparation for life and work, life and work must first evolve so that education can be moulded by them. While the Fourth Industrial Revolution has opened an unprecedented gap between technologies available and those deployed in schools, the Covid-19 pandemic has fuelled a significant headway in education in a very short interval, an unimaginable feat for normal times.

According to UNESCO, in 2020 more than 1.5 billion students were affected by the pandemic, the equivalent of 87% of the world's population of students. Education has never witnessed the interruption of face-to-face classes on such a scale. When schools had to shut their doors, there were no immediate and effective actions that could be taken to continue the management of teaching and learning processes. Negative outcomes involved interruption of studies, school dropouts, losses in social and emotional developments, increased abuse at home and even food insecurity. This unprecedented closure of schools will account for a significant rise in social inequalities worldwide.

On the other hand, the constraint of being forced to stay at home has fostered unprecedented progress in digital literacy and infrastructure to manage e-learning. Besides the aid of education programs broadcasted on television and on radio, countless students found a way to enter online classes either through a desktop, a tablet or a mobile phone. Politicians and school maintainers invested heavily in infrastructure and connectivity for students and school buildings. But, the greatest legacy of this period will probably be the substantial increase in digital literacy by educators.

Meanwhile, teachers were forging ahead with computer skills, and to further complicate their situation, they also had to deal with a dramatic drop in student engagement. Afar from the school environment and with reduced social contact, students found many reasons to disperse during remote classes. Teachers had to be creative to retain students' attention, and several of the teachers resorted to the use of EdTech startups as innovative forms to conduct online learning. That is to say, besides discovering new digital tools, many teachers deepened their abilities to implement Active Learning methods and to develop 21st Century Skills, demonstrating considerable progress in technology and education.

EdTech is a branch of startups working hard to innovate in the education market. Although the pandemic propelled them into the spotlight, before 2020, EdTech startups were already dominating several aspects of education, from content generation to knowledge consumption to assessments. Besides enhancing classroom learning and improving student outcomes, they also work with institution management, communication among communities, scholarships, security control in schools, and market intelligence, in the form of software and hardware development.

The conventional concept of education is a K-12 system - kindergarten through to elementary schools to middle and finally, high schools. The EdTech market also embodies higher education, corporate training, and various non-regulated courses. Business models address final consumers (B2C), other businesses (B2B), clients of other businesses, mostly students (B2B2C), governments (B2G) and investors (B2I). The range of diversity and extensiveness of the EdTech market allows for a greater complexity when analysing the problems EdTech addresses through viable solutions.

There are countless ways to categorise EdTech roles, and the internet is flooded by frameworks attempting to accomplish such goals. One noteworthy endeavour is Holon IQ's Global Learning Landscape. This consultancy firm specialised in education has deployed machine learning to analyse 60,000+ educational organisations worldwide, with results being interpreted by their international network of experts. The outcome was an open-source taxonomy for the future of education, licenced under Creative Commons, whose report lists 1,250 EdTech startups grouped in 50 categories. A more comprehensive database of EdTech startups can be found on the EdSurge website with over 2,500 EdTech products available.

## 2021 Global Learning Landscape

**Holon**

With classroom doors closed and conventional methods of education incurring a setback, summed up with the need for upskilling courses for working-class individuals, the EdTech market gained sudden momentum. According to EOS Intelligence, before the coronavirus pandemic, the EdTech sector was estimated to reach a value of US$ 342 billion by 2025. The forecast revisions accounting for the impact of the COVID-19 pandemic increased the prediction by 18%, expecting the global EdTech market to reach US$ 404 billion by 2025.

The number of EdTech unicorns is also a good thermometer to understand how the market is trending. A unicorn startup is a private company with a valuation of over US$1 billion. As reported by Holon IQ, before 2020, there were 14 EdTech unicorns around the world. As of May 2021, the count has soared to 25 unicorn startups. Collectively, these unicorns have raised over US$16 billion of total funding in the last decade and are now valued at over US$74 billion.

A short-term rush brought by COVID-19 is expected to give headway to increased adoption of what is known as emerging technologies. Apart from online content and interactive activities built into online platforms, some technologies largely undeveloped in their potential are progressively being integrated into core education delivery. Among others, they embrace artificial intelligence, expanded reality (AR, VR, MR), robotics, blockchain, internet of things, and nanotechnology. When matured and disseminated, these technologies are capable of completely changing the status quo of education known today. EOS Intelligence expects them to cross the US$ 22 billion mark by 2025 from US$ 4 billion in 2019.

Although a large number of players in the EdTech sector were able to capitalise during the pandemic, uncertainty looms of how the market will react once educational institutes reopen completely. Even if by a small percentage, the demand for online learning is likely to shrink, and players without a clear-product concept or a well-defined monetisation policy may fall out of the global competition. When the surge slows, EdTech startups that based their entire business around remote learning will have to find ways to maintain the post-pandemic value. In spite of that, the growth accelerated by COVID-19 is likely sustainable, benefited by a significant change in the mindset of the market.

In 2016, Thomas Frey, a world-renowned futurist, predicted the largest internet company of 2030 would be an education-based company unknown at the time. If that were to become true without a pandemic in the way, COVID-19 surely added strength to his prediction. 2020 disrupted the education system and acted as a catalyst for change that was already underway in the sector, helping close a massive innovation gap between education and other industries.

## Time And Space

Education's systems emerged concurrently with the First Industrial Revolution, and the latter played a major role in shaping the former. Deploying machines to expand the efficiency of manufacturers' production implied some well-known arrangements, for instance assembly lines which divided labour, allotment of products according to the date they were fabricated, and sirens to signal when to start and when to stop working.

Schools mirrored factory-style structures, submitting students to common curricula as if in an assembly line, with teachers specialised in school years and in subjects. Students were also divided in groups, according to the year they were born, regardless of their academic affinities or the pace they learned. What is more, maintaining standardisation involves coordinating the beginning, the pause, and the end of classes. These mechanisms account for the duration of non-negotiable learning cycles, in detriment of respecting students' individual progress.

A second phenomenon in place when education systems arose were the complications that resulted from war. National States figured a unified population with a shared language, history, and religion demonstrated better outcomes during conflicting times, because citizens were more likely to agree to die defending their homeland. Nationalism fostered investments in education and forged schools to serve military purposes. Discipline was a praised key value and cited as the foundation to educate a universal population with few teachers, in moulded classrooms with one small stage and rigidly lined school desks.

Again, through the advancement of technology and education, these inflexible time and space arrangements have become out-dated. Ominous information availability exempts the need for students to wait to receive information from teachers. Allowing students to guide their own learning, respecting their interests as much as their rhythms, fundamental elements of Active Learning, contradicts the use of sirens and standardised learning cycles. There is enough technology to aid personalised paths and assessments, so that the amount of time dedicated to each topic can vary from one student to the other.

Time relativisation allows for regrouping of students according to proficiency level in each subject, rather than by their age. Although a simple idea of how to group students, which is grounded in literature (i.e. Teaching at the Right Level), most schools still prefer to separate students according to age and grade levels. This allows for easier classroom management and legal regulations. But, these new paradigms are progressively gaining notoriety within institutions.

Next is the issue of how space is utilised. When teachers cease to act as gate holders of knowledge and allow their students' collective intelligence to flow, reforms in space utilisation are created. Applying Active Learning and developing 21st Century Skills largely involves working with peers, either in pairs or in small groups, therefore breaking the classroom traditional arrangement of desks in rows. The more modular the arrangements, the better for promoting the two dimensions, Active Learning and Twenty First Century Skills. Moreover, taking students outside their classrooms to green areas and even away from school boundaries to explore their city's spaces can significantly enrich the learning process.

Notwithstanding different desk arrangements and classroom field trips, the greatest disruption in learning spaces has been brought on by technology. A couple of decades ago, having a class geographically distanced from the teacher seemed unfamiliar, if not inconceivable. But in 2020, hosting classes "on the cloud" became the norm, with students accessing them from anywhere. The widespread phenomenon of e-learning was a volte-face for time and space in education. Besides instant access to classes from any location, students can study at any hour.

Another noteworthy, looming change in space is the one brought by Virtual Reality, an already widely accessible technology. With a cheap cardboard headset, a mobile phone and a connection to YouTube, students can search for VR videos and go through countless immersive experiences, many of which are educational. Virtual Reality instantly transports users to anywhere they wish to go, from different cities to the Solar System to a visit inside the human body. It is even possible to gather with colleagues in the same virtual location.

Changes in Time and Space mostly stem from the three trends, Active Learning, Twenty First Century Skills, and Technology. To treat students as protagonists and develop their Soft Skills, illustrated both in Active Learning and in 21st Century Skills, both time and space need to be reconceptualised to address students' diverse learning needs. Technology, in turn, not only provides aid to personalised paths, but also enables digital meetings and virtual teleports, completely disrupting the traditional face-to-face spaces at schools.

## Conclusion

The COVID-19 pandemic caused leaders to respond quickly to how students could continue learning, which triggered thorough renovations from teachers and brought innumerable innovative endeavours into the spotlight, accelerating much needed transformations. But the intricacies of an industry as diverse as education can be quite troublesome to be decodified. If successful, this chapter should have brought to the forefront an understanding of the diverse direction education is taking in a simplified model. With some additional hope, it may help guide the implementation of innovative learning processes.

Overall, what is trending in education is the required actions to properly prepare individuals to tackle the third millennium, considering how the world is becoming multidisciplinary, interconnected, nonlinear and exponentially unpredictable. The Active Learning approach aims at augmenting students' learning efficacy, while the development of 21st Century Skills gives the foundations for individual sustenance throughout incessant changes in life and work. Students' performance of both Active Learning and 21st Century Skills improves through the use of technology, synchronizing education with financial, health, transportation, and communication industries, among others. At last, Time and Space reforms are necessary to accommodate the evolution of the three previous trends.

With so many challenges expected to continue in the future, such as increased unemployment, overpopulation, terrorism, climate change, new pandemics and even loss of control of artificial intelligence, more than ever educators worldwide need to effectively and democratically educate its population. The quicker that instruction evolves in tandem with students' learning needs and curiosities, the higher the odds of positive outcomes for the next decades. Changes can be stressful, but they are awfully pressing in education, the grassroot sector for developing all the others.

# We Don't Want No Education

## Denise Wong Wai Yan

Venture Builder and Co-founder of fail ventures

EdTech is a super interesting space. Given my experiences, as an ex-/always student, a tutor and an EdTech entrepreneur, I've picked up a couple of observations I want to share here. Please note, whilst my notes aim to be general, I have primarily been involved in K-12 education.

### Introduction

Let's start from the beginning - what is the goal of education? This answer informs how we should think about disruptions in technology, because hopefully these disruptions should accelerate us towards this end goal. I think the point is to vaguely prepare children for (their, our, your) future.

### Pain Points

Given that, we can start to see some issues with the current education system. Both are probably a reflection of 2 things: 1) when education was first conceived, it was designed to be a mass production machine of cookie cutter workers for the Industrial Age, and 2) times are changing faster than education.

### Problem 1: The Wrong Content

Unfortunately, education may not teach anything important. We teach things academically, but not practically. Our curriculum is to real life, what classical economics is to behavioural economics. We don't teach children generally how things work in the real world, but teach them precisely how we think things *should* work in the world. For sure, there is a place for English, Maths and Art. But the application is missing - i.e. we don't teach how to apply maths to investing, or saving.

Moreover, we miss out on fundamental lessons in being human. For example, we don't teach psychology or the heuristics of the mind - perhaps the most important thing we should teach people is how our brain sabotages us, and how we should avoid that to think clearly. Even worse, we teach our kids the wrong things. For example, in schools, we spoon-feed people the "right" and "wrong" answer, without teaching them how to find and solve problems. We use only one yardstick to measure students, instead of letting kids develop what they're good at. Indeed, (in more traditional educational systems like Hong Kong) we punish creativity and initiative. Indeed, in local schools, we punish people for being attacked by other students. We inoculate people against innovation, which cannot be the right thing. We mistake elite education and memorisation with real learning and understanding. Though of course, an argument can be made that these teach us transferable skills, but then why don't we teach the real skill itself?

**Problem 2: The Wrong Delivery Method**

Not only do we input the wrong things, we do so in the wrong way.

For starters, we don't seem to cater to psychology. There are studies around Bloom's Two-Sigma problem, memory hacking spaced repetition and the Pygmalion Effect that could all have incredible applications in the classroom. In fact, education functions as a factory: they take in students, and churn out standardised employees. Our current models of education were built during the industrial age, to churn out **standardised** workers. Our current teaching systems are still one size fits all: there is little tailoring of content, attention and testing, and there is little care for each individual's talents or interests. It's just not very joyful. Moreover, doing so means that each student's potential isn't maximised, we just aim to get them across an arbitrary line.

Lastly, on a macro/systems level, education can be scarce and expensive.

**Disruption**

None of the above are new, or really interesting. What's interesting about education is that, though its flaws have been known for a long, long time, very little has actually changed. Disruption is inevitable and welcome. The question is, what form it will take.

**The Story So Far**

Let's start with what existing disruption we see, and where we think it'll end up. I've structured the disruptions below chronologically, where possible. Many disruptions also are combinations of the below.

**Existing Trend : Old-School Education Archetype**

- Groups of students taught by teachers, sitting standardised tests

The below three trends really all come down to improving student's performance in the education system. If traditional schooling is a road between birth and employment, then these interventions are wheels, so students can move faster and easier.

**Existing Trend #1: School-Performance Enhancing Solutions**

- The most obvious disruption has been old-school supplements. This has obviously come in the form of tutors, revision books and notes, fuelled by parents who are willing and able to pay people for more.

**Existing Trend #2: Moving The Above Online (Mooc/Youtube)**

- Obviously, though incredibly slowly, we have made marketplaces or online versions of all of the above.
- Standouts include VIPKID and Byju in the online tutorial space, as well as Quizlet in the educational study tools space

### Existing Trend #3: Personalisation And Data/Ai Driven Education

- Increasingly, we are seeing new online tools to personalise, and thus make learning more effective. For example, we see spaced repetition flashcards, or learning visualisation tools. Standouts include Anki.

The first paradigm shift is, moving outside the demands of traditional school. Increasingly, people see that extra-curricular activities are useful. If traditional schooling is a road between birth and employment, then these interventions may be seen as shortcuts or side roads branching off from the main road.

### Existing Trend #4: Extra-Curricular Learning (+ Online)

- In more developed economies, especially in Asian cultures that prize education, we are increasingly seeing extra-curricular classes, e.g. music lessons. These usually teach a "hard skill" like being able to play music, often done due to a) traditional values, as many English style boarding schools that rank highly stress this, b) transferable skills, or c) university admissions boosting effect.
- Within this trend, we're now seeing a move and focus on "soft skills", e.g. critical thinking skills. People are becoming increasingly comfortable with skills that may not be immediately measured or shown, due to a) increased need in the new economy or, b) the demands of international facing schooling, e.g. IB or AP style that lead to better university admission outcomes.

The second paradigm shift is replacing the demands of traditional school. If traditional schooling is the road most travelled between birth and employment, then these solutions offer an alternative path entirely.

### Existing Trend #5: Technology Bootcamp

- Already near and around Silicon Valley, coding bootcamps arise for people who want to pursue jobs in technology. Essentially, these act as a replacement for traditional education.
- Standouts include Flatiron School.

### Existing Trend #6: Alternative Schools

- Interestingly, new schools aim to replace traditional pre-college education, with their own curriculums/teaching formats.
- Standouts include Sora, which allows for student directed learning. Standardised curriculum content is broken down, and reassembled into projects and areas of reasoning the student cares about.

The third paradigm shift is towards lifelong schooling. If traditional schooling is a road most travelled between birth and employment, then these solutions are similar to a discovery that the road never ends.

### Existing Trend #7: Lifelong Up-Skilling

- Increasingly, we are moving away from a one-company, rank-climbing career arc, to multiple life changes during this new stage of technological innovation and change.
- People in my/the new generation are expected to see automation/technology, creation of new industries, fluid working, globalisation and dramatic career switches. Traditional education is not preparing people for this.
- Standouts include Blinkist, or MOOCs.

The fourth paradigm shift is outside of a strict binary of "learning" vs "not". If traditional schooling is a road most travelled between birth and employment, then these solutions represent the realisation that learning is not just a road, but also the trees that line the path.

### Unbundling The Campus

- Increasingly, interventions acknowledge how education is more than book/school/tuition learning. We see education comes from others - mentorship and alumni, our peers or on projects.
- Special mention to Handshake and Facebook Campus.

### Another Way Of Looking At It

A VC recently described to me how he sees EdTech progressing. Interestingly, it coincides with the "shifts" I described above, only he suggests three waves instead of four shifts. The three waves are 1) dumping content online, e.g. Khan Academy and YouTube, 2) online marketplaces, e.g. VIPKID and 3) now the shift towards community based EdTech.

### Why Haven't Things Changed?

Being at the leading edge of a field doesn't mean you have to be one of the people pushing it forward. You can also be at the leading edge as a user. It was not so much because he was a programmer that Facebook seemed a good idea to Mark Zuckerberg as because he used computers so much.

This seems obvious, but the next big disruptions have to be something people *demand*. Remember how we said the point of education is to teach things for the future? Well, that remains true but it is not the whole story. Education also serves as a *necessary step to be completed*, and a *signal/credential*. In terms of the "job to be done", education is deceptive: it doesn't just have to educate, it has to signal.

### Status Games Are Zero Sum

If you were the dean of Harvard and you said, "Hey, Harvard is doing so well that we're going to 100X our enrollment," you would have a revolt. The reason Harvard is powerful is that it's a zero-sum status signalling game of locking out everybody except for legacy people who did really well in school. But, in order to have a school that really scales, you have to rely on something other than just the signalling. I think schools are learning that.

This leads us to the roadblocks so far: because actually, as a product, education isn't just responding to consumers' demand for better-quality education. They also need to respond to the need for a parent to complete a task, and for credentialing. Parents (as the primary decision maker) have a lot of subconscious, unmet needs.

**The Parents' ...**

**Apathy**

As I said in my YC interview, it's interesting how education isn't really something parents devote brainpower over. It's just a tick on the conventional list, to get things done. In the face of this, almost apathy, it's hard to usher in change.

**Need To Measure Favourably Against Conventional Metrics**

Moreover, because it's just a step to get completed, parents aren't really motivated to try anything new. They're not trying to maximise gain here, just check off a step.
For others, they care a lot. But they also need to feel like they've tried their best, according to prevailing social conventions. They judge themselves by existing social metrics.

"We spend on the best schools as insurance that we've tried our best."

**Lag Behind**

The above two even assume that parents see a problem. The truth is, education is a game that depends on keeping up with changes 10 years into the future, whilst selling to consumers who may be 20 years in the past.

**Credentialism**

Related to the above, the reason for new educational models, which can deliver 10x value, is because we haven't yet unbundled credentialism. So long as getting into certain schools or getting some qualifications serve a *signalling* effect, and the vast majority of employers accept this, we will hurt the case for a new model education.

We've already discussed how modern education in the West has its roots in serving a post-industrial economy. Now, to discuss EdTech internationally, we need to layer onto that an understanding of the Eastern education system. Historically, and in very broad strokes, credentials were a method in which institutions controlled who rose to the top. To pass the gruelling exams to get access to social mobility, one had to have sufficient social and economic means to do well, which limited serious competitors to a certain pool. Inequality in education is a feature, not a bug.

### Future Of Work Is Still In The Future

Inertia. Without wide scale changes to employment forcing the above, humans automatically adopt past models of schooling, without thinking about psychology, technology or what the future will look like.

### What's Next?

We've discussed above some trends of education, and the outline of change.
Many of these trends are evolving, and three big ones are beginning to form a flywheel: 1) the Future of Work/Creator Economy 2) Web 3 and 3) the Future of Education.

### 1) Future Of Work/Passion Economy

This Future of Work is symbiotic with the creator/passion economy. Increasingly, one's passions are as monetizable as a career. Web 3 is a perfect accelerant and complement to this. Whilst Web 2 was mostly about our relationships with large, centralised platforms. Web 3 is all about decentralisation allowing value to remain with creators, further fuelling the Creator Economy. Moreover, the decentralisation of Web 3 means that when we organise, it is in the form of DAOs. Not only do the creators retain power, not the platforms, but these DAOs build community in a peer-to-peer ideological way not previously seen.

### 2) Future Of Education

This plugs into some trends from the future of education we discussed above.
Web 3's increased ability to monetise drives the creator economy to create more high quality, alternative sources of education (trend 2, 4, 5 and 6).

DAOs are an ideal implementation of trends 7 and 8. DAOs are, by sheer virtue of their construction, fit well for community based education: which is a great unbundling of the non-academic education experience (8) and lifelong learning (7).

### 3) Future Of Education: Fow/Passion Economy

Moreover, as Future of Education grows, we will increase the supply of people that prefer or prosper in the Passion Economy. Not only do they serve as evidence that EdTech can work, and thus create social acceptance for the future of education, it's likely they will be change agents advocating for the Future of Work. These Future of Work employers will ignore credentialism, and increasingly demand for skills far away from traditional education. This growing gap allows for a greater pain point, allowing startups to plug the gap and further fuelling this acceleration.
All the above grows the Future of Work, coming full circle. In other words: I make good money via the creator economy. I make even better money with Web 3. My money making allows me to create great education resources, and creates demand for these resources from people aspiring to be me. These people learn especially well with my Web 3 community. As these people learn, they become creators. They become successful in the creator economy. Others see this and more accept the creator economy and alternative schooling. Together, us creators hire more,

and demand for skills different from traditional education rises. This increased demand for non-traditional skills creates demand for alternative schooling, which may be plugged by startups, who finally gain social acceptance, or by us creators. If plugged by creators, I make good money via the creator economy. And the cycle starts again.

The future of education is super exciting. This flywheel means that, when change occurs, i.e. when we hit a critical mass of demand for alternative skills that overwhelms the roadblocks identified above, change will happen *increasingly* quickly. This means that startups have an exciting opportunity to position themselves at the critical mass tipping point, and quickly roll up the market, creating meaningful change. I look forward to seeing these developments occur.

## Using Tpack To Inform E-Learning Product Build

### Dr Leila Khouja Walker

### Co-Founder/Chief Product Officer At Persona Education

In this section we look at how Mishra and Koehler's (2006) Technological Pedagogical and Content Knowledge (TPACK) framework can be central to the development of an effective e-learning resource. This is illustrated using the example of the Persona Life Skills social-emotional online learning platform, developed by the UK based EdTech company Persona Education.

### The TPACK Framework

The TPACK framework builds on Shulman's (1987) description of Pedagogy, Content and Knowledge (PCK) that described how teachers' understanding of educational technologies and PCK can interact with one another to produce effective teaching using technology.
There are seven components to the TPACK framework:

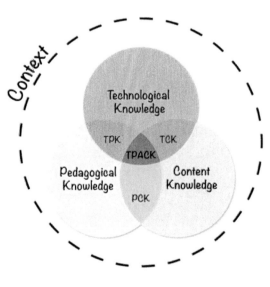

Source. TPACK.org

The TPACK framework is rooted in the interplay of three types of knowledge: Content Knowledge (CK), Pedagogical Knowledge (PK), and Technology Knowledge (TK).

TPACK goes beyond seeing these three knowledge bases in isolation, shining a spotlight on the intersections between the different types of knowledge involved: Pedagogical Content Knowledge (PCK), Technological Content Knowledge (TCK), Technological Pedagogical Knowledge (TPK), and ultimately, at the intersection of all three, Technological Pedagogical Content Knowledge (TPACK).

The rationale behind TPACK is that technology should not act as the "lead" when designing a lesson or learning journey for a student. Instead, effective technology should enable the integration of the Content Knowledge required and the most effective Pedagogical Knowledge available to support the learner's ability to gain specific Content Knowledge.

In other words, specific subject matter (Content Knowledge) requires developing sensitivity to the dynamic, transactional relationship between best teaching practice (Pedagogical knowledge) and then the technologies, if any, that may support the desired learning journey and outcome (Technological Knowledge).

TPACK is a constant reminder to all technology enthusiasts working within education that it has an important role to play, and that its involvement should be subject to a development pathway that sees it placed after Content and Pedagogical considerations.

**Interpreting The Persona Life Skills Theory Of Change**

Persona Life Skills is an online learning platform that uses a personality insights framework to inform, improve and accelerate the acquisition of 22 social-emotional life skills associated with greater wellbeing and employability among secondary students. The platform delivers a unique learning journey aimed at teenagers, with the objective of countering the downward trend in wellbeing with age and over time, as self-reported (OECD 2018), and at the same time building social-emotional skills in preparation for the workplace.

The Persona Life Skills software was designed using the TPACK framework. The learning pathway and long-term user journey are reflected in Persona's Theory of Change model:

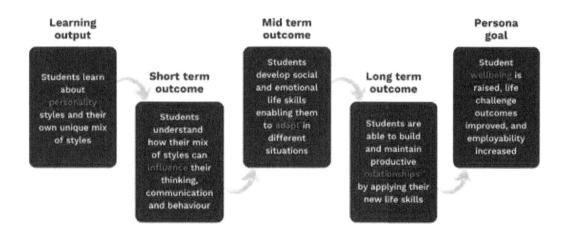

Source: www.persona-life.com

Persona Life Skills introduces students to the concept of personality styles. It provides an adaptation of a scientifically proven framework, empowering students to gain insights about their own mix of styles – their 'Persona' – as well as other people's. Students learn how their Persona can change over time, as well as how it may differ in social, learning and work contexts.

Using a learning metaphor of exploring islands representing life challenges such as managing social media, working in a group and speaking in public, a scaffolded curriculum matched to stage of development guides students in using personality insights to help develop social-emotional life skills. Improving these life skills, including self-control, empathy, communication and resilience, helps students to make better decisions about self management and their interactions with others, building more effective relationships and leading to greater wellbeing and employability. The learning outcomes are monitored as modules are completed.

So how was the development of Persona Life Skills guided by the TPACK framework?

**Content Knowledge (CK)**

*"Teachers' knowledge about the subject matter to be learned or taught....As Shulman (1986) noted, this knowledge would include knowledge of concepts, theories, ideas, organisational frameworks, knowledge of evidence and proof, as well as established practices and approaches toward developing such knowledge." (Koehler & Mishra, 2009)*

The first step in the design of the Persona Life Skills online learning platform was the development of the personality insights framework that lies at its heart. This unique framework was co-created with young people aged 13-19, representative of the end user group.

As part of their initial learning journey, student users respond to a series of 'Persona Insights' questions about how they think, communicate and behave in various situations. This data input is then converted by an algorithm into personalised data output, providing them with Content Knowledge (CK) about their unique mix of personality styles (Persona Insights), in the form of visuals, word clouds and textual commentary.

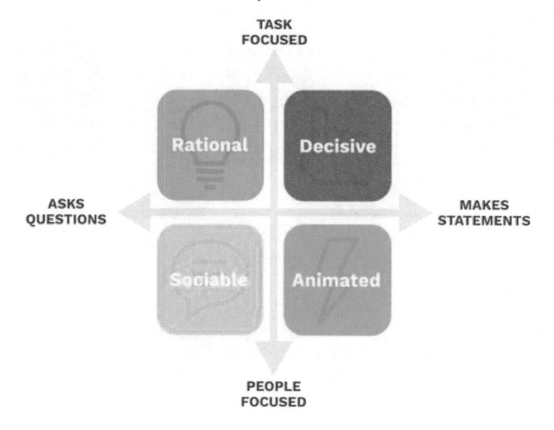

Source: www.persona-life.com

This Content Knowledge (CK) is used by the student as a reference as they then work through a series of 'life challenge' learning modules – such as Preparing for Exams, The Unexpected and First Job – that invite them to apply and learn from their newly acquired Persona Insights knowledge.

For example, a student may discover that their main personality style is "Decisive". They are provided with insights into how this might affect their thinking, communication and behaviour in different contexts (social, learning and work), including positive characteristics, as well as growth areas to consider.

Additional Content Knowledge (CK) is gained when a student takes one of the many life skills modules, where they are provided with tools and strategies to support development of their individual social-emotional life skills.

22 life skills across six skill sets provide structure for Persona Life Skills users on their journey towards improved wellbeing and employability.

Source: www.persona-life.com

## Pedagogical Knowledge (PK)

*"Teachers' deep knowledge about the processes and practices or methods of teaching and learning. They encompass, among other things, overall educational purposes, values, and aims. This generic form of knowledge applies to*
Cooperative learning is a perfect complement to flipped le understanding how students learn, general classroom management skills, lesson planning, and student assessment." (Koehler & Mishra, 2009)

The second step in the Persona Life Skills design process was to determine the most effective pedagogical routes to support users in gaining the Content Knowledge (CK) outlined above. In other words, to develop Pedagogical Knowledge (PK).

Not yet considering technology, the product development team at Persona Education was informed by three strongly evidence-based pedagogical methods for supporting effective learning:

i) Flipped learning

An instructional approach that directs from a group learning space to the individual learning space, with the resulting group space being transformed into a more dynamic, interactive learning environment.

Well before COVID-19 and forced school closures, many schools had begun to adopt a flipped learning approach. The benefits are stark. With curriculum time limited and teacher resources at a premium, the flipped classroom allows teachers to instruct students to carry out activities that do not require a teacher at home, followed up by activities that do require a teacher such as group discussion and Q&A (whether in class/or remotely), to facilitate deep learning.

Persona Life Skills provides in-app 'Teacher Guidance' reference resources with each learning module. Within a module, teachers are able to set students on a path to complete tasks on their own (or in small groups) without the teacher being physically or virtually present. Other tasks are marked as best completed with the teacher present, to guide the student user further and often to bring a wider group of students together to discuss and share their learning.

ii) Cooperative learning

Sometimes called small-group learning, an instructional strategy in which small groups of students work together on a common task. The core benefit of cooperative learning is showcasing the positive effects of interdependence while underlining the importance of personal responsibility; students work collaboratively with one another, but they all have a different task to accomplish or concept to explain.
arning. As mentioned above, the flipped classroom allows students to learn independently as well as prioritising activities best done with a teacher and the rest of their class or group. When a class is brought together, cooperative learning is then applied.

Within Persona Life Skills, Kagan cooperative learning structures are promoted. For almost two decades, Kagan has dominated the cooperative learning market.  Research clearly shows the impact this instructional approach has on student motivation and engagement.

Five common Kagan structures used in Persona Life Skills, and their impact on developing interpersonal skills as well as academic learning – or Content Knowledge (CK) – are illustrated below:

| Structure Functions | Classbuilding | Teambuilding | Social Skills | Communication Skills | Decision Making | Knowledgebuilding | Procedure Learning | Processing Info | Thinking Skills | Presenting Info |
|---|---|---|---|---|---|---|---|---|---|---|
| | Interpersonal | | | | | Academic | | | | |
| RallyRobin | | | ★ | ★ | | ★ | ★ | ★ | ★ | ★ |
| Timed Pair Share | | ☆ | ☆ | ☆ | | ☆ | ☆ | ☆ | ☆ | ☆ |
| RoundRobin | | ★ | ★ | ★ | | ★ | ★ | ★ | ★ | ★ |
| RallyCoach | | | ☆ | ☆ | | ☆ | ☆ | | ☆ | |
| Stand Up, Hand Up, Pair Up | ★ | | ★ | ★ | | ★ | ★ | ★ | ★ | ★ |

Source: www.kaganonline.com

## iii) Imagined contact

An indirect contact instructional strategy for promoting tolerance and more positive intra-group relationships. This is achieved by stimulating positive interactions between perceived different people, prior to any actual future interaction.

The development of social-emotional life skills is often seen as something a student must do in real-time and with others, especially those skills that require an understanding of others and their own uniqueness. Such life skills include empathy, respect and open-mindedness. However, studies conducted in conflict regions, such as Northern Ireland, have shown that a better approach may in fact be a simulated learning activity. The rationale behind the use of a simulated (or imagined) learning activity is that for many students this is a 'safer' starting position from which to counter any prejudice against difference.

Persona Life Skills is premised on the importance of understanding self and others, underpinned by the idea that everyone has a unique mix of personality styles. Personality is an external expression. In other words, it is defined by how other people see us rather than how we see ourselves. Understanding their own mix of personality styles, and that of others, helps students to make better decisions when dealing with other people, and therefore form more positive relationships and achieve more mutually beneficial outcomes in different situations.

Persona Life Skills learning modules use scenarios to help students place themselves in 'someone else's shoes' so they can consider different situations and interactions. This imagined activity provides students with a safe place to observe, reflect and potentially adapt their thinking, communication and behaviour when faced with similar real-life scenarios in the future.

Source: Persona Life Skills

**Pedagogical Content Knowledge (PCK)**

*"According to Shulman (1986), this transformation occurs as the teacher interprets the subject matter, finds multiple ways to represent it, and adapts and tailors the instructional materials to alternative conceptions and students' prior knowledge. PCK covers the core business of teaching, learning, curriculum, assessment and reporting, such as the conditions that promote learning and the links among curriculum, assessment, and pedagogy." (Koehler & Mishra, 2009)*

Persona's personality insights framework acts as the initial Content Knowledge (CK) driver to inform the Pedagogical Knowledge (PK) required to transform knowledge of personality insights into the acquisition and application of social-emotional life skills. This user journey is followed up by capturing student progress data, including self-reporting against perceived skills gained, and making it available on a dashboard within the app.

Broken down, this user journey can be seen to comprise steps towards gaining Content Knowledge, with Pedagogical Knowledge acting as the stepping stones to facilitate the journey.

For example:

i) Understanding personality insights (CK) – students are taken through a series of imagined contact scenarios (PK) in order to gain this new Content Knowledge (CK).

ii) Development and application of life skills (CK) – students are taken through learning modules that use a flipped learning approach (PK) whilst adopting cooperative learning when the flipped classroom is working as a dynamic group, facilitated by the teacher.

iii) Reflection of knowledge gained (CK) – students are asked at the end of each learning module to reflect on the progress they have made, enabling them and their teachers to determine (via student profile and dashboard screens) which learning module journey (PK) they would benefit from next.

## Technological Knowledge (TK)

*"Knowledge about certain ways of thinking about, and working with technology, tools and resources. and working with technology can apply to all technology tools and resources." (Koehler & Mishra, 2009)*

The use of technology in education is fraught with assumptions about what works and what does not. Often, the blame for lack of technological adoption has been laid at the teacher's feet. However, the COVID-19 pandemic school closures and online learning has shown that the teaching profession is, in fact, highly capable of adopting technologies that meet their teaching and learning needs.

The use of technologies in Persona Life Skills was informed by the Content Knowledge (CK) and Pedagogical Knowledge (PK) that had first been established.

i) Online learning platform (web app)

The need to provide schools with teaching and learning journeys online is a given in the post-pandemic world. As we continue to support those who work to close the digital divide that still affects millions of students around the world, the truth is that the now and future for receiving education support and resources is, for most, through digital means.

With this in mind, Persona Life Skills was created as an online learning platform that provides easy personalised access for teachers and students. As the platform is hosted in the cloud, provided they have access to an internet-connected device, users can access the learning journey equally well in school, at home or even somewhere else such as a library or café – enabling flipped learning.

ii) Probability density function algorithm

The application of a probability density function (PDF) algorithm – only possible thanks to software handling complex back-end data processing – enables a detailed and nuanced analysis of an individual's mix of personality and communication styles, based on their responses to a set of questions presented in the app. This technology amplified what would otherwise be a 16 data point output if manually calculated, to a 10,000 data point output (625 fold increase).

In other words, with the application of technological knowledge (TK), Persona Life Skills can differentiate between users with 10,000 unique combinations of personality styles.

iii) Natural language generation

Each student is provided with a set of Persona Insights data in the form of a textual commentary about their thinking, communication and behaviour characteristics, determined by the statistical distribution of their PDF data. Using natural language generation (NLG) technology, each commentary is compiled from a library of statements, and this correlates with the user's unique mix of personality styles, giving them personalised insights and recommendations.

The NLG within the Persona Life Skills app provides thousands of possible output variations. These variations include data on the user's mix of personality styles, positive characteristics, growth areas to consider, what to watch out for when under pressure, behaviours to be mindful of, self-insights compared with friend's insights, and three different contexts: social, learning and work.

iv) Data visualisation

Persona Life Skills also represents the personality insights visually in two different formats: word cloud and heatmap.

The use of adjectivalword cloud and heatmap visuals, in addition to the NLG text commentary, provides each user with additional representations of their unique mix of personality styles, supporting comprehension and deepening understanding.

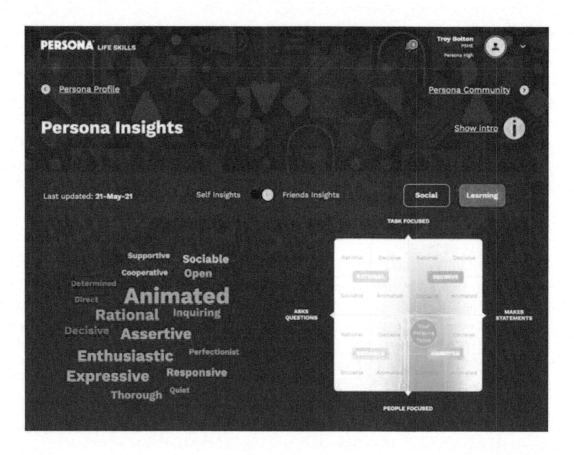

This type of technology-enabled multi-modal output helps to promote accessibility for the full range of end users.

## Technological Content Knowledge (TCK)

*"An understanding of the manner in which technology and content influence and constrain one another. Teachers need to understand which specific technologies are best suited for addressing*

*subject-matter learning in their domains and how the content dictates or perhaps even changes the technology—or vice versa." (Koehler & Mishra, 2009).*

Personality insights data generated through the use of a probability density function algorithm (TK), natural language generation (TK) and data visualisations (TK), as described above, comprise the critical content knowledge (CK) for students to use as they are taken through a series of life challenge learning modules, learning about and applying social-emotional life skills.

Combined, these TK elements deliver personalised reporting (CK) for each student.

## Technological Pedagogical Knowledge (TPK)

*"An understanding of how teaching and learning can change when particular technologies are used in particular ways. This includes knowing the pedagogical affordances and constraints of a range of technological tools as they relate to disciplinarily and developmentally appropriate pedagogical designs and strategies." (Koehler & Mishra, 2009)*

Providing schools and students access to Persona Life Skills as an online learning platform or web app (TK) is a critical feature of enabling the use of a flipped learning approach as pedagogical knowledge (PK). Flipped learning requires student users to be able to access content anywhere and anytime.

The use of various data visualisations (TK) provides students with alternative learning routes to understanding their Persona Insight data (CK).

## TPACK – Heart Of Innovation

*"Underlying truly meaningful and deeply skilled teaching with technology, TPACK is different from knowledge of all three concepts individually. Instead, TPACK is the basis of effective teaching with technology, requiring an understanding of the representation of concepts using technologies; pedagogical techniques that use technologies in constructive ways to teach content; knowledge of what makes concepts difficult or easy to learn and how technology can help redress some of the problems that students face." (Koehler & Mishra, 2009)*

Technological Knowledge (TK) has been applied in the Persona Life Skills online learning platform to find the best way to deliver personalised Content Knowledge (CK), through the most impactful Pedagogical Knowledge (PK) practices.
Although the build of Persona Life Skills was carried out focusing on the three separate components (CK, PK, TK), the build was also informed by the prescribed TPACK order and intersections between each - CK - PK - PCK - TK - TCK - TPK.

Following this order of development, the cumulative effect (TPACK) is the creation of the desired user journey resulting in optimum teaching and learning outcomes. In other words, TPACK is the means by which the Persona Life Skills Theory of Change is realised fully.

**TPACK – Context**

The TPACK framework is enveloped within a wider context. It is an important reminder that every learning experience is unique to its setting and users, regardless of any EdTech product or service's ability to provide effective teaching and learning – when all three knowledge components (CK, PK, TK) intersect.

Persona Life Skills was designed to apply across a range of contexts, and the in-app characters, scenario settings and life challenges were chosen to be as widely representative as possible of a global audience. This of course does not remove all contextual variables, but is an attempt to establish a common ground from which students are empowered to build the targeted social-emotional life skills.

i) Life challenges for Teens

Each learning module within the Persona Life Skills platform focuses on a life challenge typically encountered by 13-19 year olds, from dealing with unexpected events (eg. pandemics, moving schools/home), to managing homework, preparing for exams or getting ready for their first job.

ii) Different contexts – social, learning and work

Various learning modules focus on different contextual settings – social, learning and work. This enables Persona Insights data (CK) similarly to be contextualised across these three contexts, providing users with the means to cross-reference their thinking, communication and behaviour. For example, a student may find the aspect of their mix of personality styles that is most evident is very different in one setting compared with another.

iii) Self insights vs 3rd party insights

As mentioned earlier in this section, personality is an external expression. How we see ourselves (Self Insights in Persona Life Skills) is a helpful reference point to compare with how others view us (Friends Insights).

Persona Life Skills allows and encourages users to invite friends, peers or colleagues to answer a set of Persona Insights questions about them. Users can then see Persona Insights data (CK) based on the 3rd party insights, as well as their own self insights.

The more people who answer the questions, the more accurate and representative the user's mix of personality styles reported in the app will become, as any impact from statistical outliers isreduced.

**Measuring TPACK Impact**

In closing, how can EdTech measure the success of using such frameworks as TPACK, so that an iterative process of improvements can be applied? These improvements are critical for the sustainability as well as scalability of any EdTech product or service that aims to achieve its mission, and become a success in a crowded marketplace.

Although providing a theoretical framework (TPACK for example) is essential for guiding the integration of technology with educational systems, the real value of any framework lies in its ability to make sense of the real world. To this end, reliable and valid research instruments to gather feedback from users are fundamental for assessing consistency between theory and practice of TPACK.

There has been significant improvement in research methodologies and rigour in assessing TPACK over the years. Regardless, current approaches commonly focus on identifying TPACK components in isolation, although TPACK represents a dynamic relationship composed of the connections between the three core categories: CK; PK; TK.

Persona Life Skills relies on an expert student user group – the Persona 'WiseCrowd' – to co-create, test and help iterate isolated learning journeys. The WiseCrowd members advise on quality, personalisation and comprehensibility of the personality insights framework, considering their own unique Persona Insights data (CK). They suggest life challenges (CK) within which to set life skills development (CK), take learning modules (CK) in order to provide feedback on accessibility and engagement (PK, TK), and self-report on their own life skill development progress (CK, PK).

The collection of data for measuring TPACK impact is achieved by a) providing the WiseCrowd with access to the e-learning platform, b) setting unique user journey tasks, and c) providing an e-survey for reporting their experience against each task completed. In addition, one-to-one sessions are set up to allow researchers to observe and measure first-hand the extent to which the use of Persona Life Skills achieves the desired learning outcomes.

It is important to note that Persona Life Skills makes the assumption that positive user feedback from the three core components of TPACK individually, is correlated to meeting the requirements as laid down by the whole, i.e., the intersection where all three components meet (TPACK). This assumption is founded in the belief that true isolation of each component is misleading, since the most desirable user journey requires all three to be in action for it to be successfully completed. Users then self-report against this user journey within the web app, enabling a TPACK success feedback loop.

The Postcard helps you to reflect upon how much you have learnt in each Island. Your teacher will be able to see how you respond.

**In this Island, I have learnt how to get better at:**

**1.** Stress management. Managing my stress in different situations.

| Disagree | Agree | Agree strongly |

**2.** Being adaptable. Able to adapt my thinking, communication and behaviour, to achieve positive outcomes in different situations.

| Disagree | Agree | Agree strongly |

**3.** Staying positive. Maintaining a positive attitude and believing things will work out well.

| Disagree | Agree | Agree strongly |

Previous          Leave this Island

Source: Persona Life Skills web app

The Persona Life Skills online learning platform was predicated upon TPACK as a guiding framework for its initial build, and the team behind it continues to rely on TPACK in their iterative approach to making improvements to the platform, as well as pivoting to new user groups and markets.

As with all theoretical frameworks, assumptions were made to enable practical steps to be taken. However, a continuous loop of user co-creation, testing and feedback serves to mitigate any inaccurate assumptions, and helps to create an EdTech product that evolves to meet market needs, both now and into the future.

# 6 Governments

# How Can Governments Foster EdTech Systems?

## Melanie Debattista

Edtech lead, Malta Enterprise

There is no need to emphasise the link between a good quality education and personal / national prosperity. Investing in education is not as straight-forward as it sounds, especially in the 21st century with rapid changes in digital technologies and the demands of different industries.

The definition of literacy has changed. Whilst in the 20th century we understood literacy as the ability to read and write, today we think of the ability to read and write as not only with pen and paper but also using digital technologies like computing devices and the internet.

It is without doubt that there is a need to invest in this digital literacy. It is estimated that last year [2021], approximately US$1.6 million dollars was spent in e-commerce, 197.6 million emails were sent, and 500 hours of new video were uploaded on YouTube every 60 seconds (European Commission, 2021). Yes, every single minute.

The Covid-19 pandemic has accelerated the transition to digital platforms, and the question is no longer whether they are used or not, but whether we can maximise their benefits while addressing the challenges like misinformation, privacy and cybercrime.

For education to thrive in the digital era, a robust technology infrastructure, a sound education technology (EdTech) policy framework, and a workforce with the right skills and competences, will make it possible for entrepreneurs and investors alike to take the digital leap with confidence. A well-designed and sustained education ecosystem will make such a transformation both easier and more effective.

But, what are the approaches that a national government needs to take to attract both new and experienced EdTech players that can help develop this new economic niche in a particular jurisdiction? Through this article, we will navigate different approaches and methods that are starting to get traction with EdTech operators.

### A. Enablement Through Regulation: Education Certification And Licensing

Countries that lack natural resources but are dependent on their human resources tend to invest heavily in their population as a key economic contributor. Therefore, a sound education strategyfit for the 21st centuryremains crucial.

### The European Qualifications Framework (EQF)

In the EU, following the so-called Bologna Process, all signatories have agreed to move towards a curriculum that is built on learning outcomes, a range of learning experiences, and a qualifications framework that facilitates student progression and mobility across signatories. This gave rise to the harmonised European Qualifications Framework (EQF), to which the EU member states look for guidance and alignment.

This is also the case with Malta. Through the Malta Qualifications Framework (MQF) (see figure 1) the harmonisation of the European Credit Transfer System (ECTS) with the European Credit System for Vocational Education and Training (ECVET) is achieved.  In this respect, students who progress along the framework – from whichever path taken – can move on to more challenging academic levels within their area of study.  This may range from diploma and higher national diploma levels in vocational or academic subjects, up to vocational degrees at bachelor and master's level, to professional doctorates and /or Doctor of Philosophy.

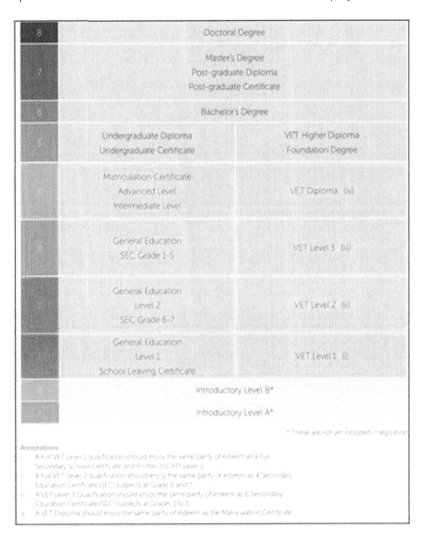

*(Figure 1- The Malta Qualifications Framework*. Source: Malta Qualifications Framework, 2021)

The recognition of the European Union's EQF allows for harmonisation of qualifications, whichfacilitates progression to its students from a level to another during their education and training. In the case of Malta, it provides for progression within the framework and sets the tracks for both academic as well as vocational types of education and training. With respect to primary and secondary (K-12) education, a National Curriculum Framework (or equivalent) provides general direction and operational parameters for all accredited compulsory education, whether provided by for-profit or not-for-profit providers (see figure 2).

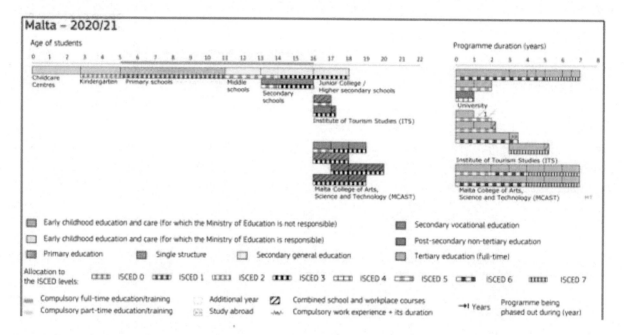

*(Figure 2 - Structure of the Maltese National Education System. Source: Malta – Eurydice – European Commission, 2021)*

### Certification Of Non-Formal Education

As new trends in 21st century education increasingly recognises the value of experience and learning from outside the traditional formal channels, various countries around the world have adopted policy that has put in place the necessary mechanisms to appraise non-accredited education.

This may be done through processes such as the Recognition of Prior Learning and the Validation of Non-Formal and Informal Learning. These education toolboxes are not only bridging education and training, but are also making it easier for the workforce to re-skill and up-skill.

Private segment investments in non-accredited education can be seen from multinationals in the technology sphere, such as Microsoft, who create courses that are sector specific and appeal to targeted audiences. The recognition of sector-recognised qualifications is done through the European Network of Information Centres in the European Region and the National Academic Recognition Information Centres in the European Union (ENIC-NARIC), which encompasses a network of national information centres that provide information on mobility and the recognition of academic and professional qualifications. The ENIC-NARIC network shares the secretariats of UNESCO, Council of Europe, and European Commission.

## Licensing Education Institutions

Licensing is one of the major barriers to entry. Each respective jurisdiction holds a different set of requirements for the setting up and managing of new education institutions. It can, however, be generally observed that the most barriers to entry come into effect in further and higher education licensing. These types of institutes are typically subjected to peer reviews in both quality-assurance, as well in terms of academic work.

Education sector professionals observe that there are two countries in the European Union that have the least barriers to entry, and are typically referred to as being the destinations of choice for new registrations. Estonia and Malta are the two most efficient jurisdictions in the EU that have developed a licensing regime that enables quality-oriented checks and balances, yet an agile adaptation for new market entries.

Within the EQF system, the European Association for Quality Assurance in Higher Education (ENQA) acts as a common baseline for higher education. This network stretches across all European countries and its regular auditing work ensures a high level of compliance that translates into good quality education.

Accreditation and licensing of educational institutions across the European jurisdictions have been updated to cater for the requirements presented by the rapid adoption of e-learning, with its pedagogies and methodologies that in some respects are distinct from traditional education. With the case of Estonia, one can see that the licence is provided for education within the territory (Republic of Estonia Ministry of Education and Research, 2019). On the other hand, Malta allows for a wider provision of the services, providing a series of quality checkpoints which the Malta Further and Higher Education Authority imposes on its licensees (Provider Licences - Malta Further & Higher Education Authority, 2021).

With the introduction of e-learning, one can also observe an increase in interest in e-certification. At the Institute of Tourism Studies in Malta, DLT-based certifications are issued to all full-time students. Be it digital or traditional, certification is also regularised by the jurisdiction, and the country-dependent model may be observed from the respective legislative regime.

## B. Enablement Through Regulation: Technology Certification

Regulators must prepare themselves for new segments and set-up a framework that allows new technologies to thrive. Through a robust, reliable and transparent ecosystem, businesses and entrepreneurs can safely develop products and services that can reach international markets. Startup regulation needs to support the entrepreneurial vision and allow for innovation.

Looking beyond the pandemic, government expenditure in the area of education and technology is expected to grow. There is no turning back as the importance of online learning, meetings and business have now been realised. However, only those countries that will harness innovation that is supported by the right regulatory framework and proper incentives to established and start-up businesses will thrive in this digital society.

In the case of the Mediterranean island of Malta, startups are supported with their endeavours through the Malta Digital Innovation Authority (MDIA), which has been set up to assist investors with sandbox opportunities. As an Authority within the ecosystem, it aims to promote the development of innovative technology, as well the development of the regulatory process to support business and consumers. This process is regulated through two main legislation frameworks: the MDIA Act and the Innovative Technology Arrangements and Services (ITAS) Act. Additional regulatory frameworks cover other digital components such as Digital Ledger Technologies (DLTs) and iGaming, with the latter being primarily regularised under the Malta Gaming Authority.

## C. National Business And Start-Up Contact Points

Foreign Direct Investment (FDI) is key to many of the European Jurisdictions, who all seek to support the introduction of new providers in various types of market segments. Estonia and Lithuania are very strong with the support provided for new business, particularly in the technology sphere. Other countries such as Ireland (Department of Trade, Enterprise and Employment), Portugal (Agency for Competitiveness and Innovation or IAPMEI), the Business Support Office (OAE) of Barcelona, Spain, and the Lithuanian Business Support Agency (LVPA) have all created incentives for startups. However, the Island of Malta provides for a well-defined, focused and attractive approach through the government's investment arm – Malta Enterprise (ME).

Although the hand-holding exercise from such investment companies helps entrepreneurs to accelerate their growth, in a tiny country such as Malta, this support feels more personal and efficient. Partly due to its size, the ability of this island to reach regulators and policy makers in the effective development of the infrastructure is noticeable. ME boasts of a 'red carpet'treatment to foreign investors, which suggests that all FDI is considered as a VIP. This approach by the Maltese agency is dictated by the country's vibrant but small economy.

The agencies in different countries provide information regarding investment and include schemes that support the setting up of the business, the financing of the start-up and business development support to grow accordingly. In the case of Malta, a good place to start exploring the offering is through http://www.startinmalta.com/.

The schemes offered by these agencies take different forms, from loans to grants to fiscal and infrastructural support. Others, which may form part of the larger dimension of the European system of funding, will be negotiated by each respective country, subjected to its priority areas, and the respective vision that that would entail to the hosting country. Malta provides three basic schemes for start-ups as explained in startinmalta.com: a seed and growth funding of up to 200,000 that also covers the business planning stage; a repayable advance of up to 800,000; and a scale-up grant of up to 200,000 in tax credits and cash grants.

Having one point of contact for the various needs of a business has served much of the economic development, and similar entities are worth looking for in any country, as these enabling bodies support an entrepreneur's delivery through their wide access to European, regional and local prospects.

## D. Beyond Hard Cash: Soft Support

Governments typically invest directly in their workforce through initiatives that support up-skilling and reskilling, to incentivise the workers to adapt to new and developing skill sets.

Moreover, through an attractive corporate taxation regime, a country's commitment to research and develop new technologies and a robust legislative framework make a jurisdiction friendly for new product development.

Around 250 iGaming companies are situated in Malta, including some of the major players like Betsson, Tipico and Kindred. Other companies in FinTech have also pursued, which have resulted in a workforce pool with transferable skills within the digital sphere.

In Malta, the Maltese language is the national tongue of the natives but the English language is used as the *lingua franca* of business. This is a strong asset of the Maltese islands when presented as a potential host to new business. The English Language remains Malta's key to the rest of the world and the British cultural heritage is still rooted in the country, despite its 60 years of independence from the UK. British tourists remain the biggest incoming segment, accounting for 24% in pre-Covid-19 figures, more than next-door neighbour Italy which, geographically, is only 90 km away (NSO, 2020).

## E. Small Is Nimble – Jurisdictions That 'Get' Start-Ups

When considering the partners with whom one goes into business, it is certainly essential to note the competence and enthusiasm that can be brought to the table. Through the determination and support of the involved parties, businesses will find the required input from relevant stakeholders. In this sense, small might not be a hindrance. Relatively small jurisdictions like Malta, Ireland, and Lithuania may be effectively nimble – an element which can play a vital component for the development of new products and as a digital test-bed, which may be scaled further to the piloting phases.

## F. Tech As A Given: Shaping The Classrooms Of The Future

If digital technologies have become an integral part of our lifestyle and our country's economy, the question begs: how can technology be best integrated into our educational systems to provide for both digital literacy and prepare the workforce with the necessary skills and competences to design, produce, implement and support the vast and critical digital technologies infrastructure on which our world is built upon?

EdTech ventures can only benefit from a holistic approach to both technology and education policy development. However, the sector needs to be ready to take on such changes, through infrastructure and service support. The EU has been at the forefront in the promotion of digital technologies in education with its various initiatives and programmes like IMPACT Ed-Tech (impactEdTech.eu/) and the European EdTech Network (www.eetn.eu). These are inspired by the EU's Digital Education Action Plan (2021-2027). Individual member states also take initiatives at national, regional and local levels. These include, the *National Digital Learning Repository (NDLR)* in the Republic of Ireland, the *Value of Knowledge, Strategic Agenda for Higher Education and Research 2015-202*5 in The Netherlands, the *Mission de la Pédagogie et du Numérique pour l'Enseignement Supérieur* or MiPNES (Mission for Pedagogy and Digitalisation in Higher Education) in France, and Malta's 'One Tablet Per Child' initiative (European University Association, 2018).

Malta stands at the forefront in terms of investment in ICT in education. This is confirmed by the fact that the country scores above the EU average in almost all categories, especially in the availability and the productive use of digital technologies in schools, and the positive relationship of both educators and learners with technology (2nd Survey of Schools: ICT in Education (2021).

Being sector-ready is indeed an important consideration, and for this reason, finding a country that provides internet access and a digital screen in all the classrooms, equips all educators in public schools with a laptop, and provides both educators and learners with free online productivity and communication software, is worth noting. Malta has gone a step further and provided its students with a free tablet computer (including independent schools) in the upper primary school levels with its 'One Tablet Per Child' initiative (Digital Malta Strategy, 2021).

This type of investment in a relatively small society sets the scene for the impact of technology when adopted by the whole ecosystem. Provided that a society sample size can be scaled up in a way that makes sense in larger numbers, the choices made, and the existent infrastructure are worth noting. This modelling is typically implemented in the United States, whereby a county or a state may be selected based on demographics, the readiness, and the adaptability of the social fabric to act as a testbed of a particular product or service. Once the necessary studies are collected and the product is refined, the entrepreneurs typically commence penetration in new markets, whilst adjusting and adapting for each respective state law unless otherwise regulated through the federal government.

Similarly, technology use in education is a key foundation that lays the ground for technology proficiency of students and learners across all ages. It is worth noting, however, that the tiny island of Malta was one of the first in the world to issue formal qualification certificates both in print format and in digital format through 'blockcerts', digital certificates based on the blockchain (DLTs). Every compulsory education school leaver and successful student at the Malta College for Arts, Science and Technology (MCAST) and the Institute of Tourism Studies (ITS) receives this. This goes to show that the technology adaptations may happen across an education programme life cycle, and beyond into industry.

The adaptability of the market remains a key component in product development and testing, as this allows business to research and explore the consumer behaviour accordingly.

**F. Teacher Training**

Although technology has helped different societies reach out to new territories to conduct studies, it is worth noting that there should exist a solid fabric within the local market that caters for teacher training. This should be present within the higher education structures; however, it should also be supported through solid foundations. As technology develops, so does teacher training, which in certain countries, governments allow for a budget to be allocated to teacher learning in the form of work resources.

This is typically allocated for the purpose of continuous professional development as well as other professional needs. Such schemes are derived from collective agreements made with education providers.

## Conclusion: Beyond The Pandemic

The COVID-19 pandemic has, however, brought new opportunities to the market, as it has accelerated the transition of education provision towards virtual platforms. Much of it has been readily available for years, but their potential has not yet been maximised.

Online classes were not the answer to all types of learning, and the Vocational Educational Training (VET) sector was particularly hit with the closure of schools, labs and workplaces that hosted apprentices. Hospitality was also hit hard with the closure of not only schools, but also training restaurants and the hospitality sector outlets for several weeks (CEDEFOP, 2021). This has created more awareness of what AI, Augmented Reality and Virtual Reality can bring to education to take it to the next level.

These two sides of the coin have been represented in all parts of the world. However, many successful transitions have been made amongst universities. Others have started to adopt a blended approach to synchronous and asynchronous types of learning, and we are expected to see more of it soon. The challenges however are still there, particularly those related to internet and technology accessibility in certain parts of the globe, such as Indonesia, according to OECD data ("The COVID-19 pandemic has changed education forever. This is how", 2020).

GOVERNMENT

The forced push to digital through COVID-19 has taught us that online education has a potential, and a place, in our society. Probably not across all age groups, for studies have shown a different type of engagement. In the case of young children, a more structured approach has proven to be more effective in view of distractions.

The resilience of the Maltese education system, thanks to its highly qualified human resources and significant investment in technology, was proven with the publication of the exam results of the Secondary Education Certificate (SEC), the end-of-compulsory education exams comparable to the English GCSE, in August 2021. These results were comparable to the 2019 pre-COVID-19 results, proof that the Maltese students and the Maltese education system withstood the challenge of closing schools and going completely online.

The continued investment in digital technologies and human resources for those countries who have done so within their education system, saw their dividend paid during the pandemic when all schools switched from in-class to on-line learning within a few days. However, adaptation from the people is still to be seen. Culture change has always been an issue with any new technology.

One thing is certain however, that in a worldwhere people prefer to lose their wallet than their smartphone, national governments need to provide a regulatory framework and supporting services for entrepreneurs and investors, as the faster new and better technology emerges and is widely adopted, and the quicker we shall all reap the benefits.

GOVERNMENT

# 7 Technology

# Supercharging Modern Learning Environments Through IOT-Enabled Education

## Guneet Kaur

Co-founder Finnex solutions, Technology Editor at Cointelegraph& DEA Fellow

### COVID-19 And Disruption In The Education Industry

The outbreak of coronavirus (SARS-CoV-2) pandemic has caused the suspension of teaching and learning processes at the university level, as well as changes in course schedules and reduced attendance, which has resulted in poor test outcomes and, in the long run, will likely have a negative impact on students' future. Steps taken to tackle the virus' spread have hindered the educational process, reducing students' and lecturers' opportunities for training and mobility worldwide. Despite these challenges, the unusual situation opened up new possibilities, spurring the advancement of distance learning and interactive educational technologies. Almost every country in the world has taken measures to adapt to this changing world of education. For instance, the digital transformation of higher education has been a focal point of the European Union's growth strategies through the implementation of new information and communication technologies. The European Commission's policies support the transformation of education and learning processes in a time of rapid technological change by providing funding for training developments. Therefore, under pandemic conditions, high-speed internet connections and widespread use of digital technology for training provide students worldwide with fast and secure access to educational material.

One such technology that contributes to the transformation of contemporary education is the Internet of Things (IoT). The Internet of Things (IoT) is a technological development that allows objects, people, and environments to communicate in real-time. Physical environments are becoming more innovative and integrated than ever before due to the IoT's introduction and development. The Internet of Things is being used by governments and educational institutions to exploit data, streamline processes, and encourage sustainability. In several universities, the use of smart objects and devices is well known. Chips, sensors, and other wearable devices have become commonplace in education. It is evident that technology in the classroom has many advantages, including saving teachers time, allowing for personalised, project-based learning, and providing students with the digital skills they will need in 21st-century employment.

*"The Internet of Things is all about going from being reactive to constructive and even predictive".*

### How Does IoT Help In Supercharging Modern Classrooms?

The Internet of Things (IoT) was first coined in 1999 (TEM Journal, 2022) as an expansion of the use of Radio Frequency Identification (RFID) to allow physical objects to communicate with one another and with their environment. This principle has been improved over the last ten years, new realistic solutions have been implemented, and it has become the foundation for the most recent advances in information technology. The transformative role of technology in today's educational institutions has revolutionised education from a knowledge-transfer model to an active collaborative self-directed model. Many organisations have been forced to reconsider how they teach and learn as a result of this. Technology affects education in many ways, from student participation in learning and curriculum development to assist teachers in delivering customised content and enhancing student outcomes. The fundamental goal of implementing IoT in education is to create an atmosphere that promotes learning in a modern, standard, and productive manner that meets the needs and expectations of students. IoT systems make it easier for educational institutions to gather large amounts of data from wearable devices and sensors and take action based on that data. Students may use QR codes, embedded sensors, and other technologies to explore an environment with these systems. According to Statista. com's research, IoT is currently expanding at a rapid rate, with 27 billion connected devices worldwide as of 2019 and 75 billion by 2025. (TEM Journal, 2022)

*"IoT supercharges modern education by encouraging smart education, which facilitates smart teaching and smart learning, intending to build a smart classroom and a smart campus."*

The components of smart education are explained as follows-

**a) Smart Teaching:** Smart teaching is a unique teaching technique that differs from the traditional chalk-and-talk method. Here, the teacher uses electronic devices to provide education in a variety of ways. It aids the learner in understanding the various aspects based on the numerous options available. It also offers high-quality content 24 hours a day, seven days a week.

**b) Smart Learning**: Smart learning is a form of learning through the use of electronic devices. Based on the learner's availability, the learner can undertake specific coaching/ training. It promotes individualised learning.

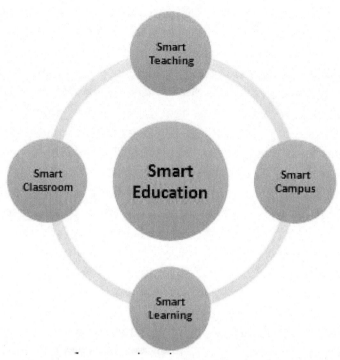

Figure1: The components of Smart Education.

**c) Smart Classroom**: A smart classroom is an intelligent space that is fitted with various hardware and software modules. Modules that track different parameters of the physical environment or students' attributes such as efficiency, focus, and achievement include cameras, video projectors, sensors, and face recognition algorithms.

**d) Smart Campus**: With the aid of smart technology, school vehicles can be tracked and handled effectively. IoT sensors can be used to monitor traffic movements around campus, providing helpful information that can help schools identify which areas need additional safety measures, such as lighting, to protect their students and visitors. IoT can also help in ecosystem monitoring and energy management on the campus.

In recent years, the use of IoT in the education sector has received a lot of attention. Smart education offers a considerable forum for the e-learning process. Smart education is a more efficient and effective method of increasing productivity. It significantly affects the learning process by radically altering the conventional learning process and making it even more engaging.

**Applications Of IoT In The Education Sector**

By bringing learning centres closer to the virtual world, IoT will make schools and universities smarter and more connected. The potential areas where IoT can help in upgrading the quality of education are explained in the sections below.

**Secure Campus, Eco-System Monitoring And Campus Energy Management**

Some of the problems that could be solved by introducing modern technology into education include creating a healthy and secure environment in universities by controlling students' access to labs, classrooms, and other areas. NFC (Near Field Communication) and RFID (Radio-frequency Identification) are two IoT enabler technologies that can be used to improve university security and simplify access control. For example, Bournville College has implemented Cisco Physical Access Control Technology to manage access to various campus areas.(Shura, 2022) This technology has made handling access simplified to 400 doors on the main campus, including offices, classrooms, and other communal areas. Similarly, the Internet of Things can be used in energy storage and ecosystem tracking to improve energy production and create a more sustainable future. As a result, many national governments have implemented Smart Grid, a particular IoT energy management application. Universities may use the same principle to build a green campus environment by lowering $CO_2$ emissions, tracking and regulating energy and water usage, and providing a safe teaching and learning environment.

## Enhanced Teaching And Learning

By offering a more prosperous learning environment and real-time actionable insight into students' success, IoT will help institutions improve the quality of teaching and learning. It has the potential to build a smart learning environment in which students can tailor environmental variables, such as room temperature, to their preferences. In the modern education environment, IoT devices such as fitness bands, tablets, sensors, laptops, e-books, and virtual and augmented reality headsets are being used to track and control students in various ways to recognise and analyse students' learning habits. IoT can be deployed in following ways to improve learning and teaching:

**a) Learning management system (LMS):** As more students use laptops and tablets in the classroom, teachers have begun to rely on tracking tools to keep their students on track. Teachers may use learning management systems to monitor, administer, and record how their EdTech devices are used in real-time. Data monitoring and reporting functionality in the more advanced frameworks can help recognise learning gaps and support asynchronous lesson plans. Furthermore, during an assessment, data from IoT sensors can be analysed to identify anomalies in the students' actions being tested. The lecturer receives messages from the device and can identify which students are engaging in deceptive acts. Then, the lecturer may issue a warning and dismiss cheating students from the exam.

**b) Automated attendance tracking systems:** Mandatory student IDs have become more common as school safety concerns have grown. If wearable IoT and cloud computing are applied, they could revolutionise how faculty members monitor their students' attendance and on-campus location. Educational institutions can also use real-time communication systems to inform parents on their children's development, and IoT sensors can help parents monitor their child's class attendance in real-time.

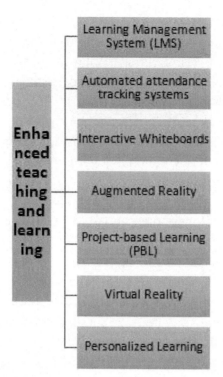

Figure2: Ways in which IoT can be deployed to improve teaching and learning.

**c) Interactive Whiteboards:** Since the mid-90s, interactive whiteboards have become the most common EdTech tool, allowing educators to streamline in-class assignments without disturbing their teaching strategies. Recent advances in embedded technologies and wireless networking have greatly expanded the capabilities of interactive whiteboards, allowing educators to integrate audio and video-based materials without the use of external hardware. Teachers can use modern digital whiteboards to present multimedia lessons, display student presentations and projects, and foster collaborative problem-solving activities.

**d) Augmented Reality:** Augmented reality technologies are steadily gaining popularity among educators, despite being less common than other EdTech tools. By integrating 3D models and animated content into classroom assignments, AR will increase interaction and support visual learners. This will assist teachers in making science topics more approachable while also stimulating their students' technical interests.

**e) Project-based Learning (PBL):** PBL is a student-centred teaching approach that focuses on developing student interdisciplinary skills, teamwork, interpersonal communication, critical thinking, and project management abilities. Students use project-based learning to engage with their peers, rather than only listening to and reading about abstract ideas. IoT encourages PBL with the aid of flipped classroom apps, allowing students to arrive with a thorough understanding of the topic to be explored. The flipped classroom replaces in-class lectures with interactive, hands-on exercises and allows students to preview course materials outside of class. Pre-class learning planning, in-class learning events, and post-class learning consolidation are the three phases of flipped classroom work. Students participate in self-directed learning using online learning tools to prepare for class. The students and the instructor complete participatory learning tasks during in-class learning activities. Students study materials to improve learning outcomes during post-class learning consolidation. Students will learn outside of the classroom, apply what they have learned in class, interact with other students, and receive direct input from their teachers.

**f) Virtual Reality:** For students who identify as disabled, the Internet of Things could be helpful. Students who are deaf or possess any hearing loss may use a system of linked gloves and a tablet to translate sign language to speech (i.e., verbal speech). Providing educational assistance to disabled students through the use of IoT devices and systems is a positive way to do so.

**g) Personalised Learning:** Educators can personalise education for each student by gathering data about their success during lessons and exams and by understanding their learning styles and preferences. This is especially important for higher education, where students have a greater chance of finishing their studies if the path is tailored to them. Connected sensors can act as intelligent tutors, detecting student distraction and disinterest in real-time. More engaging material can then be offered to the students for continued learning.

## Health Monitoring

Since a student's health is such an essential factor in deciding his or her overall academic success, having access to a high-quality healthcare programme is vital in any educational setting. Wearable technology is a popular application of IoT in healthcare. In a non-invasive and unobtrusive way, a wearable interface tracks physiological signals over long periods. The most common use cases for these wearable devices are fitness bands and smartwatches. Such devices can be used to record various types of data such as students' medications, medical history, blood pressure, oxygen level, and other vital signs. Moreover, since online students are more likely to experience neck pain, back pain, and other related issues, the wearable device can warn students to get up and walk after long periods of sitting, intending to improve their overall health.

## Summary

The benefits of integrating the Internet of Things in education include the ability to keep track of educational supply management, not having to fill out a lot of paperwork, and correctly distributing funds. IoT strategies lay the groundwork for a more risk-free, effective, and interconnected decision-making process, where all stakeholders (parents, teachers, and students) can improve the facility's condition. Additionally, IoT processes terabytes of data simultaneously, allowing educational institutes to track students' progress, safety and oversee teaching specialists' professional training. Stakeholders can use real-time data to improve testing and grading efficiency or when looking for new ways to enhance classroom engagement. IoT in education makes educational institutions operate more effectively, lowering long-term maintenance and storage costs. Facility managers may also use connected IoT devices for education to ensure that energy consumption is efficient. The Internet of Things has several security technologies that can help parents and students feel more comfortable in their learning environment, foster good behaviours, and make it easier for facility managers to maintain order in the organisation.

## Limitations Of IoT-Enabled Education

Despite the above advantages, IoT in education has several disadvantages. The most challenging aspect of the IoT-education relationship, or the critical obstacle, will be security and privacy. Data collection is, of course, an unavoidable part of this partnership. Many educational characteristics, such as students' learning background, location, and personal data, are collected here. As a result, protection and privacy concerns about IoT in education are among the critical issues that must be carefully addressed. IoT in education also faces a high cost of implementation problem. These costs include software licences, hardware purchases, and maintenance costs.

Furthermore, there is a risk that the software will be compromised, exposing users' personal details. As a consequence, the customer is responsible for all safety risks. Attendance monitoring, temperature sensors, interactive whiteboards, and other smart IoT technologies are currently being used in the education field. Some of these devices and applications are incompatible and have limited interoperability with other intelligent systems, making it difficult for the company to develop an IoT system that is both reliable and open to all users. For effective implementation, an educational institution must ensure that both its IT equipment and teaching methods promote IoT in the classroom. These roadblocks can have a significant effect on the future of digitalised education.

## Future Trends

In the future, the Internet of Things will boost both the teaching and learning process. Students will learn more efficiently, and teachers will be able to complete marking their assignments more quickly. IoT tools are expected to provide a more appealing, versatile, interactive, and quantifiable educational environment that meets a large number of students' diverse needs. However, as there are billions of IoT devices and objects. A massive amount of data (big data) gets stored, analysed, and sensed by these sensors, and it has become difficult for non-technical and technical users to process this data. The problem of collecting and processing sensed data is a significant concern in the Internet of Things, which should be addressed in the future. Furthermore, to eradicate safety concerns, users should be taught to turn the devices off while not in use and adjust the default passwords or other security settings.

## Conclusion

The education sector is currently regarded as one of the underserved markets with untapped technological adoption opportunities. Nonetheless, the COVID-19 pandemic and the resulting social constraints have dramatically altered how learners and instructors teach, read, interact, and collaborate in just a few months. As a result, lecturers were forced to rapidly reorganise their courses into an immersive digital framework and formulate a technique for accurate remote analysis and assessment due to unforeseen circumstances.

However, the Internet of Things (IoT) plays a vital role in the distinctive transformation by filling this void. As a growing number of educational organisations use similar gadgets to promote e-learning, IoT in education is poised to be a distinct advantage. Moreover, economic growth and long-term sustainability can be achieved by using IoT. By 2025, roughly 2-3 billion people will have access to the internet, and IoT-related economic growth is expected to range from $2.7 trillion to $6.2 trillion.

The IoT is a rapidly evolving technology that links virtual and physical objects. It is a critical component of the internet's future as it integrates everyday objects with artificial intelligence. Since the world is changing rapidly, it is essential to keep up with it. The Internet of Things (IoT) assists educational organisations in this process by making day-to-day tasks uncomplicated for universities and colleges.

Using networking sources such as the internet, IoT allows objects to be sensed and managed. As a result, the Internet of Things enables everything and anyone around the world to be linked. IoT was created primarily to relieve human burdens, as controlling objects through networking is much more difficult. It is also fast and straightforward to use, with fewer bugs and errors. This method enables connections to multiply, resulting in the creation of a whole new network of interconnections. IoT will become a reality in the near future due to significant investments and improved protection for the massive amounts of data stored in clouds, which will be available to all students at any time. An education provider can face numerous challenges in successfully integrating IoT devices in a classroom setting, including dependable Wi-Fi connections, network bandwidth, web analytics, security, availability of devices for teacher training, students, and equipment cost. These challenges should be addressed in the future to improve the education sector.

# Enabling Technologies – The CASE For EdTech

## Surinder Sharma

Founder and CEO of Smart Kidz Club

### Introduction

Education is essential for both the individual and for society. Literacy and reading proficiency are the very root of, and the first steps in, an individual's educational journey. If someone cannot read proficiently, their future education faces multiple and consistent challenges. According to the U.S. National Adult Literacy Survey, 70 percent of all incarcerated adults cannot read at a 4th grade level, "meaning they lack the reading skills to navigate many everyday tasks or hold down anything but lower (paying) jobs."[1] Considering the future of work, the ability to read and educate ourselves and reskill for rapidly changing workplaces is extremely important. Education impacts the progress of an entire society and the world's economies. According to Montenegro and Patrinos, the global return on investment (ROI) from schooling is highest at the primary level at approximately 10 percent, compared to secondary education (five percent) and university education (6 percent).[2]

Lack of education and growing disparity in education systems are a threat to nations, creating wide gaps in workplaces and socio-economic status. Despite millions of dollars spent on various initiatives around the world, an unimaginable illiteracy rate still exists. Among children one year younger than primary school entry age, more than one-third are excluded from pre-primary or primary education. The number of out-of-school children in this age group (around 47 million) has shown no progress since 2014.[3] In fact, for primary grade children the number of out-of-school children has increased by 1.7 million since then.[4] Of the world's 694 million children of primary school age, 387 million fail to achieve a minimum level of learning.[5] Globally four out of 10 children fail to meet minimum learning standards.[6]

Socio-economic factors play a large role in determining access to pre-primary education. Though education systems have been sufficiently developed in some countries, this is not the case for all. In many developed countries, you can see disparity among education systems based on geographical area or economic classes. The real challenge is to sufficiently develop education systems across all of these. Moreover, education's focus needs to shift to the primary level, as clearly evidenced by Montenegro and Patrinos findings on ROI cited above. Failing to include a certain population pulls the whole nation backward and entails spending millions on patchwork or **"band-aid solutions"** rather than addressing the problem at its core.

More recently, the COVID-19 pandemic has created severe disruption to global education systems, by forcing more than 1.6 billion learners in over 190 countries out of school at the peak of the crisis.[7] School closures due to health crises have a multi- layer impact on learners. They lead to more school dropouts, leave learners at a higher risk of abuse, loss of confidence and self-esteem, and contribute to a decline in quality teaching and learning. While the result has been a scramble to online learning and the use of assorted EdTech tools to prevent disruptions in learning, the biggest challenge has been the lack of equitable access to internet or online connectivity. By far, the most devastating factor for both teachers and parents has been the inability to reach the learner populations who do not have online access. COVID-19 and the need for remote learning have thrown a glaring spotlight on the digital divide—the fact that internet and mobile network access varies greatly in low- and middle-income countries. Internet access is as low as 39% in Vietnam and some African countries. Online learning will be easier only for those with access; excluded will be large groups of disadvantaged learners who may not have electricity, who may have a radio but not a television at home, others with basic feature mobile phones but not smartphones, and those with only low-bandwidth internet available with high data costs.8

In addition, teachers have been burdened with having to adopt and use new and often complicated technologies, having to reinvent lesson plans and relying on teaching and learning approaches that do not work well. They may face a complex learning curve with these unfamiliar education technologies, without having a chance to evaluate their effectiveness in remote education settings. Despite global non-profit and research organisations such as The EdTech Hub9 and UNESCO, who have partnered to launch a filterable database of available teacher resources, many teachers are still overwhelmed and burdened with evaluating the tools suitable for their specific educational context.

## The CASE For EdTech

While EdTech can be a great equaliser and game changer in the future of delivering education to millions, it needs to be designed so as to be impactful in reach, accessibility, collaboration, and power to both engage learners and empower teachers. We must build and uncover enabling technologies that conquer the barriers preventing millions of learners from accessing educational materials and resources.

An "enabling technology" is defined as an innovation that can be applied to drive radical change in the capabilities of a user or culture. And in order for any EdTech solution to be truly transformative for learners across the world, it needs to consist of four key components that I call the **CASE for EdTech** (Figure 1)—**C**onvenient **A**ccessible **S**calable **E**ducational.

The CASE Diagram

Figure 1: *The diagram shows the four critical components for any education technology to be transformational and drive radical change.*

**Convenient**—*If It Isn't Convenient, They Won't Be Using It.*

Convenience and ease of use are at the heart of human innovation across all industries. Technology is driven by the quest for more efficient, easy-to-use platforms and tools that eliminate human bias, inefficiencies, or complexities. Over the past decades, technology has integrated itself into virtually every industry—FinTech (financial), MarTech (marketing), HealthTech, and EdTech. Startups, a majority tech-driven, have exploded in 2020-21. In 2020, 4.4 million new companies started worldwide—the highest increase startups have seen over the past decade at 26.9%.10 The COVID pandemic has forced us from our former routines and prompted us to re-examine the way we work, live, and do business. With work, school, and even socialising going partially or fully remote, technology has been leapfrogging its way into our new normal, reimagining easier, more efficient and safe ways of working together.

The largest example of technology integration into our daily lives has been the way we are communicating. Zoom, Google Meet, and Microsoft Teams have become an essential part of our daily life and work. The very fact that all these platforms offer the convenience of communicating safely from our home has made them widely applicable and accepted around the world. Though these platforms have a learning curve as users explore new features, had these been inconvenient or complicated, they would not have been as popular. Take, for example, Zoom, which offers the convenience of a video meeting with one or multiple participants from a desktop, mobile phone or other device via a mobile app. The Zoom app became the most popular video conferencing service of the pandemic. Its daily downloads increased from 56,000 in January of 2020 to 2.13 million two months later.11 Zoom's popularity gives credence to the fact that convenience and ease of use are defining factors in the adopting and scaling of any technology. In a similar vein, EdTech has been another industry that has seen a surge during the pandemic. With prolonged school closures and uncertainty over the pandemic that still continues to rage in 2021, teachers, schools, and parents have all been scrambling to find solutions that will help keep their students and children learning from home.

Despite – or perhaps because of – the pandemic, EdTech startups have experienced a significant surge. According to EdSurge, which tracks such funding, U.S. education technology startups raised over $2.2 billion in venture and private equity capital across 130 deals in 2020, a nearly 30 percent increase from the $1.7 billion invested in 2019 across 105 deals. The $2.2 billion marks the highest investment total in a single year for the U.S. EdTech industry.12 Countries and education departments around the world are using EdTech to support remote learning—online, or via radio, television, texting, or apps—during the pandemic.13 Despite all these investments during the pandemic, however, both teachers and parents have struggled with the complicated platforms and tools thrust on them without much evaluation on their effectiveness, convenience, and safety. Many are so cumbersome, incorporating extensive modules and features in the software that teachers and students find it difficult to use the applications. Studies show that three-quarters of teachers say the internet and other digital tools have added new demands to their lives and have dramatically increased the range of content and skills about which they must be knowledgeable. Nearly half say it has increased their workload.14 It is straightforward that any education technology that is not convenient or takes too much time to learn will simply not be used. Keep in mind the variations in the user profiles and skill levels of the users across all demographics. EdTech solutions need to be designed keeping in mind all these profiles. In order for any EdTech solution to be adopted at an extensive scale, the first key ingredient is for it to be convenient to use, easy to access, and simple to master.

## 2. Accessible— *There's No Progress Without Access.*

Even though rapid progress has been made in improving connectivity for citizens, especially after the obvious gaps exposed by remote learning, internet connectivity is still a huge challenge, even in developed countries like the United States. More than 50 percent of students in some states were unable to access online lessons and learning due to connectivity issues. Around one in 10 of the poorest children in the U.S. has little or no access to technology for learning.15 Mark Lieberman at Education Week cited reliable, high-quality internet experiences for all as the big pandemic tech challenge.16 The challenges fall into one of three areas:

a. **Lack of digital devices or hardware for at-home learning**— While schools have turned to online and virtual learning environments, they often assume that all students will have access to some kind of a digital device, laptop, desktop, or smartphone at home to partake in virtual learning. This challenge can most easily be met by providing hardware, tablets, and digital devices to students who do not already have some sort of setup at home.

b. **Lack of steady high-quality at-home connectivity** —This second challenge is slightly more difficult to address. Learning for school students has gone virtual, either completely or in some sort of hybrid scenario. Steady, high-quality at-home connectivity forms a key element in this kind of educational scenario. However, what many households have witnessed is that although the internet is available, the burden of several devices simultaneously vying for bandwidth affects the quality of access—i.e., video freezes or audio drops off. With families stuck at home working and attending school at the same time, access to uninterrupted high-quality connectivity causes a severe disruption in the student's learning process. In addition is the added stress of not being able to attend a lesson and losing out on active instruction, all of which eventually leads to learning loss. This is exacerbated for young children with limited attention span who have a hard time sitting in front of an online screen.

c. **Lack of internet connectivity**—The third challenge is the most devastating and has been the bane of online and virtual learning during the pandemic. The EdTech digital divide has been magnified under a spotlight during the pandemic.17 Most EdTech solutions and online learning require internet connectivity. However, even in developed nations like the United States, a disproportionate number of school-age children lack home broadband access. An estimated 21.3 million people were lacking access in 2019, according to the Federal Communications Commission (FCC).18 This lack in internet connectivity is more pronounced in rural and low-income households. According to a PEW research study, low-income households tend to be more smartphone-dependent and lack access to multiple internet-enabled devices (tablets, PCs, or laptops) to get online.19 According to the broadband advocacy group EducationSuperhighway, 21 million U.S. students and nearly a quarter of all school districts are not meeting minimal bandwidth goals for digital learning.20 This digital divide is even more pronounced in developing and medium-to-low-income countries. With few exceptions, African countries have been ranked at the bottom third of countries in terms of internet availability and affordability.21 In addition, for most nations that do have connectivity via telecom networks, massive data costs prevent them from taking advantage of online learning tools. Many national governments and ministries of education have had to rely on radio and text messages to continue educational lessons for their students during school closures. The lack of internet connectivity has severely impacted the continuation of learning from home and exacerbated the education inequities and learning losses in young children.

While national governments have focused on expanding broadband access to all populations, EdTech solution providers should not rely on the presence or absence of this critical yet unreliable component in delivering education. EdTech tools need to be designed and developed by incorporating offline functionality that does not rely on continuous streaming of the internet for delivery of educational content. EdTech solutions that can deliver high-quality education, both content and delivery, without the need for internet connectivity are the ones that can actually transform the learning landscape by bridging the digital divide and making learning truly accessible to all.

EdTech companies like Smart Kidz Club, Inc. use the power of mobile technology to make their digital library of educational, nonfiction content accessible to all without the need for continuous streaming internet. They have incorporated offline access of content as a core component of their design framework. A part of the company's mission is to make high-quality educational content accessible to all children irrespective of their Zip Code. They have seen a surge in demand for their early education apps around the world, with a nearly 1100% increase in new users in 2021 alone. Thus, accessibility of and to an EdTech solution without depending on availability of broadband access or continuous internet forms an integral part of future enabling technologies.

**3. Scalable**—*If You Fail In Scaling, You Aren't Enabling.*

In order for any EdTech product or solution to make a radical change in the performance of learners, it needs to be globally scalable, both in its tech capabilities and applicability, especially within the segment it addresses. Here are two important components of scalability:

a. *Application*—Many EdTech products are available for schools and teachers to use in the classroom with students and for parents to use at home with their children. It is important for such products to be applicable across a wide range of demographics, socio-economic statuses, and geographic locations, both urban and rural. A product designed to cater only to a specific target audience will most likely not be scalable. While designing the framework for such a product, it is important to first identify your target audience, whether in terms of age, grade level, demographics, ethnicities, socio-economics, or geography. A product designed for a narrow and specific audience cannot be scaled for a wider implementation. It is important to get early feedback from potential users across different demographics while designing the technology framework, to ensure that you understand their unique needs, gaps, and challenges and incorporate them into your product. Payment gateways and processes are another factor to be considered and researched before you build your product. How do the existing users pay for other similar tech products? What are the challenges they face? How can these be improved and streamlined for a smoother transaction? All these are questions that form the basis of how scalable your product will be in terms of its widespread applicability.

b. *Technology*—The other important component of scalability is technology. An EdTech product that has far-reaching and widespread application around the world will most likely buckle under the pressure of rapidly growing new and daily active users if the technology infrastructure has not been designed to handle a high volume of users. With a large volume of users, EdTech solutions need to be configured for onboarding, data storage, data processing, data handling, and data management efficiently with minimal costs and without excessive delays in processing time or poor user experience.

Many educators and parents are now realising that most online learning tools and technologies are highly expensive and available to a certain limited segment of the population. Many other EdTech products and tools are restrictive in their application and cater to a specific segment of the population, whilst others cannot scale rapidly or onboard millions of users quickly. It is imperative that enabling education technologies are scalable both in terms of their tech capabilities as well as their widespread applicability and adoption.

**4. Educational**—*Education Should Be The Leading Intention.*

The fourth critical component in my CASE for education technology to be truly transformational is for it to have a high educational context. Many EdTech tools, especially those for parents to use with their children at home, appear fancy, with top- of-the-line features and latest tech tools incorporated within their solutions. They qualify as technology solutions seemingly for "education," but do not incorporate all the components of a meaningful one. These are extremely appealing and exciting to incorporate in classrooms and at home, but students and children often gain nothing substantial by using them. In effect, they are brilliant packaging with empty contents. Several other EdTech products incorporate complex tools and use distracting bells and whistles that make the product cumbersome to use and may actually hinder learning. A classic example of this are the myriad children's apps that claim to be educational but actually incorporate harmful animations and games that have shown to be detrimental to young children.

A 2018 study conducted by Dr. John Hutton, a researcher and paediatrician specialising in "emergent literacy," exposed children in and around the age of four to three forms of story narration:22

a. Audio only
b. Audio with static illustration (picture books)
c. Dynamic animation (cartoon)

After observing the children's brain patterns in a functional MRI machine (non-invasive and safe), what emerged was termed the "Goldilocks Effect" by Dr. Hutton. The dynamic animations and cartoons, according to Dr. Hutton, were "too hot." In this condition, the children's brain scans showed a great amount of activity, but they were having a tough time figuring out what was happening as their mind was being over-stimulated. The audio-only version was described by Dr. Hutton as "too cold"— the children were having a tough time understanding what was being said because of a lack of visual clues to give them context. The picture books were the "just right" condition where the children's understanding of the story was maximised. In this condition, children were being challenged just the right amount while also learning a lot more than from the other two methods. This clearly demonstrates the distracting and harmful effects of animations and cartoons on young children. Yet you will see thousands of EdTech solutions incorporating animations in their learning tools for young children. Their focus is more on engagement through entertainment rather than educating through engagement.

EdTech solutions, especially for young children, should be based on the latest education research and conform to the science of learning and development. A grid developed by a group of children's researchers (Hirsh-Pasek et al), can help evaluate educational technology apps that can offer truly deep learning.23 EdTech solutions need to score high on educational context of supporting exploration, questioning and discovery in relation to well-defined goals as well as on these following four pillars (Figure 2):

**Pillar 1**.*Active Learning*—This is where the learner is actively involved and in control (minds-on) of his learning experience.

**Pillar 2**.*Engaged Learning*—This occurs when a learner is encouraged via continuous motivation and feedback, without any distractions or peripheral elements. Many educational apps have bells and whistles so ingrained in the learning process that it takes away the focus and distracts the learner from the learning process. It is imperative to ensure that the fire-alarm syndrome is avoided within the learning process.

**Pillar 3**.*Meaningful Learning*—This is one that stimulates the learner's mind to think about the learning and eventually connect with things in their real life.

**Pillar 4**.S*ocially Interactive Learning*—This is one that offers high-quality social interaction, incorporating praise and encouragement.

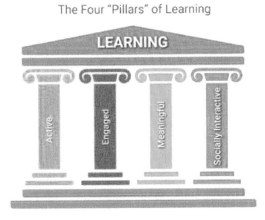

The Four "Pillars" of Learning

Figure 2: *These are the four principles or "pillars" representing the core of the learning sciences that are essential for any meaningful learning to occur by an educational technology. (Hirsh-Pasek et al.)*

EdTech solutions that appear on the top right quadrant of the grid (Figure 3), scoring high on the four pillars and in their educational context are the ones that will move the needle enough to make a large impact on students and learners and can be termed as enabling technologies capable of being game changers.

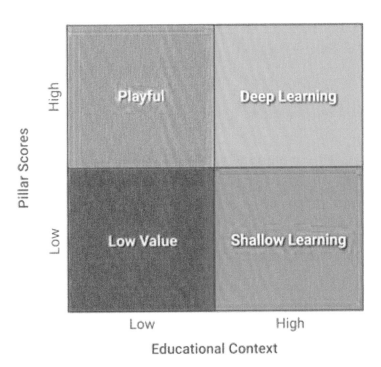

Figure 3: *The grid for evaluating the pedigree of an app. (Hirsh-Pasek et al.)*

## Conclusion

In conclusion, considering the current world scenario, with the pandemic, political unrest and so many displaced populations, education technology is here to stay. With educators, parents, and students all becoming more familiar and comfortable with technology for learning, it is very likely that it will become an integral part of the education system.

According to a survey of 386 teachers by the Education Week Research Center in March, nearly half of teachers — 49 percent — said their ability to use technology had "improved a lot" during the 2020-21 school year and another 39 percent said it "improved a little." Only 13 percent said it remained the same or had gotten worse. Moreover, educators' attitudes towards technology have also improved. Almost 60 percent of 855 US teachers, principals, and district leaders surveyed said their opinion of educational technology has become more positive over the past year, while just 11 percent said it had become more negative. In addition, 74 percent of those 855 educators said they expect that teachers will be expected to integrate devices more deeply into their lessons going forward, due to the widespread purchases of Chromebooks, laptops, iPads, and other devices over the past year.24 (Klein, 2021)

EdTech is undoubtedly the future of education and, if designed properly, can be impactful by way of its reach, accessibility, collaborative potential, and power to engage learners and empower teachers. The only caveat is to evaluate EdTech solutions for their effectiveness with the **CASE** elements that should form the core components in the design and implementation for these solutions to be undeniably enabling. Such education technologies can serve as powerful tools that are game changers and great equalisers helping nations address their most pressing problems in education and literacy. EdTech and mobile education, if done right, can be the backbone of the future of education.

# The Edufication Of Gaming – Moulding Minds In The Metaverse

## Dr.Andrew Dahdal

Associate Professor
Centre for Law and Development
College of Law, Qatar University

Video gaming has often been considered anti-social and harmful to young minds. Some countries, such as China, have even introduced laws to stop children playing online games beyond set time limits. The educational value of video games has long been recognised by pedagogical experts and those in the gaming industry alike. The direction of this synergy, however, has often been one where educational objectives are devised first and then the games are built around them. Rather than gamifying education and creating purpose-built video games for educational purposes, what if existing popular video games were used to enhance the educational experience. Instead of creating an educational universe through a game, recent trends have emerged where educational objectives are brought into and leverage pre-existing gaming worlds. The philosophy behind this view is that educators must meet students on their own terms. The old mantra that educators should 'go out and teach' should also include going online. As the so-called 'metaverse' evolves, and people engage in more and more activities in virtual worlds, this edification process will likely become the norm. From an economic point of view, it is not viable for new worlds to be created when existing worlds already prevail.

### Game Design First

Disingenuousness is obvious – especially for kids. Young people know when there are ulterior motives behind a given reality. Designing a game where the object is to indirectly push an educational agenda suffers from this stigma. One may call it the 'Where in the World is Carmen San Diego' syndrome. In the mid-80s, a video game released for various platforms (including the Apple II and Commodore 64) sought to teach kids about geography through a mystery game. The idea was termed 'edutainment' – and the logic was: kids are hooked on video games, so why not get them to learn through that medium? The intentions were good, and indeed the franchise continues to this day in one form or another (i.e. Google Earth Carmen San Diego), but kids instinctively knew this was not actually a *real* video game and it never really reached any great levels of popularity.

Video game technologies are now quite unbelievable. Developing a video game is a multimillion-dollar investment and often involves everything from script writers and actors to marketing experts and financial consultants. Software engineers are no longer the sole creators of video games. Any education project that seeks to leverage the video game platform will have little to no chance of genuinely engaging actual gamers. It would be akin to trying to sell a 2007 Toyota Camry to a Car enthusiast already driving the latest Ferrari.

The proposition here is rather than gamifying education – why not 'edufiy' gaming. The gaming 'infrastructure' is already well developed. These virtual worlds are vibrant and intricate, and best of all; millions of avatars – linked to real people, already populate them.

## Educational Games

There are plenty of educational video games that have been developed in the past four or five decades. On the Wii, XBOX and PlayStation, for example, there are titles such as 'Sesame Street: Once Upon a Monster' (for the younger children), 'Smarty Pants' (a trivia game from EA entertainment – makers of the FIFA series), 'Reader Rabbit', LittleBIGPlanet 2 and Portal 2 (both problem solving games). For handheld devices, such as the Nintendo Switch, there are titles such as 'Bookworm', 'BrainQuest', 'Animal Genius' and 'Learn Science'. Additionally, educational games on mobile phones and tablets are being added all the time.

What these games have in common is that they were designed with education in mind. Whilst this approach ensures that learning outcomes are reflected in the game play, there is an inescapable sense that the gaming experience is second-rate and contrived. Games are supposed to be fun. As such, these educational games are perhaps better described as 'electronic educational activities'.

Admittedly, some of the open-ended games such as SimCity and Civilization have huge player bases for their fun value, rather than their intrinsic educational attributes. Those games involve city-building activities that promote planning and foresight perspectives among players – both important cognitive skills.

So, whilst an educational gaming sector already exists, the true revolutionary innovation presently emerging is the leveraging of already existing games with massive popular appeal and inserting into those gaming universes (within the delimitations and rules of that universe) educational dimensions.

In general, one of the most effective pedagogical approaches is that of *experiential learning.* That is, students learn by having experiences and reflecting on those experiences.

Modern games such as Fortnight, Assassins Creed, Call of Duty, Roblox or Minecraft are all immersive experiences of varied intensity. Players 'lose themselves' in these virtual worlds and the things they do or see in the games have an emotional and physiological impact in much the same way they would in real life. The process of using existing non-educational games for educational purposes is termed 'Game Educfication'. This is a phenomenon that is already happening and accelerating. Below, several prevailing examples are presented.

## Examples Of Game Edufication

### 1. Assassins Creed 'Discovery Tour'

Assassins Creed, released in 2007, is an 'open-world' game where players control characters who are part of an age-old conflict between 'Assassins' and the 'Templars'. The game is beautifully rendered with stunning graphics and motion engines that depict realistic movements of people's bodies and objects in the virtual world. The storyline is also philosophically sophisticated. The two opposing sides, Assassins and Templars, both desire to bring peace to the world – although the Assassins seek to do this through 'free will' while the Templars believe that 'order and control' are the paths to peace. The story is much more nuanced than plain good vs. evil.

The Assassins Creed franchise, produced by gaming house Ubisoft, now includes movies and action figures. What makes the game particularly appealing, beyond aesthetics, is the way in which fictional characters and true historical events are intertwined.

The makers of the game soon realised that the worlds they were (re)creating were not only hugely detailed, but also very immersive in and of themselves. Players in the game would often just wander around the world exploring. Therefore, the game-producers decided that Assassins Creed would be an ideal game for the 'edufication' process.

After 3 years of research and work, the Ubisoft team released the Assassins Creed Discovery tour in 2018 as a spin-off from the actual game. Although players do not go on a violent quest as part of a grand battle – they are taken on a journey through Ancient Egypt, Ancient Greece or through the Viking Times. The level of detail in the virtual worlds gives players a very realistic look at life, work and leisure in these ancient, historical eras. As technology changes and on-screen visuals are replaced by virtual reality headsets, experiences will become even more realistic.

## 2. Minecraft: Education Edition

Minecraft is another 'open world' game where players can collect materials and build structures with little or no boundaries in a 'sandbox' manner. Unlike Assassins Creed, however, this game is not premised on a grand narrative and players are not required to pass levels or missions. Minecraft has various modes of play including 'survival mode', where players must mine resources, build and create in an environment that can be hostile and 'kill' their characters. Alternatively, players can play in 'creative mode' where they have all the resources they need and all they have to do is experiment with tools, structures and their environment. The other two modes, 'hardcore', and 'adventure' are additional variations.

In November 2016, Mojang Studios, the creators of Minecraft, released Minecraft: Education Edition, as a resource educators could use to engage students in various subjects. In addition to the game, the resource also included pre-prepared lesson plans. For example, young students studying maths could measure the perimeter of a given space within the Minecraft environment. The collaborative nature of the game, where multiple players can inhabit the same world, is also an important educational element that Minecraft encourages. Minecraft continues to be a versatile platform that, although lacking in sophisticated graphics, is highly malleable to educational innovations.

## 3. Roblox

Roblox was first released in 2006. In 2021, the Roblox Corporation floated on the New York Stock exchange (RBLX) and has a market cap of around $70 billion. Similar to Minecraft, Roblox is not a sophisticated game with high-end graphics. It is a humble virtual platform where real people can meet, interact and play games through avatars. On average, Roblox has 43 million active daily users. Users within the Roblox world can play various games within the game. That's right, as a virtual world, Roblox allows players the freedom to play other games within the Roblox universe. Currently, there are more than 35 million games that players can play within Roblox. Many of those games are educational.

One of the most prominent areas where Roblox is a vehicle for education is in the context of coding. Companies such as IDTech, Code Kingdoms and Code Ninjas provide coding lessons and modules through the Roblox platform. One of the priority areas of some of these programs is to keep children interested in STEM (Science, Technology, Engineering and Mathematics) subjects – especially girls.

In late 2021, Roblox announced its vision to bring virtual classrooms to millions of children across the world, and established a $10 million community fund to support the growth of educational initiatives on its platform. Roblox is the closest manifestation of the Metaverse we have today.

**Education In The Metaverse**

The idea of making learning fun is not a new one. There remains an underlying truth that children, and indeed all people, have the most fun when they are interacting with others. Presently, the online world is the conduit through which digital social interaction is mediated. The world that exists online has now become known as the 'metaverse', denoting an existence above reality where geographical distances, physical disabilities and other challenges disappear.

It is estimated by the Roblox Corporation that by 2030, 100 million students will engage with high quality learning in the metaverse. This new virtual frontier is where commerce and socialising are headed. It is inevitable that education will soon also be through some version of an online world. Companies such as Roblox and Facebook are positioning themselves to be the leaders in this space by investing billions in building and owning the metaverse.

**Immersive learning**

Technology is developing rapidly and immersive virtual reality goggles (such as Facebook's 'Oculus') are becoming more accessible to the mainstream. Indeed, Facebook's recent name change to 'Meta' speaks to the perceived potential virtual worlds hold. As existing game franchises on PC and console platforms migrate into VR, there is great potential for improved and immersive gaming experiences. Even without the VR element, existing games hold great learning potential. Today, you can delve into Roman history through a real-time strategy game and anyone who has ever played a Zelda game will also know the amount of reading involved! Less dramatic objectives such as simple arithmetic, geography or even physics can also be incorporated into games that children love such as Minecraft. This is already being explored with Minecraft Education Edition.

EdTech can learn from one of the main lessons emerging from the fintech phenomenon – user experience comes first. Rather than developing games for learning – the 'edufication' idea that we are seeing emerge (and will likely dominate the online education space in the next decade) is leveraging existing gaming platforms for educational objectives. There is no need to press reset on something that is as rapidly developing as the modern gaming industry. Let the game developers do their thing, and when these massive open online worlds are populated - educators should come in and ask: 'can we play, too?'.

# The State Of Education In South Africa And Africa

## Mangaliso Sean Mbusi

EdTech Entrepreneur, Founder atKamvaEducation and a member of and contributor to Future Africa Forum

In South Africa, 20000 of our 25,000 schools are considered dysfunctional. That's 80% of the system. Almost 50% of students will drop out by the time they reach grade 10.

Generally, the matric pass rate (the percentage of children that graduate high school) is based on the number of students that sit the Grade 12 final exam. However, current debate argues that this methodology does not accurately reflect the state of our education system. In 2009, 1,072,993 children enrolled for Grade 1. In 2020, only 578,468 sat for the final exam. What happened to the other 494, 528 children? Have we forgotten them?

Pre-COVID-19, global statistics showed that 262 million children did not attend school, and that 617 million children and adolescents cannot read or do basic maths. Less than 40% of girls in sub-Saharan Africa complete lower secondary school and some four million children and youth refugees are out of school.

According to the Facing Forward Schooling for Learning in Africa Report by the World Bank, an estimated 54.6 million African children of primary and lower-secondary school age (averaging 24 percent of this age group) remained out of school in 2015, accounting for 45 percent of the global out-of-school population. Many of these children may never attend school. The three most populous Sub-Saharan African countries account for about 40 percent of children who are out of school: 10.5 million in Nigeria, 7.5 million in Ethiopia, and 3.2 million in the Democratic Republic of Congo.

### Dysfunction

The dysfunction in our education system is characterised by dilapidated infrastructure, lack of parental involvement, lack of motivated and well-trained teachers and poor education outcomes. Most of these schools are under-resourced and exist in communities that are crippled by poverty, unemployment, criminality and service delivery protests.

These protests tend to result in the vandalism and burning of schools by angry residents to voice out their discontent with local municipalities. During the hard lockdown, theft and school break-ins were prevalent. This was largely due to the adoption of EdTech tools, meaning schools were now equipped with laptops and tablet devices to support online learning.

The public schooling system is riddled with innumerable challenges of governments working with limited resources and capacity, as well as infrastructure backlogs, including pit latrines, dilapidated buildings, teacher shortages, low academic standards, and low levels of adequate numeracy and literacy skills. As a case in point, grade 12 learners in South African public schools obtained a 34% bachelor pass rate (required to study a bachelor's degree at university), compared to 91% at private schools.

Unfortunately, we are not as efficient as the likes of Finland in our public education, where a child can be enrolled in any school in their neighbourhood and the quality is the same across the system. Here, parents enrol their children in expensive schools, far away from their homes, in the hopes that their children will obtain a quality education. For this reason, a lot of families, or at least those who are lucky enough to have relatives in the economic hubs of the country such as Johannesburg and Cape Town, migrate to these cities in the quest to obtain a better education. This demand puts a lot of pressure on the local government to build schools and recruit more teachers.

This has opened a gap in the market. There has been an exponential rise in the proliferation of low-cost private schools such as Spark Schools and Curro. These schools offer a price point close to what the government spends per child for public schools (roughly between R23000-R25000), at a quality level that far exceeds that of our public schooling system. Parents are scraping together whatever resources they can to enrol their children. Parents should not take the blame for voting with their feet by enrolling their children in schools where they perceive quality is, as opposed to no fee or "affordable" public schools.

In spite of all the challenges our education systems face, the rest of the world has not stagnated. Like every industry, education has been greatly affected by the pandemic in that the need for technology is both clear and urgent. Taking into consideration that Africa is currently trailing most developing and emerging markets in educational outcomes and in meeting goal 4 of the SDGs, national governments need to accelerate the provision of basic infrastructure, water, sanitation, electricity and qualified teachers. We should worry about a new emerging inequality: the digital divide. If we don't fix our education quickly, Africa might get left behind.

## The Context Of Most SA Schools

South Africa's schools are mostly in the rural areas and townships. As the most unequal country in the world, quality education, functional schools and economic prosperity sit on one side and dysfunction, deprivation and poverty sit on the other.
South Africa also has a high unemployment rate of 28.48%. University students are graduating into unemployment in droves. The jobs shed by the pandemic has added more people into the unemployment basket. In Zulu there is a saying, "Indlalaibangaulaka" which, loosely translated, means *hunger causes, unrest, anger and violence.*

Our communities also have a theft problem. Schools are particularly vulnerable as they house devices meant to aid them with online learning. Criminals see an opportunity to take it. This is made easier due to the fact that parental and community involvement is almost non-existent in some areas. Schools do not make provision for professional security personnel like their counterparts in more affluent areas. This leaves schools more vulnerable to vandalism and theft, leaving them perpetually under-resourced. A total of 1,577 schools were vandalised during the hard lockdown in May 2020, causing damage that ran into millions of Rands.

## Two Education Systems In One Country

South Africa is largely made up of two education systems. The first are private, affluent public schools with high fees and high academic standards. The exorbitant fees they pay are able to fund devices, software and training required to support online learning and are helped by an active and highly involved parent community

The second education system is largely dysfunctional. It caters to the majority of students and families and is characterised by non-fee paying, low fees, the working class, a big student to teacher ratio and a school feeding scheme. For this reason, the acquisition of hardware, software and connectivity are funded by corporations (through their CSI Corporate Social Investment programme spend) and NGOs. These devices and connectivity are the fundamental requirements for running EdTech services and products, at least at school level. However, what became more apparent during the pandemic was that students lacked access to devices and connectivity at home, meaning that it was difficult to continue with some form of learning whilst schools were closed.

These disparities, however, existed long before the pandemic - it just amplified their existence. EdTech joins a long list of priorities that still have to be met, and all are equally important.

EdTech should aim to solve these disparities at scale as a prerequisite for learning and teaching. Learning platforms and apps will not gain traction if the systemic issues have not yet been solved.

## Learning During COVID-19

Since the COVID-19 pandemic struck, our Department of Education, together with the private sector and NGO stakeholders, undertook "online" learning interventions to prevent lost classroom time. In her first media briefing since schools were forced to close in March 2020, the minister of Education indicated that, since the country-wide lockdown and subsequent closure of schools, the impact of online learning interventions were less than 20% - meaning the majority of learners were left behind.

If some semblance of equitable access to education through EdTech is to be realised, it will only be achievable if the private sector takes a leading role in investing in computer labs, training and connectivity in the most under-resourced schools.

The challenge, however, comes when students have to return to their homes in townships and rural areas, where they lack mobile devices and internet connectivity. To combat this, the private sector will have to provide Wi-Fi hotspots and telecoms providers will have to offer discounted data bundles.

As much as EdTech offers new avenues to learning, in a developing and unequal country such as South Africa it has the potential of creating a new inequality: the digital divide.

The digital divide not only relates to lack of student access, but also to the incompetency of teachers and parents in using digital tools. Yes, parents are using Facebook and WhatsApp to communicate with family, friends and colleagues - but that does not mean they are able to use tools such as Google Classroom to help their children navigate their learning.

## A Mixed Approach Low Tech And High Tech

Because of our low internet penetration and lack of affordability, according to a report by Cable. co.uk, a UK price comparison website, South Africa ranks 148 out of 228 countries on the price of mobile bandwidth. The average price of 1GB in SA is R88 or $4.30. For this reason, a mix of television, radio and internet should be adopted to deliver educational content. However, low-tech interventions such as TV and radio also come with their own unique challenges. They are neither adaptive nor personalised and they cannot measure progress or collect data.

Lessons notes have also been shared via popular messaging apps such as WhatsApp and Facebook. However, the fragmented use of different messaging platforms and tools has opened up the education system to plagiarism. This was evident when a final maths and physics examination paper for grade 12 was circulated on WhatsApp. There were calls for students to retake the exams but, after consultation with stakeholders, the final decision was for students to not re-take, due to fears that the matric exams of 2020 would be compromised.

## Teacher Experience

Learning under COVID was a baptism of fire for many teachers, as not all schools were equipped with tech solutions or teachers competent to use them. Suddenly, teachers were sending work via WhatsApp and uploading work onto Google. Those without prior technology training were thrown into the deep end and had to figure it out as they went along.

## Parent Experience

For parents, it was a harsh glimpse into the work of educators. Pre-COVID-19, parents were accustomed to between 20-30 minutes of helping their children with homework, but as lockdowns commenced, this changed into entire school days. Parents were also under financial stress, as job losses threatened many industries.

Just a couple of days into lockdown, teacher admiration was at an all-time high. This should now be followed up with better pay, working conditions and support. Some parents were even tweeting that teachers should be paid R1 million each, judging by all the work that they do.

## Student Experience

Initially, it seemed like manna falling from the sky; an extended holiday. However, in his book "Learning under Lock Down", Professor Jonathan Jansen shared children's stories of how they coped with learning from home and explored the emotional toll this took on them. The idea of a prolonged holiday soon wore off, and students shared examples of having to share devices with siblings, being distracted with chores, taking care of their younger siblings and missing the interaction and attention of a teacher.

## Looking Forward Into The Future

As the first phase to solving education in South Africa and the developing world, EdTech should strive to improve the socioeconomic and school climate challenges that most of our schools find themselves in. EdTech should be aimed towards cultivating a sense of belonging, school connectedness and a positive school climate. It could play a pivotal role in turning our schools from dysfunction into learning organisations in which parents, students and teachers feel a sense of belonging.

The direction towards EdTech should be inclusive. EdTech should meet students, families and schools where *they* are. Different distribution methods should be able to cater for all. Students that cannot afford connectivity should be able to access it through their school's reception, download worksheets from a device made available by the school and should have access to ballot-type boxes, where students can drop off their assignments in the case that the school must close. And, those who can, should continue to use the online avenues that are available.

The reality is that most public education systems lack the capacity to provide basic education. As the Facing Forward Schooling For Learning in Africa report states, "managing even the basic functions of the system is a challenge. They (governments) must plan and manage the training, deployment, accountability, and payment of teachers; oversee the choice of location for new schools as well as the construction processes; supervise the procurement and timely delivery of textbooks and learning materials; and ensure the collection, analysis, and use of data on a regular basis." The provision of quality education is a task that governments cannot do alone. Now, they must oversee the rollout of Education Technology. Governments and corporates should prioritise EdTech and adopt policies that place internet connection as a basic human right. It is incumbent for all of us to prevent a looming Digital Divide that will exclude many of Africa's children from economic participation.

# 8 Future

# The Opportunity To Reshape Education

## Gil Almog

VP of Customer Experience at Guesty and previously CEO and co-founder x10ed, CEO and founder LearnSights

Much talk and endless digital ink have been poured lately about the opportunity that COVID-19 has brought to our footsteps to reshape education.

In my home country of Israel, as elsewhere in the world, horrified parents were suddenly exposed to what actually happens in school, as Zoom provided an online peeping hole into the classrooms. The reality was that teachers were left to define the "new normal". For lucky children with great and technologically savvy teachers, the experience offered the opportunity to explore the vast offerings that EdTech and digital content has to offer to education. But - for many children, the experience was, to put it bluntly - quite bad, compounded by confused teachers, baffled principals, and overwhelmed ministries of education.

### A New Medium

What happened with the "zoom classroom" reminded me of other occasions when a new medium presented itself, and it took some time to adjust and use the new medium as it should be.

In a talk by Guy Vardi, my former CEO at Matific and a brilliant innovator in many fields, in the early days of TV, many shows were "dressed-up" radio skits - the popular format of the time. One of the first TV broadcasts of the BBC was a group of voice actors who stood in front of a static video camera and read a scripted play, very similar to how actors were reading scripts on the radio. The actors' instructions before the broadcast were "dress nicely - this is a visual medium." TV evolved to filmed plays and live events and soon after, the new TV industry invented new formats - sitcoms, TV dramas, soap operas, game shows, reality TV, and the list goes on and on.

Similarly, the first-ever TV advertisement was an innovation purely because it combined two widely used formats: radio and print advertising. The ad displayed a luxury watch (print), and a voice in the background hailed the product's properties (radio).

Fast forward 50 years and internet advertising is born. The very first ads were essentially a simple banner ad with a call-to-action (click). It took a few years for rich-media ads, video ads, targeted ads, and more. The past decade has demonstrated an ever-increasing sophistication in the exploitation of the capabilities of the internet medium.  Today, there are many internet advertising formats, ranging from highly engaging to website-banning annoying.

While awkward and, in some cases, utterly depressing, the Zoom (Meet, Teams, etc.) lessons of 2020 are a significant breakthrough. Why? Because the main barrier to the adoption of EdTech (I will discuss later on why this is important) was that (most) teachers, rightfully so, refused to deal with technology. It's quite a horrifying experience for a teacher to be in a classroom with 20-30 personal devices when a few kids have a problem with their device, forgot their password, or have an opinion about the quality of the EdTech relative to Fortnite or some other highly engaging game.

The first Zoom sessions were at best, not great. Teachers were simply taking the old school lessons and delivering them through a new medium. But as time passes, there is an opportunity to use the internet medium to transform education.

Once teachers crossed this barrier, they were suddenly open to many more EdTech products that could help them solve various problems or deliver value and thankfully, we started to see the evolution of the Zoom classroom.

The hope for the education system is that EdTech will stay in the mainstream even after humanity learns how to keep schools open, with the COVID pandemic under some degree of control.

## Technology In Education

The use of technology in education is certainly not a new concept. Several innovations, as described by AviWarshavski of MindCET, from the gramophones,film projectors, personal computers, and of course, the internet were hailed as what will finally change the education system and allow for it to evolve. Ultimately, it's all about the adult in the room (or Zoom room) that decides about what, how, and when technology enters the classroom. When teachers and educators are open to embracing technology, it opens the opportunity to use the technology for a wide area of applications. According to HolonIQ, by 2018, there were over 15,000 funded EdTech startups in the world. These startups were offering solutions for easier administration of schools, communication with parents, new methods for teaching existing subjects, and products that help develop essential skills, to name a few. These new skills are, in many cases, not part of current curricula. Examples include personal finance, data literacy, social-emotional skills, executive functioning, and higher-order thinking (i.e., computational thinking, problem-solving, etc.). Some of these products broke through the early adopters' phase, are on their way to scale, or are already contributing to the inevitable disruption of the education sector. Others are still struggling to find a good product-market fit. Either way, it's just a matter of time. The COVID education crisis is helping accelerate this disruption - precisely because teachers were forced to embrace remote teaching technologies to maintain some form of educational continuity.

There is a slight problem with leaving the EdTech decision with teachers. It's not that they are not capable of making EdTech purchasing decisions and in many ways, teachers are the best positioned to make these choices. However, there are a couple of other factors. Firstly, teachers are not responsible for the budget. Perhaps they should be, or at least get a portion of the budget allocation at their discretion. Second, the education systems are not sure what to spend their budget on, and the main reason for that is that schools usually use budgets to maximise some metric or reach some goal. With or without this in mind, an important question to ask is "what is the purpose of education?" - especially in the K-12 system. While up to 10-15 years ago there was a systematic progression from kindergarten to primary, Jr. High, high school, to university (if you are lucky to get accepted) and then to a career, today, the purpose of school is somewhat more elusive.

For one, children are born with a device in their hands, meaning that their teachers are no longer the single source of information. But, a more critical aspect is that children are starting to ask very directly why they need to go to school and "what's in it for them."

Many young adults can get great jobs or work as freelancers using self-taught skills learned on their own. On the other hand, many young adults who bothered to get degrees are unemployed. The school has become, unfortunately, and not categorically, of course - a place where you can hone your social skills and somewhere to hang out whilst your parents are at work.

It's not a surprise that there is a growing movement of new formats at schools. Some of these schools throw away traditional pedagogy and focus on teaching skills such as SEL, collaboration, project management, and data literacy - all critically important for the rapidly changing world. In countries such as India, the best schools are promoting "upskilling and reskilling". They understand that to attract students, they need to give a promising future prospectus.

## COVID-19

Enter COVID-19 to the scene. School shutdowns forced education systems to rethink the physical format of the class, how to use technology, how to provide access to a device, and how to ensure a good internet connection for all students. However, how to maintain the emotional bond between the teacher and students was arguably the main remaining reason to fight for some sort of structure in the education system.

I need to pause for a second to explain the last sentence. Technically, you can place children in front of screens, alone or with their "classmates," and teach them almost anything. There are so many great EdTech solutions out there that you can (with good curation) create a great learning experience for any child with a device and a broadband connection. The only reason why this "vision" is a dystopia rather than a utopia is that the teachers are the ones that provide the structure and bond that is so necessary to guide children in their learning. In many places around the world, the teachers create new content and lesson plans that can work interactively, and for many, this is daunting, time-consuming, and utterly frustrating.

The utopian version of this vision is great apps, dynamic content delivered by the best "superstar" teachers, with AI systems that help the "regular" teachers realise the potential hidden in every child. Instead of "no child left behind," we will help every child maximise their potential, learn with curiosity, and build skills that will allow them to understand who they are, what they like, and how to define their future path. EdTech brings this vision to reality by providing a surplus of tools that teach new skills (including a great one named Plethora that teaches computational thinking) and infrastructure such as Google Classroom to help teachers manage through this abundance and not get lost.

Education systems in many countries are now exploring new models that were once considered experimental or anecdotal. Models such as flipped classrooms, blended learning and station rotation are now the "new normal". Education systems are now also much more open to spending budgets on EdTech since teachers have been forced into a new reality where they have to

FUTURE

use technology to teach. Once the logistic issue of device and connectivity was (or will be) be removed, there is suddenly an opportunity to change the whole system. In Israel, several high-tech companies led by WD and NGOs (such as IATI, the Economic Social Forum, Atidim, Pitchon Lev, and others) came together to collect used devices, upgrade the devices, and distribute them to families that needed them for their children.

## From Vision To Reality

To make this vision a reality requires coordination and execution. The very first step that needs to happen is to redefine the goal of the education system.

In the past, there were variations of 3 common goals to most education systems : (1) gaining social skills, (2) social "indoctrination" (this is true in almost all societies - schools teach values that are specific to that society), and (3) getting good grades to get accepted to a good high-school or university, or kick start a vocational career. Nowadays, the third goal is becoming less and less relevant and should therefore be revised. A heartfelt recommendation heard by Education leaders such as the late Sir Ken Robinson and OECD's Andreas Schleicher is to make this goal all about allowing children to attain skills that will help them achieve their version of success in the future. For some, this version of success may be finding a job, but for others, it may be fulfilling a dream and gaining expertise in a particular area that a specific child is passionate about.

The goal of the educational system for children in their early years is to allow them to explore and tap into their endless curiosity. In later years, it should help each child find out their unique path in the world. By the time these children reach high school, it should be about achieving critical skills and life experiences that will help these young adults tread successfully in this path or have the skills needed to switch paths quickly in a rapidly changing world.
This "unique path" may very well not yet be known. It may be a laser-focused direct path or a wobbly jumpy path with multiple areas of interest. This is the challenge that education systems must embrace - to allow each child to find their path and unique voice in the world and gain the skills required for a rich and fulfilling adult experience.

Personal learning paths may have sounded like science fiction a couple of decades ago. Today, with the use of machine learning, data mining, and the richness offered by the thousands of EdTech products already available or currently being developed in someone's garage, it isn't such a far-reaching concept. It's viable to foresee how we can collect data from all the EdTech products that children use, analyse this data, and come up with a set of recommendations and insights that can help teachers deliver personalised education. In the same way that Amazon can recommend a product, EdTech solutions should guide what to learn next. Students and their parents should have much more control over their learning path and achieve their version of future success.

The EdTech World needs to develop a standard way to collect data without infringing on a child's privacy, allowing students to own their data while providing access to solutions that benefit them.

## The Teacher's Role

Another essential element of the school system that needs to change is the teacher's role. Until recently, teachers were the source of knowledge, and they were the ones that faced the challenging task of creating the content they delivered in their classroom. Today, content is abundant, and teachers can save a lot of time and effort by curating most of the content instead of creating it. Suppose we start to treat the teacher's time as the scarcest resource in the education system. In that case, we can find multiple ways to eliminate or reduce administrative work, allowing teachers to be mentors for their students, and focus their time on the kids who need help the most. Turning teachers into mentors is not a new idea, but it's a key component in changing how the education system operates. Teachers may very well resist this change, although from speaking to hundreds of teachers from all over the world, it's clear to me that teachers will significantly benefit from such a change. Their role will not necessarily be more straightforward, but hopefully more impactful and fulfilling.

It's critically important to understand that education is not like other industries. Unlike industries that went through disruption by taking away the middleman (Booking.com and Kayak taking out the travel agencies, Gett taking out the taxi station, Netflix taking out the video rental shop), in education, it is not so simple - and also not advisable. Teachers and educators are critical players in any change in education, and unless they find value in a solution, they will not embrace it. Without an adult in the picture who creates the opportunity for learning, EdTech solutions will find it very hard to impact. This understanding creates a considerable challenge for EdTech solutions, but it also presents an opportunity for the EdTech companies that understand the teacher's mindset.

## What Is Killing Curiosity?

I have four children, and I can attest that it was an utterly frustrating experience to see how my kids were super excited to start school when they were in 1st grade, and how by 3rd grade, they were already cynical about school, homework, and tests. Essentially, they see the primary value of school as a place where they can meet their friends. It's not that school is not teaching them anything, but it quite systematically killed their natural curiosity. It became all about grades and submitting homework. I seriously don't see the need to give tests to anyone in primary school, but until the whole system recalibrates its approach, I don't have many good options as a parent.

By the time most kids reach Jr. High, fear of failure is such a decisive factor in the school experience that, once combined with adolescence, school becomes the enemy.

Games are an excellent way to enable learning while reducing the fear of failure. In video games, your character can die, but it's not so traumatic - you just start over and try again. In a captivating series of photographs, photographer Philip Toledano captured video gamers in multiple expressions - from frustration to exhilaration. However, there was one emotion he couldn't capture - boredom. Children (and adults for that matter) are so engaged in good games that they "forget" themselves and can play in deep concentration for hours on end.

In the reality of homework and assessments, getting a wrong answer or failing in a test promotes fear of failure, killing curiosity, and undermining all the excellent work teachers and educators are attempting to do. Children today are more afraid of failing in an exam than being bullied in school.

We can use games (at least the good ones) to teach almost anything. Games can keep kids engaged, reduce the fear of failure and provide practically an unlimited amount of data that can help teachers understand their students better.

## Kids As Teachers

We can all probably relate to when we taught something to someone - a colleague, a new employee, or a student. Teaching a particular topic promotes a much deeper understanding than learning in the traditional way. By allowing students themselves to be responsible for teaching various subjects, they will become better learners. This phenomenon is commonplace on YouTube. Young, extremely proficient "YouTubers" teach other children very sophisticated things. Examples include building a Minecraft server, using sophisticated design and video editing tools to create engaging video clips, and growing their social network community using sophisticated tools that businesses typically use for the same goal.

## The Role Of Data

Data can play a considerable role in this transformation. Teachers can get insights about students who have difficulties or about lessons or assignments that were difficult for many of the class. The way children use EdTech products, and especially educational games, can teach us a lot about the students. We can learn about the child's play style, how they approach a challenge and how quickly they give up or ask for a hint. These are all indicators of how they will face real-life challenges and provide an opportunity to hone essential skills. Parents can get very detailed insights about their children and have the ability to mentor them, be more involved, and more aware of their struggles and success. Not all parents want to be involved, but many do, and in many cases, don't know how to ask the right questions to find out vital information for their children's future success and present well-being.

Finally, suppose an education system has a good definition of the skills and learning outcomes they expect. In that case, data can play a crucial role in tracking progress across these skills and outcomes. Tracking is a significant outcome of using data since it will reduce the need for constant testing and assessment, reduce the fear of failure, and bring back the curiosity that is fundamental for learning.

## The Opportunity To Reshape Education

The irony is that "all" that policymakers need to do is to decide that they want to reshape education. In an OECD education ministers meeting held in 2016, Mr. Naftali Benenet (then Israel's Minister of Education) said:

"The leaders in this room have the power to transform the world to make people more tolerant, more mindful, more creative and to provide a real opportunity for the children of the world."

There is no need to invent anything - educational games, new teaching models, technology, and finally, the awareness is all there. Policymakers "just" need to decide, define the goals, allocate the budget and focus on executing this opportunity. There are tremendous barriers - teachers that may fear the change and not necessarily embrace it, budget allocation, politics - and a dozen others. But the timing is perfect. There is public support, a greater understanding of the need, an abundance of solutions, and (generally speaking) teachers have ridden themselves of their initial resistance and started to see the benefits of EdTech. Let's not miss this opportunity to prepare our children for the challenges of the future.

## Acknowledgments

I would like to thank Sarit Firon, Gal Trifon, Ofer Zadikario, Shahar Bar-Or, Mart Aro, Dr. Avi Washavski, Dr. Ilan Ben-Yaacov, Dr. Cecilia Waismann, Dr. Trisha Calella, Guy Vardi, Prof. Shimon Shocken, Prof. Raz Kupferman, Shmulik London, Harris Goodman, Yovel Badash, Dr. Yaron Jacobs - you have all been inspirational figures that helped me shape my views - in general, and specifically on education.

I would like to thank my wife Yael for being a tolerant, patient, wise, and infinitely loving partner.

Everything I do in education (and in general) has to do with my four incredible kids - Itamar, Talia, Yonatan, and Uri - I hope I will continue to learn from you on a daily basis.

# Informing Education: A Data-Driven Evolution

## Graham Reed

Founder, Omega Pegasus

Spring 2014: After a conversation with my colleagues at the Department for Education for England & Wales; ideas cultivated from another project I was working on led me to begin playing with some designs of a new school database (MIS) concept. That utopia: a truly dynamic and modular platform allowing one to plug in any additional system from any vendor, from any area of the school ecosystem, into a core hub. The best visual representation of this would be a bucket of Lego bricks, allowing you to build a house, or a car, or a holistic flexible school database.

The idea never got past the initial concept; commercially it would have been exceedingly difficult to grow without cooperation of a vast number of disparate, often competitive vendors. However, one aspect of this pipedream has never left me: the varied topology of data within education. From attendance, conduct, attainment and exam results to nutrition, wellbeing, local environment, health, home communication – the depth, breadth and volume of data collected about an individual child during their school life is staggering, and these examples are just a small part of the overall, fragmented digital picture of a young individual. What we have today is a fuzzy analogue image distorted by a storm outside.

Skipping to the end and having spent years immersed in education data, I am discovering a wealth of unexplored analytical possibilities that provide critical insight into the circumstances surrounding that young individual and the outcomes they achieve. The usual things schools are monitoring are attendance, conduct, attainment.

It is only possible to examine these insights by combining data and datasets from previously disparate, siloed processes and systems, often never considered to be connected. This chapter explores the possibilities of a truly holistic, interconnected data analytics concept; what the data landscape looks like now, how this will change, what can this data do for both today's students and tomorrow's, and how we can drive change at a national and even global level with EdTech data. How can we get that crystal clear ultra-high-definition image of a child's education life?

### Information Busting At The Seams

The sheer volume of data held within a variety of systems through all areas of a school about a single student is extraordinary. To best explore the scale of this, let's walk through a typical day of a student.

As we do, think for a moment about how many systems and data points might be in a school (if you work or have worked in a school, you definitely should do well here).

*Our fictional student arrives at school, perhaps on the school bus (this is recorded). Their attendance in the morning and in every lesson throughout the day is recorded, as would any absence or lateness (which may or may not trigger an alert if a pattern has emerged or a threshold reached to take action, as well as requests for explanations as to any absences from parents). Their homework has been scored as it was submitted electronically last night (or perhaps not, and so this is noted, perhaps triggering another warning). Their meal choice for lunch is recorded (or perhaps this was done the previous week, and paid for, or perhaps the family owes the school money), or perhaps the school operates a canteen and so the order there and then for what is on the tray and is recorded, and similar alerts may show. What has been ordered may be checked against any health or allergy concerns recorded against their core school record (in the MIS – Management Information System) and alerted to the servery. Perhaps the nutritional value of what was ordered is recorded and compared against their previous orders to understand trends of how healthily they are eating. Their behaviour, either good or bad, in each lesson may be recorded, which may trigger a good merit certificate, or require intervention if consistently poor or involved in a severe incident. Graded assessments will be recorded and analysed against past, forecast, and predicted grades in preparation for exams. Library books taken out or handed back will be recorded. Access to online services and resources will be logged. Communication home to parents about the upcoming parents evening, which can also be booked and recorded through linked systems, will be sent, recorded and responses monitored...*

How many did you identify? How many extras did you identify? There are so many!
Did you notice the various mentions of analytics being performed on many of those data items? This is where the present starts to meet the future – not all these data items are being regularly analysed uniformly across schools. If this were a real school, many of those analyses would still be fictional.

Where we take a giant leap into the future would be where new insights come – extrapolation - when these data items are used together.

## Data Silos & Data Heroes

Data within education settings is naturally siloed within different software systems, provided usually by different vendors – commercial organisations that are there for profit – and rarely do they work together or share data easily. Efforts over the years to overcome this have met with some success via data integrators (other commercial vendors), supplying connections between platforms to allow the data to be shared and synchronised, usually FROM the school MIS TO the third-party platforms the school has purchased. But a lack of cooperation between vendors who see no commercial value in making data sharing easy, let alone proactively working together for the benefits to schools, has limited efforts to provide a holistic collection of datasets from which to use as the basis for any good quality analysis.

This is usually left to a 'frailty of heroes' – I had to look that up - within schools to take these collections of data, mash them together and, through grit and determination, discover insights they can act upon to help their students. The problem here: heroes are not moulded, mass produced and provided to each school – every one of them is different, with a different analysis technique, a different focus and often leading to slightly different outcomes and insights.

A quick checkpoint then: Aside from the data outcomes mandated by local or national government departments (and even they are often a little suspect), there are few established standards by which educational data is analysed for good, or any, purpose. There is extraordinarily little by way of an established and defined focus within the sector to be making better use of this data in any robust or meaningful, impactful way to improve the education being delivered, whether locally or nationally. This in no way diminishes individuals who have done some fantastic analysis with their education data, many of whom I have consulted for or with over the years. But the sector is spinning its wheels.

So, where SHOULD we be aiming for with education data analytics, and why?

## A Big Data Mash-up

Earlier in this chapter I described a fictional student in a fictional school, where data was being collected, and analysis was being done – some analysis regularly done for real; some is still fictional. We analyse the data to understand a variety of different statistics, but at its core we want to see progress, improvement or basic patterns, so that we can take the best action based upon the data.

For areas such as attendance, this is rudimentary at best for most establishments, and is always looking backwards – students attend or do not, and we only see any patterns much later, and then try to take corrective action even later. But why was the student absent? Was it related to illness, bullying, funds (to get to school), a lack of interest, worry for a particular lesson? Tackling the effect (not attending school) does not solve any cause, and so prevent it from happening further – and we cannot tackle the cause because we do not know what the cause is. Further, individual events (a single day off school), despite OfSTED, MPs and education commissioners saying differently, makes little difference in the long run and not something schools would routinely be looking for as an instance to remedy. Recurring events however, are. But as we have seen already, most data available on students is at the extreme end of a causation scale – a student is not attending regularly is the last act(s) in a potentially long line of triggers and events that led to here. In a utopia, we would understand what all those causes are, and individually either prevent them from occurring in the first place (unlikely without a time machine) or quickly support those before they lead to the next event, and the next, ultimately resulting (in this example) in long term absence. However, without assigning an adult to every student individually to follow and watch their every move (or dare it be said, cameras everywhere, 1984 style) and be an expert in every aspect of physical, emotional, mental, economic, and social wellbeing to spot and support when something happens, what can we realistically do? And what can we do without recording even more information about a student than is already being done by an already overworked front-line education system?

The answer is we use what we already have better; more efficiently, and more holistically.

Where the future of school data lies is not only in a greater breadth of individual analysis on these traditionally siloed datasets, but combining them together to understand what patterns, correlations and trends exist that will shine a light on the causation of outcomes we want to avoid, or, aim for. Only then can we begin to construct viable models to predict the impact of a singular event, and also understand how an emerging pattern of behaviour and incidents starts to align to some established trajectories for our key school outcomes (attendance, behaviour, wellbeing, etc).

## Traditional Datasets

Let us first explore traditional datasets already available in schools that are not currently routinely analysed and monitored for important insights into student and/or family actions. We will explore a couple of examples to start to understand the scale of the opportunity for each in terms of wider causational analysis – what we might investigate further to add greater context to these outcomes.

Fair warning at this point: this author is not advocating for any specific analytics or data collection/use from the following or any explorations, this is intended to illustrate through example the possibilities and potential benefits if used for beneficial reasons – the examples are not necessarily balanced against the distasteful possibility of them being used for harmful, discriminatory, illegal or other negative reasons. This also focuses on analysing information that is mostly already in the school's domain and authorised to collect; returning to the theme of using what schools already have to greater effect. Schools have a legal directive to use data they collect for the purposes of providing education to students. There is a clear purpose for analysing the data for a clear and understood purpose and with clear goals that would be shared with student's families.

### Attendance
Usage: Students attending/not for what days and lessons.

Patterns and Trends: Is a student always absent or a particular day, part of day, lesson?
Wider Causation Analysis: What occurs on those days specifically in school, in a lesson, outside of school, at home? What fellow students share the same lessons, routes to school. What is on the school lunch menu that day usually? What teachers teach that student on those days? Are other students displaying the same attendance patterns?

### Conduct
Usage: Students performing well; taking notable part in events; student involved in behavioural incidents. For brevity, this example will focus on 'negative' behaviour/conduct.

Patterns and Trends: Is a student routinely behaving poorly on a certain day, certain time of day, in a certain lesson or subject (or type of subject), with or against a certain student or group, or against a certain staff member?

Wider Causation Analysis: Where is the poor behaviour occurring? At school, outside, in the playground, canteen? With other peers, are those peers older or younger, a different gender/race/religion? Is there a pattern based on times of the day? Is it poorer just before lunch? Just after? What are they eating for lunch? Is it affected based on what they eat day-to-day?

You may notice that many of the causation analysis items are already recorded in some fashion by schools in one or several systems, depending on the processes in place within the school. Schools do record what a student eats for lunch via orders at the till, or via dinner orders from parents for younger children. Therefore, we can know from that what they are eating, how much, and what nutritional value (OK, it is much harder to know if they ACTUALLY ate the meal without extra effort). We largely know when this is based on the timetable. If there are behavioural incidents, usually schools will record who was involved, whether directly or indirectly. When, where, what happened.

As you can see, just with these two important measures for students in education, there is so much that can be explored to understand why events occur: The causation analysis. If we can identify and understand the causes that lead to the outcomes, then we have the capacity to intervene a lot earlier, and either prevent or mitigate the changes of poor attendance, behaviour and more, from occurring.

Sound simple?

**Finding Patterns And Trends**

Well, not really. We do not know yet, within this example what the various causes are or can be that lead to poor attendance (I will continue to use this example for illustration), what they all are, how they impact on attendance, and what interventions need to occur at the right time to be able to course correct. The possible causes mentioned earlier are just that - possible. However, they are all causes we as experienced professionals working with children for many years, 'just know' will be contributing factors, without having implicit research or statistical analysis. How do we 'know'? Individuals use past experiences, past instances where similar students were in similar situations and had a similar set of outcomes, and the causes were similar (or later identified). With attendance specifically, there has been significant research done over the years to understand and identify poor attendance causes, with many robust and justified conclusions, but what is missing is the ability to spot and be alerted to multitude of combinations of causes, to allow action to be taken even earlier.

Conceptually, this is exactly how we will start to define trends, patterns and correlations leading to actionable insights and interventions – by looking at what has happened before; by using the information of the past (of past students) to identify trends to help future students. By and large, this is how all forms of predictive analysis, all the way through to machine learning and AI, works – by knowing some baselines, rules and standards (in this case, what we have learnt from past students) these systems could predict what any given student could achieve.

There are of course many caveats to this, and this is a simplistic concept to a complex, challenging, and still emerging field of study, almost to the point of embryonic within education.

Firstly, this does assume that all children are equal at the point of entering education, which of course will never be true.

Secondly, the volume of data is going to be important – the more data there is to inform the prediction models we are generating, the more accurate the predictions will become; if the same things keep happening with lots of students, that result in the same outcomes (e.g. absence from school) then we can accept that this is a more likely outcome for anyone with the same initial events.

Thirdly, there is the accuracy of such predictive analysis in relation to the length of time to any extreme, end outcome (e.g. absence from school) – the earlier a causation event is picked up and dealt with, the less likely that a previously predicted outcome will now occur. This is mostly because there are likely many contributing factors to that outcome and taking some of those away will alter the outcome, but also by intervening even on a small event, the previous prediction in theory will now not occur in the same way, follow the same path... At this point, I will step back before I start to veer into topics such as destiny and timelines. I am certainly not qualified to hold any sort of conversation on prediction accuracy studies and time. But this all makes logical sense – If I help a student sooner, the quicker they can get back 'on track' with less intervention, and potentially with less subsequent events.

And finally, returning to a cautionary note on ethics, these concepts do not attempt to deal with any form of cognitive or algorithmic bias inherent in any analytical system – where the patterns and outcomes are skewed based on established perceptions and expectations, and the base data used to generate the algorithms in the first place. Examples cited in the 2020s include early wide-scale use of facial recognition favouring certain race or gender in matching.

As a recap of our story so far (in our emerging future), we are using measures from all areas of school life to inform when a student is involved in a particular event or incident (positive or negative). Our analysis will take this event into account, and it may throw up some outputs or predictions about where this student is predicted to 'end up' in terms of the key outcomes that schools need to track, based on this new information.

Taking this one step further, and as useful tools for educators, our systems would likely also suggest a range of suitable interventions here and now – corrective actions that would be predicted to be most useful for the individual to help them, now, get back on track. It is fine to be able to predict where a student may be in 1, 3 and 5 years' time, but unless we can make a difference now, the predictions do nothing to improve the life of the individual and give them the best education and preparation for the working world as possible.

**Educators Call The Shots**

But our cold analysis systems can, and should, only present the information and offer possible suggestions – it should not be making decisions for our educators. Our teachers will combine the crunched numbers from the vast, interconnected datasets with their continued qualitative knowledge, compassion and understanding for each student in their teaching care to decide what action to take and apply as they see fit. This is absolutely nottaking any decision making away from front-line staff, it is enhancing their decision-making process by doing all the heavy lifting, identifying aspects that otherwise would not be noticed, even thought to be explored, and allowing them to focus more time interacting with students and doing what they do best: Teaching, supporting, enhancing.

Our analytics systems should spot opportunities for intervention, alert when certain thresholds have been hit (e.g. number of absences in a term), show where the trends are pointing to, and eventually suggest corrective action. I say eventually specifically, because even with several years of collating information and analysing outcomes, setting predictions, and working back to find the causes, knowing what interventions to take when and how will need considerable time to identify and test. And this cannot be done as analysis is done now – school by school, hero by hero.

## A Data-Driven, Ethical Evolution

The future depicted here needs a national initiative with a centralised, research-led grounding and cooperation of the education system, health professionals, social care systems, EdTech providers and government departments (children's commissioners, etc). Noting that improved analysis and prediction accuracy comes only with increased volumes of data to spot and continually refine trends, a superior endgame would be to have school data, suitably anonymised, and available to a central research institute. Such an institute would be tasked with not only understanding and testing possible trends (remembering that many we still do not know as of today), using not just hundreds of student records, but millions, but also using what it learns to provide a baseline for all schools throughout the country - to measure against at best; understand just what should be analysed together and what to look for, at worst.

This, of course, is a tall order. We live in a world where analysing personal information, regardless of the good intentions, is met with severe scepticism, not helped by scandals involving some of the biggest tech organisations in the world, as well as government departments – which in itself raises significant concerns given they will ultimately be trusted, or at the very least a trustee, of such a potentially dangerous system. This is also a long-term investment. Years of data is needed, and continually added to, to refine and adjust to how the world changes around us. Governments are not known to make such a sustained investment, particularly on a brand-new concept, and one that does not come without some potential controversy.

This future can be achieved with focus, determination, and cooperation. Ethically however, we must ask ourselves: should we? This article has explored some fascinating concepts of the art of the possible, with tangible, tantalising possibilities to do some real good with data on children's lives. But we must not get carried away without stopping to think about how such extrapolation, pattern matching, and (eagle-eyed critics will have spotted the tell-tale signs of) *profiling*, could be used for reasons we do not yet understand – or even, based on attempts over the years by governments and corporations around the world, we do understand. Various laws are in place to protect the use of personal data, namely in Europe the GDPR and others worldwide, amongst other important things to ensure that data is collected and used for the purposes that are stated, which is clearly extremely important here. Collecting data about children to help them get the best education possible by ensuring they are attending school is a clear, positive, and acceptable aim to state. Using the same information to understand how an individual might fall into criminal activity for example, is a very different aim and one that many, if not all, would object to.

But far wider than this, is the concern of where ethically does a system draw the line. We are already using technology to crunch the numbers to show patterns in a student's attendance, or attainment, to pick out where to help them improve and we appear to be happy with this so far. How much more do we analyse, together, collectively, holistically, nationally, before it becomes too much. How many patterns do we look for, and use to predict behaviours, before we start to make judgements on an individual's future before it has happened, despite numerous before them having fallen into the same patterns and outcomes. Judgements that suddenly may not be for the benefit of the individual, but for society.

How wide a remit will public bodies, from schools to governments, be given, with or without oversight? And will individuals, and parents of those students, be given the freedom to consent, or to remove their consent.

This writer is confident on the technology to deliver this future, but far less confident on those leading the future.

# Can AI Learn To Teach?

## Thabo Miles-Matli

Head of A-level Computer Science at Ark INA

The last two decades have brought major change in the use of AI technologies. AI approaches already save the banking industry billions in fraud detection, change the results of elections and beat human players at games like Go. These advancements have led to excitement, reflection on human ability and curiosity about the frontiers of automation.

AI has already entered EdTech in a large variety of applications. The gamification of language apps is now commonplace. It is easy to overlook that the decisions to give you rewards and bonuses are being made based on huge personalised datasets with cutting edge AI. Education research, particularly meta-studies, are making use of big data technologies that would have been impossible 30 years ago. More subtly, natural language processing is correcting your grammar as you write your thesis.

The above are some of the applications of the past and present but the future is equally exciting. The purpose of this article is to convince you that the AI revolution is only at the beginning in education. We will look at some of the state-of-the-art applications in EdTech with the purpose of projecting those trends out into the future.

More generally, AI research and cognitive science is having its enlightenment moment. Every year, remarkable books are being released that make the future easier to see. In most sections, I will recommend one of the books that could act as a starting point in that field. The speed of change in cognitive science makes it possible to become a relative expert very quickly. Anyone claiming to be a product manager or entrepreneur in AI should be reading a lot.

### What Is AI?

An AI system is a system that can create effects that we typically associate with human decision making such as "image recognition" or "machine translation". The Stanford professor Andrew Ng has claimed that we can now automate almost any decision that it takes a human a second or less to make. This includes the decisions that have traditionally been made by experts. There are some systems that go beyond the one second rule but they are the exception not the rule.

The tools of this exciting not-so-new field are techniques such as machine learning (automatic discovery of trends in numerical data) and other statistics. However, it is the behaviour of the system as a whole which we would describe as AI.

An example of an AI system is Alpha-Go Zero, the currently unbeatable Go playing system developed by DeepMind. Any amateur Go player can understand the behaviour of the system but to know what it is actually doing you would need to grasp Deep Learning and many other approaches. It is this high level that concerns the EdTech entrepreneur but knowledge of the details is always a bonus.

## What Is An AI Company?

Another key term is the "AI company". This concept was also introduced at Stanford and is the best way to think about AI innovation and business. An AI company is simply a company that has enormous structural data flows, the means of harvesting that data and the core competencies to apply AI techniques. There are many obvious examples of this such as Facebook but also some less obvious examples, such as Walmart as far back as the 1980s.

Education is an enormous and exciting frontier for the AI company. Education is a data rich environment, its systems of data collection are very well developed, and there have been many research studies looking at the practice of data collection at multiple levels from classroom to national. However, education presents unique challenges to the AI business and we will look at those challenges in the next section.

The Deep Learning Specialization on Coursera [1] is an incredible source of innovation, insight and technical detail. It is accredited by Stanford University and taught by world leading specialists. It requires reasonable maths and programming skills but it is worth the effort.

## The Educational Landscape For AI

At a subject level we already have some clear best practices for both educational AI and the AI company within EdTech. In this article, we will look at chess education, which is *the* mature AI EdTech product and is likely 10-20 years ahead of other similar products for other disciplines. We will also look at the potential for STEM (Science, Technology, Engineering and Maths) which is the next logical crossover for AI because of both potential revenue and the opportunities that huge technological progress has created.

Additionally, AI has huge potential at the national policy level. Here, it faces many of the challenges that face education research more generally i.e. the wrong incentives and spurious correlation of data. However, this may be where the unicorn startups of the future come from and are likely to be similar to what firms like Palantir are doing for national security. The amount of data already being collected and the very rudimentary management of that data leaves some large and important opportunities. We will look at AI for systemic educational reform in the final two sections.

## Chess And The Future Of Expertise

More people play chess than ever before and there is more money in the industry than ever before. At least part of this is due to the accessibility of outstanding tuition from AI.

Chess is also where AI technologies claimed its first human conquest by defeating the reigning world champion Gary Kasparov. Since then, no human has beaten the state of the art in chess programs. However, the story that is less well known is that AI has become integral to chess education and has fundamentally changed the global chess landscape and created some truly remarkable products.

At the same time the science of expertise has been born that allows us to study human skill. Anders Ericsson's book Peak is a must read for any educator. His work on expertise combines education with cognitive psychology and neuroscience and shows clearly what it is to master something. His work is the origin of the "10000-hour rule" and chess is the jewel in the crown of his work. Many of his recommendations for nurturing a great talent are things that AI can help with and things that it is already helping with in chess education.

Three ways AI has created value added chess services:

1. Some products provide a full analysis from beginning to end of all your tactical play (moves with a short time horizon) against what the best computers would play in a given position. At the end of every game, I get a full report of the mistakes and blunders I made as well as points when I made the best move. I can then replay any move I want from the game till I find the best tactical move.

2. This service bears repeating because through it we see the future. The *best* tactical player in the world analyses every game I play and gives me feedback move by move. If I want to replay a sequence, she humours me. She never gets bored, rolls her eyes or makes me feel stupid.

3. The frequency of certain mistakes are analysed and courses are suggested to help. If the engine is rating you consistently badly after you play a certain opening it will suggest a specific course. This is a longitudinal analysis of the earlier analyses and is almost exactly what Ericsson describes in his research as being the primary role of a master teacher. The data asset it creates is hugely valuable to someone who is serious about their chess game.

4. "Gamification". How can you gamify a game? Using the data on wins, losses, length of game, hours spent, quality of game etc you can build a highly tailored model which promotes game play or upgrades. Online chess is way more than a board game on a device. It is a hugely addictive global computer game and community.

The final service presents an obvious conflict of interest. The optimal design of the game and the community is not the same as the optimal design of the learning opportunity. The company has to define their vision as to whether they are creating the best game or the best players. However, these problems pale in comparison to the value the products create.

Grandmasters are getting younger. Prodigies are getting more prodigious. People are playing chess more than ever before and players on balance are better than they have ever been. This is in large part the consequence of excellent AI tuition.

Deep Thinking by Gary Kasparov [2] is both an excellent source of information about the impact of AI on chess and also on AI human collaboration. He presents his excitement about the future. In hindsight, his loss to DeepBlue meant that his genius had become a commodity that could be piped around the world at nearly the speed of light.

One area that I believe will follow chess is high school STEM education which we will look at in the next section.

## Pattern Recognition For Marking

Considering the above discussion of chess, we can ask: "where are we in the journey to create AI maths tutors?"

Closer than you may think.
This year, Microsoft has pledged to enter an AI into the International Mathematical Olympiad. By the time that you are reading this they have likely done so. If this is successful then it is to high school maths what DeepBlue was to chess and Alpha-Go was to Go. It could be a world-shaking moment.

What I am personally excited about is the possibility of a Maths marking AI. A program that reviews my working in the way that the chess program reviews my game. In the UK alone the market this would create would be enormous. It would disrupt not only tuition but the exams industry as well. Take the following statistics:

- The exam market was worth £296m in the UK in 2018 [3].
- A current teacher spends at least 10% of their working hours marking this equates to £15b in government spending [4].
- Private tuition was worth £2b total in the UK last year (in my experience as a tutor marking is about 20%) [5].

The financial reward would be huge but the social impact would be even more so.
Once maths marking is solved, exams become a cheap commodity. Imagine a global mathematics qualification marked by AI. It could be free at the point of use and available as easily from a smartphone in deepest Congo as at Harrow school for boys. It could revolutionise everything from recruitment to immigration policy. We may see the STEM crisis partially solved in our lifetimes.

For an excellent book on what AI can do currently in maths and science, The Creativity Code by Marcus Du Sautoy is my personal favourite.

## Disability Support

A particularly inspiring application of this technology is for building superior interfaces for disabled students and the world of education and more generally.

One of the original examples of AI powered accessibility programs is that of Dragon voice dictation software. Using various AI techniques as early as the 1990s Dragon built the leading voice dictation suite which, in particular, supports those with challenges accessing conventional computer input methods such as a keyboard.

Their product's market position generates the data it needs to improve itself and has led to an almost unchallenged monopoly. It is a textbook AI company.

Some of the new horizons of enabling technology can be seen in the promising research into the movement of prosthetic limbs. The nervous system generates enormous amounts of data. Some of this data is used to move our body. With deep learning and other AI techniques there is now the very real possibility of unlocking these codes and with them unlocking the potential of people currently limited by physical disability.

These developments in data input lead naturally to questions of new output systems. Can AI be used to make the process go in reverse, passing data into our nervous systems in new ways? How fast could a person theoretically read if their eyes were not the limit? Elon Musk cited this as one of his world-changing problems that someone who wanted to start the next Tesla should consider.

After I wrote the above, Neurolink published their research study that allowed a monkey to play video games with nothing but its mind. I have huge respect for this work and it will be instrumental in improving the lives of physically disabled people. However, as a caveat, nothing I have seen from them has suggested that they have even scratched the surface on higher cognition. Spatial input/output will remain the state of the art for the foreseeable future.

Accessibility technology is not limited to physical disabilities. Cognitive prosthetics is a fascinating area which looks at the use of devices to help people with Alzheimer's and other mental disabilities. Dr Steve Joordens lecture series Memory and the Human Lifespan [7] is an outstanding work of cognitive science that explores his own work in this area.

## Data Mining And The Search For Excellence

One of the tasks of a great education system is to direct people towards the best future. Currently, the education systems of the UK and the USA are particularly bad at this. They direct students toward ever-increasing training which builds the elusive "transferable skills". In the end, they consign the majority to work in jobs where their education was not necessary.

The English-speaking world is desperate for a solution to this very expensive problem. In the UK, it is currently taking the form of a long overdue focus on post 16 education. The establishment of the National Colleges (like Ada the National College for Digital Skills where I teach computer science) is arguably the beginning and the recent white paper "Skills for Jobs" has outlined some of the future of this movement.

However, the development of excellence in technical disciplines needs even greater focus. It needs to identify talent early and cultivate that talent throughout the lives of the individual in age-appropriate ways.

Data-mining is a technique in artificial intelligence where insights are generated from huge datasets using machine learning. It is the equivalent of hiring a thousand analysts to look over a database with thousands of fields and entries.

If we think of the Cuban Olympic pipeline, Russian nuclear scientists, Scandinavian political futures programs, US high school and college basketball etc. What all these systems have in common is that they are fundamentally data-mining organisations though mostly organised around 20th century models.

Each of these systems have nationwide "sensors" which pick up key metrics at crucial moments. This could be the speed over a hundred-yard sprint or the quality of scientific work in primary school. That data is passed through the system until some central body is notified at which point, further analysis is carried out and if appropriate provision is made for specialist instruction.

We can use data-mining to look for talent and direct it where it belongs.
Raise a Genius [8] is a transcript of an interview with the great specialist educator László Polgár. His work is based around his belief that excellence is one of the few paths to happiness. He is also the father of the famous Polgár sisters which may be the ultimate credential.

## Leaner Passports

We carry out standardised testing at historically unprecedented levels. This is generating a huge quantity of data on each individual but it is analysed at a national, not an individual, level. There is no longitudinal record or data asset created. When the teacher throws out your old exam scripts or accidentally deletes their question analysis, all that fine grained detail that has been gathered at enormous cost to the taxpayer is gone. All that remains is the final grade - whether a number or a letter. If you fail and want to retake, you are out of luck. If one day you choose to extend your learning in French from GCSE to A level, you will be starting from scratch.

Compare that to an AI company like Facebook, that maintains such personalised data that they can predict your future needs better than you can. This is where the value can be created. This brings with it ethical challenges but I would argue that it is ethically completely unjustifiable to test as aggressively as we do and not provide a detailed record to the individual which they might use over the long term to improve themselves.

Once assets like that existed and the necessary confidentiality was ensured students, teachers and parents could use that data to optimise learning. This would give rise to enormous opportunities to add value to a learner's journey with later AI products.

## Conclusion

In this short essay, I have tried to convince you of the impact of AI technologies in education past, present and future. This impact is being felt in many disciplines beyond the few I have discussed and at the level of policy in some particularly forward-looking work. However, this is just the beginning.

When I think of the potential impact of AI on education, I think of it in comparison with the great inventions of educational technology such as the contemporary textbook. This was the biggest

EdTech innovation of the last Millennium, and influences both centralised and decentralised education. We should look at AI in the same way.

The invention of the textbook by John Amius Comenius in the 17th Century allowed for the creation of the modern classroom and universal primary education. His insight was that learning must be pleasant and easy, so that students would do more of it without coercion. His vision was one of equality of education across race, gender and religion ensured by excellent stand-alone teaching resources. The teacher's role would then be free to help the student develop as a human being.

Final recommendation is to learn about Comenius and read his writings. He was a transformative technologist and reformer whose innovations endure. His work is as provocative today as it was 400 years ago.

# The Future Of Education Technology: Opportunities And Challenges

## Tarik Bouderhem&Dr.RabaïBouderhem

Co-founders of RE-L Network

### Introduction

The global COVID-19 outbreak and its social and economic implications have challenged our society. Since the first quarter of 2020, Educational Technology has demonstrated its commitment in supporting millions of learners across the world, enabling knowledge and guidance from K-12 to Higher Education students, professionals and businesses. Technological advancements allowed traditional education to endure the massive shift in our social lives, caused by the health measures put in place by governments all around the globe. We can state that the pandemic played the role of a formidable catalyst by awakening the EdTech giant. In just a few months since the spread of the pandemic and the first national lockdowns, millions of learners switched to onlinelearning which put the EdTech sector in the spotlight of the public and gained investors' attention - despite its presence and continuing development since the 2000s. Today, EdTech is experiencing its heyday - and this trend is set to increase in the long term.

Indeed, according to latest reports, the global education technology market size is anticipated to reach USD 285.2 billion by 2027, growing at a CAGR of 18.1% from 2020 to 2027. (Education Technology Market Worth $377.85 Billion By 2028, 2022) EdTech is now a global growth sector with a surge in mega-rounds deals, rising stars and unicorn startups. Indeed, numerous EdTech companies have now accessed the Unicorn status in China, India or the US.(Holon UK, 2022) In terms of funding, VC investments globally are expected to surpass last year investments by 15%. (Terrisse, 2022)EdTech Technology is revolutionising the way we learn at school and at work: from K-12to Higher-Education and the workplace, EdTech companies are helping education institutions and businesses to reshape the learning process and is undoubtedly, one of the few economic sectors to have withstood the crisis caused by the pandemic. (Edtech in 2021: How e-learning will move beyond K-12 segment for startups in post-Covid year, 2022)The resilience of EdTech is explained by the fact that education is one of our primary needs.

In the UK, Schools Minister Nick Gibb – long seen as an EdTech sceptic– said in January 2021 that the government is looking for new avenues for a strategy to build an education system more resilient and therefore more efficient and this necessarily involves the introduction of EdTech in the national education system. (Whittaker, 2022)This position is now shared by many countries around the world. This is also the case for Morocco , which has shown unfailing resilience and has made the decision to focus on online education from the very beginning of the pandemic by asking schools, high schools and universities to dedicate themselves exclusively to online courses and in parallel with the development of a long-term strategy dedicated to EdTech.(Hibbi, Abdoun and El Khatir, 2022;Abioui, 2022)The same is true of Moroccan television channels, which still today continue to broadcast school programs to enable as many people as possible to follow their education. On this point, as we will see, access to new technologies and inclusion are challenges that all emerging countries such as Morocco must take up. The exponential development of EdTech is, of course, facilitated and supported by technological progress and new technologies (I). Thus, the gradual and certain arrival of 5G in many states will radically contribute to the development of distance learning courses, by making it easier to access information and speed up its delivery to learners. The same is true of Artificial Intelligence which, through its algorithms, will take into account the specificities and needs of each person in order to give an optimal experience to each of us. That being said, if the EdTech sector has made it possible to overcome the obstacles linked to the pandemic and to allow pupils, students and professionals to continue their courses and to continue to develop their knowledge; the fact remains that many challenges stand in the way of startups operating in this sector.

**New Technologies As A Way To Enhance Education And Support Learners**

EdTech has experienced rapid development and a certain interest since February 2020 – first by constraint, then by necessity and a recognition of its advantages and benefits in the short, medium and long terms. And this, thanks in particular to technological innovation and new learning methods, focused entirely on simplifying the dissemination of knowledge and increased fluidity such as Augmented Reality, Artificial Intelligence, the massive arrival of 5G, etc.

The current generations are fond of new technologies and have had no difficulty in adopting distance learning even if, here again, human beings can never be replaced. A people-centred approach is necessary for the development of EdTech. Specifically, what are the users' expectations? How can we ensure that the experience is appreciated and developed? How can we ensure that the learner remains focused on the online course? How can we ensure inclusion ?

Many states, such as Morocco, are considering combining face-to-face courses and EdTech in the future for efficiency and flexibility wherever necessary - so nothing prevents a recognised expert or professor from delivering online lectures thousands of miles away without leaving home. On this specific point, the development of webinars since February 2020 is highly significant, and testifies to the adaptability of professionals and learners to online interaction techniques and to EdTech in particular. 5G seems to be at the top of the innovations acclaimed by experts for the development of EdTech but above all for its democratisation.
Some of the major challenges of the decade for EdTech are how to ensure that new technologies benefit everyone and that as many people as possible have access to cutting-edge technologies for education. Here, both public authorities and private actors must work together to promote inclusive and sustainable development, so as to ensure that EdTech is not only a passing fad or a niche market, but a major and lasting asset.

As for 5G frequencies, these will increase online teaching capacities, thus ensuring extremely fast download times and allowing the largest to connect to a network – that of a school, a university or a company – without latency or intermittency issues. A higher download speed also means that it will be possible to offer much more qualitative content. (Google, 2022)

Among the new technological trends of 2021, we can also mention augmented reality: virtual classrooms, robotics, personalised and adaptive learning responding to the specific needs of students (tutoring, support, etc.), the integration of Cloud services into traditional education. (India Today, 2022)

Learning analytics will also allow students to better identify their needs. The technological tools available to us today make it possible to identify the gaps and other weaknesses of learners. This therefore allows any instructor to adjust his or her lessons with great responsiveness, by detecting the points understood and assimilated by his or her students or, on the contrary, the points which deserve to be taken up and re-explained.(Top Educational Technology Trends In 2020-2021, 2022) Digital learning, thanks to instant access and customisation, is making the learning experience smoother, more personal and in-line with the real-world work. Learners are now able to learn anytime from anywhere at their own pace with innovative tools such as gamified content and micro-learning courses. On this particular point, according to recent studies, this concise and understandable format is well appreciated by learners as it helps them to stay focus and understand more easily a given topic.  Keeping learners motivated and engaged is a challenge for EdTech as the classroom is now taking place online. As a solution, technology has to bring new tools for better practices and keeping engagement high. Live content sessions and personal supportare the perfect example of helping learners achieve despite the distance. (Tauson, 2022)

EdTech can also assist in facilitating communications between peers and enabling efficient and cost-effective strategies for teachers. Recent technology leaps such as 5G, Artificial Intelligence, Machine Learning and Augmented Reality/Virtual Reality are considered as a game changer for Educational Technology . Many believe such new trends will enhance awareness and transform the traditional techniques of teaching.

Some of these teaching methods are still in their infancy but are very promising. Artificial Intelligence and Machine Learning enables a more in-depth learning experience for learners. In fast-paced environments such as university and the workplace, AI-based individualised learning tools allow students and workers to get tailored help depending on their strengths and weaknesses. Algorithms and data can help learning platforms adjust their courses and provide a tailor-made experience.

Additionally, 5G is seen as the disruptive technology of the decade with great expectations. Many consider 5G as the Fourth Industrial Revolution , and the expectations raised by this technology are extraordinary in more than one way. An IHS Markit study estimates that $13.2 trillion in global economic value will be made possible by 2035, generating 22.3 million jobs in the 5G global value chain alone. (IHS Markit, 2019) The next-generation network will expand the capabilities of distance learning, virtual reality and robotics. More immersive learning, fast downloads and improved latency will foster the learning assimilation. Online courses with large bandwidth consumption will be enhanced such as VR/AR training, live sessions and Q&As. We can easily imagine the benefits of a truly immersive course for professionals and students: the way we learn about Architecture, Real Estate, Construction, Medecine will change more than ever.

5G promises to unlock new possibilities for the digital transformation in many industries. Today, there are so many developments available that we are only just scratching the surface. EdTech is here to stay and calls for a bigger place in education in the future despite the challenges faced especially in emerging countries where the access to networks may be an issue in some rural areas but also due to the fact that some children and adults may not have the financial means to afford a laptop or a smartphone. Here, EdTech has to find out how to tackle such issues in order to reach a certain democratisation.

## The Challenges Facing EdTech

In emerging countries, where education is a challenge in terms of quality and affordability, EdTech lays the foundations for education for all. Technological solutions such as education mobile apps can compensate for the lack of laptops in classes, especially in rural areas, and narrow the digital gap between rural and urban schools. For those who cannot afford a computer, smartphones remain the best choice for learning online at low cost. In some countries such as Morocco, we have seen joint initiatives between telecom operators and government authorities to tackle the issues related to the access to a network.Indeed, Maroc Telecom decided to combat the digital gap – which is one of the purposes of its sustainable development policy – by providing access to the internet and to temporarily offer free access to all distance education and training platforms set up by the Ministry of National Education. It is interesting to note here that companies have a crucial role to play in the democratisation of EdTech and that it is, above all, a societal issue. Therefore, corporate social responsibility would require companies to work to guarantee and ensure that the entire population has access without spatial restrictions to new technologies. The rural world must have continuous access to the internet and to a quality network.

One of the most important issues for the success and sustainability of EdTech will be the support provided to teachers. Indeed, EdTech companies and competent authorities, such as Ministries of Education, must develop appropriate training courses.

In addition, an effort should be made to provide pupils and students with access to quality computer equipment. As we have mentioned, the private sector must take part in this collective effort. Corporate social responsibility makes it possible to mobilise funds or actions intended to favour and promote EdTech, such as the Moroccan mobile operators.

Obstacles of psychological origin also exist when it comes to online education. (Terras and Ramsay, 2012) Indeed, the flow of information can be prohibitive for some people. It will therefore be necessary to ensure an effective identification of the problems encountered by each learner. Today, data analytics helps overcome these obstacles. According to some authors, learners should have the "appropriate profile of psychological (both cognitive and psychosocial) skills" in order to"maximise the learning potential of Web 2.0 technology". On this particular point, instructors and online platforms should ensure that courses are delivered adequately and in consideration of the learners' needs and specificities. A professional trying to enhance his or her skills will not have the same expectations as a young learner who may struggle with algebra or literature classes.

Limited financial means is another glaring obstacle. EdTech has a significant financial cost and requires technical resources to be implemented. Thus, schools and other universities must obtain the necessary funding in order to ensure the continuity of education. Here again, public and private actors must act together.

Finally, as mentioned previously, social inequalities are an undeniable obstacle to the development of EdTech. It will therefore be necessary for private players – platforms and marketplaces – to show ingenuity in order to develop solutions accessible to as many people as possible. Similarly, public authorities must make a concrete commitment to facilitate fair access to new technologies by supporting the companies involved through incentives such as public subsidies, the conclusion of public-private partnerships, and the promotion of research and development.

In the case of Morocco, the year 2020 was a real revelation of the added value provided by EdTech and its definite implication towards a quality education that is fairer and open to all. Thus, the Superior Council of Education and Scientific Research affirmed through its President Mr. Mohamed Tahiri that "the distance makes it possible to imagine universities accessible to the greatest number".To carry out this project, Moroccan authorities plan to soon initiate a "connected campus for all" program with a budget of 200 million dirhams (approximately 20 million US dollars). Inclusion will therefore be one of the challenges that EdTech has to address not only in emerging countries but all around the world.

**Conclusion**

In emerging countries, Educational Technology is expected to change the future of education for millions of learners, especially if the digital access to technology is adequately addressed. In developed countries, Educational Technology allows for a more personalised, modular, and data enhanced digital content. Learners are now in demand for more inclusive support and a lifelong learning process that can enhance their careers and employability. Such support is extremely important during challenging times, especially when employment is at risk. The challenge for EdTech today is to answer with the right tools to keep up the pace.

# Cybernetics As The Sixth Sense In EdTech

## Fang-ming Lim and Jenna Huey Ching

Co-founder and Managing Partner and Co-founder and CEO, both FortNynja

Is it possible to automate teaching?

You could automate the process of anything these days, including the steps it would take to disseminate information across to students. While education is more than just mere repetition, there is a baseline of competency where the fundamentals are covered. The main benefits of an automated, on-demand teaching platform are its reach, consistency of delivery and autonomy of control to the user. Instead of learning about the arts from a small country school in rural Mongolia, imagine what life could be if your tutors were Natalie Portman and Samuel L. Jackson teaching you acting; Martin Scorsese and Ron Howard lecturing you in filmmaking; and Steve Martin tutoring you in Comedy. All of this is already available on Masterclass.com.

Furthering this line of thought, a few more years into the future, an ecosystem with access to technology will grant us more believable experiences through Virtual and Augmented Reality. Imagine learning from the best tutors in any vocation you can think of and have a library of them, never ageing and always ready to teach. When another Stephen Hawking-like mind comes along, a new baseline is set and students in that field get to learn from the best. This consistent and continual approach means that the benchmark keeps progressing forward and the community of students get the best subject matter experts for their level of competency.

The current convergence towards on-demand services like Netflix, Udemy and Spotify has trained individuals to consume specific information at the drop of a hat and use Google as an ultimate fact checker. In today's classrooms, teachers get fact checked all the time - meaning they must master the areas they teach.

"Education is an admirable thing, but it is well to remember from time to time that nothing that is worth knowing can be taught." - Oscar Wilde.

With sufficient time and technology, intellectual ability will be even more valuable in the years to come. Obstacles like age, gender inequality, physical disability, living in remote areas and natural disasters will be overcome. Peer learning through this connectivity will be all the more relevant as groups form based on competency of the subject matter. Collaborations will also take place between groups where interests are aligned and its these exchanges which will yield the next advancements in humanity. Teachers are students, students are teachers; and the collective new learnings will be what is valued.

Learning cell groups will be 2-3 individuals - like-minded in their philosophies, interests, and curiosities. These cell groups form a larger nest of integrated groups whose members flow freely.

Each individual facilitates the lesson based on interest, and the predominant function of these groups would be for discussion and comprehension of ideas, thoughts, and applications they have inherited from the plethora of on-demand education options. Gone are course materials that are specifically tied to things like algebra, history, or geography. Instead, it will be replaced with more abstract concepts like logic, leadership, and culture.

The next two stages of EdTech advancement will grow concurrently. One in Robotics, and the other in Cybernetics. At this stage of evolution, robots are no longer the mindless machines that only have the ability to work on repetitive tasks. Specific Artificial Intelligence would be the catalyst for us to enable us to have a more sophisticated interaction with machines. Humans would grow up with their robotic counterparts from day one. Where in Phase 1, the "teacher" was in a virtual space, robots would be the physical manifestation of a virtual teacher in physical form. One of the side benefits of having such a companion is that parenting would be an optional thing for humans. Parents who want to remain involved in their child's development and upbringing can still do so, but the stability provided for an android that provides consistency throughout their human's development cannot be understated particularly when divorce cases are at record highs and the conventional nucleus family becomes more of an exception rather than something common. By stabilising the emotional aspects of the educational journey, the student gets to explore their curiosity free from judgement.

A majority ofwhite-collar jobs would already be replaced by Specific AI, which means that a lot of repetitive menial work like auditing, quantity surveying and structural engineering would be replaced with higher functioning jobs that emphasise creativity, problem solving and exploration. A simple analogy of this advancement would be how familiar we are with using a word processor like Microsoft Word or Google Docs. While we may not have much clue on the programming logic and code which goes on behind the program, we are more than comfortable to utilise the functions of a word processor to pen down our thoughts.

This movement forward in robotics brings to the surface many questions around the concept of humanity. When the primary caregiver, educator and facilitator is an android, how will the maturing growing human child see itself? My take on this would be that humans, by this stage, would be on a mission to explore new dimensions, like outer space and the metaverse. We would be adventurers like Zheng He, Galileo and Shakespeare, who explored and discovered vast new worlds in their own area, be it on the high seas, through a lens or through literature. With our partner Android alongside us, we would be adventurers in spaces yet to be discovered be it in the physical or metaphysical world.

Cybernetics, on the other hand, is a different phase altogether. In the world of Cybernetics (not to be confused with SciFi's definition of a cyborg), EdTech is now at a stage where humans will learn with the 5 common senses, plus their sixth - their mind. This means that physical form and intellectual ability are operating at very high levels. Whereas in the earlier phase, the physically impaired could only stimulate their mind to overcome their physical impediments, this phase of technology has allowed for the mind to fix these physical impediments on either a genetic or a cybernetic level. This will literally be a manifestation of "mind over matter", as we learn how to restore function or enhance our abilities further through the integration of some artificial component. At this stage, EdTech as a field starts interacting with others, like MedTech, as live teaching occurs at the same time as medical references and treatments are initiated.

At a Cybernetic stage of education, language will no longer be a barrier. Gone are the days of trying to comprehend what my Russian counterpart is trying to explain to me. We would be immersed into the metaverse where our mind is whole with our physical body. Imagine going into a metaverse platform that is curated to your learning. No longer do we rely on books or instructors in classes that we need to pre-register or book.

When I was pursuing my degree abroad from my home country, some of my best learning came through the perspectives I gained from interacting with my surroundings. I could immerse myself in the culture, weather, religions, languages, food, ideas, history, terrain and philosophies that made my whole education much richer. Imagine if we could experience that in perpetuity through our sixth sense via Robotics and Cybernetics. Time in effect would be *relative* not just in an equation form, but in an intimate personal form solely unique to us. We internalise lessons best when we have a tremendously intimate experience - and the metaverse would afford us that.

Beyond the compounding experiences we would acquire, we would also be more compassionate in the process. Our education would not be purely academic on understanding something "simple" like Newton's laws of thermodynamics. Instead, we could choose to understand the plight of the Mayans when faced with the Spanish Conquistadors or look behind the lens of Army Photographer Ronald Haeberle who recorded the atrocities at My Lai by GIs, or to train ourselves emotionally through the experiences of Francis Crozier as he led his crew to survive being trapped in Antarctica.

Beyond just human experiences, cybernetics would also allow us to fully understand aspects we could once only imagine in our minds. Take, for example, trying to understand the aerodynamics of how the physique of an owl allows it to glide almost in silence. In the metaverse, we can *be* the owl in a digital form and should we choose, become a physical owl via cybernetics. We would be able to feel the wind against our wings, the ruffle of our plumage just under our neck and we would have night vision better than any electronic goggles. The metaverse world will feel like it is real with the wind, temperature and waves you can pre-set to try a different environment without any danger to the user. The Cybernetic owl in this case would be akin to an online avatar getting "hurt" in an online game. Risk in trying new things is removed from the equation completely.

Cybernetics will allow us to learn without consequence. We would be gods in our own world as we venture into others. Resource scarcity as we currently understand it in economic terms would melt away in the world of cybernetics.
Not enough energy? We would learn, risk free, till we harnessed the sun.
Not enough time? We would discover how to upgrade our consciousness into the metaverse until such a time we can upload it into a cybernetic sleeve.
Not enough perspective? We would run compressed scenarios for months on end.

The mind is an unexplored world. As we explore the world around us, we come to learn more about ourselves. As we develop ourselves further, we get to surpass previous limitations set by our environment. Maslow's Hierarchy of Needs indicates Food, Water, Warmth and Rest as the most basic of our needs. As we progress forward in Robotics and Cybernetics, we will strive to increase our control on our environment. Where Neanderthals would find respite from the elements by huddling in a cave sufficient for their needs 100,000 years ago, today we see the need to build artificial islands in the shape of a palm, climate-controlled skyscrapers 163 stories high or a modular space station that orbits earth at 408km. We are ever expanding on our need to dominate our environment. With today's technology, we are also seeking to tame our mind by building virtual worlds, the precursors to the metaverse. We are at the precipice of commencement of the basic understanding of the metaverse of which we still have little clue how it all fits together. Though, given another 100,000 years of education and technology, how much more of the environment will we try to tame and how much deeper will our understanding be of ourselves?

EdTech is the catalyst to propel humankind into its next evolution. While we may struggle with its complexities and wrestle with its moralities. However, one thing we have to agree on is that the momentum humankind has built in its evolutionary learnings has accelerated us to the breakneck speed we are being pushed forward with technology now. Whether we finally end up taming the great universe or find peace in the inner workings of our minds, perhaps Robotics and Cybernetics is what's needed for us to be one with our universe.

Perhaps this is what it means to be all and one, at the same time.

FUTURE

# Bibliography

Abiloch, Harada, &Fontichiaro, (2013). Growing schools: effective professional development. *Teacher Librarian,* 41(1), (8-13.)

Alexander, B. (2020). *Early signs of fall 2020: Three paths, three scenarios for higher education.* Retrieved from https://bryanalexander.org/

Fullan, M., Senge, P. M. (2010). *All systems go: The change imperative for whole system reform.* Thousand Oaks: Corwin

Fullan, M., & Quinn, J. (2016). *Coherence: The right drivers in action for schools, districts, and systems.* Thousand Oaks, CA: Corwin.

Marzano, R. J., & Pickering, D. J. (2010). The highly engaged classroom: The classroom strategies series (Generating high levels of student attention and engagement). Marzano Research Laboratory.

Marzano, R. J., Pickering, D. J., &Heflebower, M. (2011). The highly engaged classroom. Bloomington, Indiana: Marzano Research Laboratory.

Rhoads, M. (2020). *Navigating the toggled term: Preparing secondary educators for navigating fall 2020 and beyond.* Seattle, WA: Amazon Publishing.

Rhoads, M. (2021). Navigating the Toggled Term: A Guide for Classroom and School Leaders. Bern, Switzerland: Peter Lang US. Retrieved February 12, 2021 from https://www.peterlang.com/view/title/75300

Samee, Ali. (October, 18th, 2020). *Educators teaching online and in person at the same time feel burnout: The COVID-19 pandemic has led many schools to offer both classroom and virtual instruction, but teachers say doing both concurrently is exhausting.* NBC News. Retrieved from https://www.nbcnews.com/news/us-news/educators-teaching-online-person-same-time-feel-burned-out-n1243296
Jake F. (2020) EdTech

Anne G. (2018) 6 Reasons why teachers don't use technology in the classroom- what can EdTech companies learn?

Tes E. (2018) What is pedagogy?
Origin of the Word. 2022. *Education.* [online] Available at: <https://etymology.net/education/> [Accessed 17 January 2022].

Edustaff.co.uk. 2022. *EduStaff.* [online] Available at: <https://www.edustaff.co.uk/blog/72_> [Accessed 17 January 2022].

GeeksforGeeks. 2022. *Top 7 Companies That Don't Require a College Degree - GeeksforGeeks.* [online] Available at: <https://www.geeksforgeeks.org/top-7-companies-that-dont-require-a-college-degree/> [Accessed 17 January 2022].

BIBLIOGRAPHY

Iftf.org. 2022. [online] Available at: <https://www.iftf.org/fileadmin/user_upload/images/ourwork/Tech_Horizons/realizing_2030_future_of_work_report_dell_technologies.pdf> [Accessed 17 January 2022].

Glassdoor.com. 2022. *Google & 14 More Companies That No Longer Require a Degree.* [online] Available at: <https://www.glassdoor.com/blog/no-degree-required/> [Accessed 17 January 2022].

Doucet, Netolicky, Timmers&Tuscano, 2020, Thinking about Pedagogy in an Unfolding Pandemic, UNESCO, p5 & 8
https://issuu.com/educationinternational/docs/2020_research_covid-19_eng

Edutopia, April 2020 https://www.edutopia.org/article/why-are-some-kids-thriving-during-remote-learning
McKinsey, Oct 2020
https://www.mckinsey.com/industries/public-and-social-sector/our-insights/reimagining-higher-education-in-the-united-states

Kamanetz, Anya, Oct 2020
https://www.npr.org/2020/10/21/925794511/were-the-risks-of-reopening-schools-exaggerated?t=1615395387177

Sir Ken Robinson, Aug 2020
https://www.youtube.com/watch?v=lUvNTt6crFM

McKinsey, Sep 8, 2020
https://www.mckinsey.com/industries/public-and-social-sector/our-insights/reimagining-a-more-equitable-and-resilient-k-12-education-system,

Scott, Mark, Oct 9, 2020
https://www.mckinsey.com/industries/public-and-social-sector/our-insights/reforming-public-education-in-australia-an-interview-with-mark-scott-ao

Horizon Report, 2020
https://library.educause.edu/resources/2020/3/2020-educause-horizon-report-teaching-and-learning-edition

Conversation - banning mobile phones
https://theconversation.com/banning-mobile-phones-in-schools-beneficial-or-risky-heres-what-the-evidence-says-119456

Couros, G, Medium Mar 2021
https://medium.com/@gcouros/what-are-the-basics-in-education-today-54f56def1021

Bashir-Ali, K. (2006). Language learning and the definition of one's social, cultural, and racial identity. TESOL Quarterly, 40,628–639.

Bayliss, D. &Vignola, M-J. (2007). Training non-native second language teachers: The case of Anglophone FSL teacher candidates. *The Canadian Modern Language Review/La revue Canadienne des langues, vivantes*, 63, 3, pp. 371-398.

Chun, C.W. (2009). Critical literacies and graphic novels for English-language learners: Teaching *Maus. Journal of Adolescent & Adult Literacy*, 53 (2), 144-153). doi: 10.1598/JAAL.53.2.5

Davis, B., Sumara, D. &Luce-Kapler, R. (2015). *Engaging Minds: Cultures of Education and Practices of Teaching (3rd Ed.).* New York: Routledge.

De Larios, J., Marin, J., &Murphy, L. (2001). A temporal analysis of formulation processes in L1 and L2 writing. *Language Learning, 51*(3), 497-538. https://doi- org.proxy.library.carleton.ca/10.1111/0023-8333.00163

Engelkamp, J. (1998). *Memory for actions*. Psychology Press. DOI: 10.1002/(SCI)1099-0720(199912)13:6<582::AID-ACP650>3.0.CO

Golly-Haring, C., &Engelkamp, J. (2003). Categorical-relational and order-relational information in memory for subject-performed and experimenter-performed actions. *Journal of Experimental Psychology. Learning, memory and cognition Exp., 29*(5), 965- 975. https://doi.org/10.1037/0278-7393.29.5.965

González-Lloret, M., &Nielson, K. (2015). Evaluating TBLT: The case of task-based Spanish program. *Language Teaching Research, 19*(5), 525- 549. http://doi.org/10.1177/1362168814541745

Hummel, K.M. (2013). Target-language community involvement: Second-language linguistic self-confidence and other perceived benefits. *Canadian Modern Language Review, 69* (1), 65-90. doi: 10.3138/cmlr.1152

Kanno, Y., &Norton, B. (2003). Imagined communities and educational possibilities: Introduction. Journal of Language, *Identity & Education, 2(*4), 241–249.

Leaver, B.L. (2003) Motivation at native-like levels of foreign-language proficiency: A research agenda. Betty Lou Leaver & Ekaterina Kuznetsova, Boris Shekhtman, Ludmila Tsurikova (Eds)., *Journal for Distinguished Language Studies* (59-82). California: MSI Press.

Moreno-Lopez, I., Ramos-Sellman, A., Miranda-Aldaco, C. &Gomis Quinto, M.T. (2017). Transforming ways of enhancing foreign language acquisition in the Spanish classroom: Experiential learning approaches. *Foreign Language Annals, 50*(2), 398-409. http://doi.org/10.1111/flan.12267

Morgan, B., &Ramanathan, V. (2005). Critical literacies and language education: Global and local perspectives. *Annual Review of Applied Linguistics, 25*, 151-169. doi:10.1017/S0267190505000

Olgilvie, G., &Dunn, W. (2010). Taking teacher education to task: Exploring the role of teacher education in promoting the utilization of task-based language teaching. *Language Teaching Research, 14*(2), 161- 181. https;//doi.org/10.1177/1362168809353875

Sarani, A., &FarzanehSahebi, L. (2012). The impact of task-based approach on vocabulary learning in ESP courses. *English Language Teaching, 5*(10).
https://dx.doi.org/10.5539/elt.v5n10p118

Steffens, M.C., von Stülpnagel, R., &Schult, J.C. (2015). Memory recall after "learning by doing" and "learning by viewing": Boundary conditions of an enactment benefit.
*Frontiers in Psychology, 6*. https://doi.org/10.3389/fpsyg.2015.01907 Vanderveen, T. (2018, October 18).

The Nature and Impact of Portfolio-Based Language  Assessment (PBLA). *Contact Magazine,* 5-11, from http://contact.teslontario.org/the-  nature-and-impact-of-portfolio-based-language-assessment-pbla/
Vargas Vásquez, J.M., &Moya Chaves, M., &Garro Morales, C. (2016). The roles of the instructors in an ESP task-based language teaching course. *RevistaActualidadesInvestigativasenEducación, 16*(1), 1-23. http://dx.doi.org/10.15517/aie.v16i1.21974

Yuan, F., &Ellis, R. (2003). The effects of pretask planning and on-line planning on fluency, complexity, and accuracy in L2 monologic oral production. *Applied Linguistics, 24*(1), 1- 27. https://doi-org.proxy.library.carleton.ca/10.1093/applin/24.1.1

Top Tech Innovations of the Past 20 Years. https://www.independence.edu/blog/top-tech-innovations-of-the-past-20-years

E-learning and Digital Education – Statistics & Facts. https://www.statista.com/topics/3115/e-learning-and-digital-education/

Global EdTech Market to reach $404 [Billion] by 2025. https://www.holoniq.com/notes/global-education-technology-market-to-reach-404b-by-2025/

Education Technology Market Size, Share & Trends Analysis Report by Sector. https://www.grandviewresearch.com/industry-analysis/education-technology-market

Smartnotes Platform for Buying & Selling Digital Student-Created Notes. https://smartnotes.ai/

Global Publishing Market 2018-2022. https://www.businesswire.com/news/home/20190724005328/en/Global-Publishing-Market-2018-2022-USD-20.81-Billion-Incremental-Growth-Over-the-Next-Five-Years-Technavio

University of California Will No Longer Consider SAT and ACT Scores. NY Times. https://www.nytimes.com/2021/05/15/us/SAT-scores-uc-university-of-california.html

Why Children Are Set on Becoming YouTubers When They Grow Up. Mediakix. https://mediakix.com/blog/percent-children-becoming-a-youtuber/#:~:text=In%20a%20study%20published%20 in.be%20a%20YouTuber%20(34.2%25)

Barokas, J., & Barth, I. (2018). Multi-stakeholder ecosystems in rapidly changing educational environments. In *2018 IEEE Global Engineering Education Conference (EDUCON)* (pp. 1934-1938). IEEE.

Bonk, C. (2016). Keynote: What is the state of e-learning? Reflections on 30 ways learning is changing. Journal of Open, Flexible, and Distance Learning, 20(2), 6-20.
Bravo, E., Amante, B., Simo, P., Enache, M., & Fernandez, V. (2011). Video as a new teaching tool to increase student motivation. In *2011 IEEE global engineering education conference (EDUCON)* (pp. 638-642). IEEE.

Chai, A. (2014). Web-enhanced procrastination? How online lecture recordings affect binge study and academic achievement. *Discussion Papers in Economics economics, 201404,* 26.

Chang, S. (2007, December). Academic perceptions of the use of Lectopia: A University of Melbourne example. In *ICT: Providing choices for learners and learning. Proceedings ascilite Singapore 2007* (pp. 135-144).

Danielson, J., Preast, V., Bender, H., & Hassall, L. (2014). Is the effectiveness of lecture capture related to teaching approach or content type?. *Computers & Education, 72*, 121-131.

Davies, R. S., Dean, D. L., & Ball, N. (2013). Flipping the classroom and instructional technology integration in a college-level information systems spreadsheet course. Educational Technology Research and Development, 61(4), 563–580.

Edwards, M. R., & Clinton, M. E. (2019). A study exploring the impact of lecture capture availability and lecture capture usage on student attendance and attainment. *Higher Education, 77*(3), 403-421.
Elliott, C., & Neal, D. (2015). Evaluating the use of lecture capture using a revealed preference approach. *Active Learning in Higher Education, 17*(2), 153-167.

Etherington, D. (2015). LinkedIn to buy online education site Lynda.com for $1.5 Billion. Accessed from https://techcrunch.com/2015/04/09/linkedin-to-buy-online-education-site-lynda-com-for-1-5-billion/ on 29thApril, 2021.

Freed, P. E., Bertram, J. E., & McLaughlin, D. E. (2014). Using lecture capture: a qualitative study of nursing faculty's experience. *Nurse education today*, 34(4), 598-602.
Gardner, R. C. (1985). Social psychology and second language learning: the role of attitudes and motivation. London: Edward Arnold.
Griffin, D. K., Mitchell, D., & Thompson, S. J. (2009). Podcasting by synchronizing PowerPoint and voice: what are the pedagogical benefits? Computers & Education, 53(2), 532–539.

Groen, J. F., Quigley, B., &Herry, Y. (2016). Examining the Use of Lecture Capture Technology: Implications for Teaching and Learning. *Canadian Journal for the Scholarship of Teaching and Learning, 7*(1), 8.

266

Jaasma, M. A., & Koper, R. J. (1999). The relationship of studentfaculty outofclass communication to instructor immediacy and trust and to student motivation. *Communication education, 48*(1), 41-47.

Kay, R. H., &Kletskin, I. (2012). Evaluating the use of problem-based video podcasts to teach mathematics in higher education. Computer & Education, 59, 619–627.

Kearney, M. (2013). Learner-generated digital video: using ideas videos in teacher education. Journal of  Technology and Teacher Education, 21(3), 321–336.

Kiyici, F. B., &Yigit, E. A. (2010). Science education beyond the classroom. *International Online Journal of Educational Sciences, 2*(1), 225-243.

López Osorio, D. M. (2017). The use of authentic videos, as a teaching strategy, to lower some boredom signs shown by Intermediate English students at Universidad San Ignacio de Loyola when practicing grammar, in order to improve results.

Mayer, R.E. (2009). *Multimedia Learning* (2nd ed.). New York: Cambridge University Press.

McGarr, O. (2009). A review of podcasting in higher education: its influence on the traditional lecture.Australasian Journal of Educational Technology, 25(3), 309–321.

McKinney, D., Dyck, J. L., &Luber, E. S. (2009). iTunes University and the classroom: Can podcasts replace Professors?. *Computers & education, 52*(3), 617-623.

Morris, N. P. (2012). Podcasts and mobile assessment enhance student learning experience and academic performance. *Bioscience Education, 16*(1), 1-7.
Morris, N. P., Swinnerton, B., & Coop, T. (2019). Lecture recordings to support learning: A contested space between students and teachers. *Computers & Education, 140*, 103604.

Noland, A., & Richards, K. (2014). The Relationship among Transformational Teaching and Student Motivation and Learning. *Journal of Effective Teaching, 14*(3), 5-20.

O'Connor, N.G. (2021). Tech Asia – YouTube -https://www.youtube.com/channel/UCrgVIJD4dymgvTiEcOSoyFA

O'Connor, N. G., Yang, Z., & Jiang, L. (2018). Challenges in gaining supply chain competitiveness: Supplier response strategies and determinants. *Industrial Marketing Management, 72, 138-151.*

Owston, R., Lupshenyuk, D., & Wideman, H. (2011). Lecture capture in large undergraduate classes: Student perceptions and academic performance. *The Internet and Higher Education, 14*(4), 262-268.

Payne, M. R. (1985). *Using the outdoors to teach science: a resource guide for elementary and middle school teachers.* Educational Resources Information Center, Clearinghouse on Rural

Education and Small Schools, New Mexico State University.

Scholtes, P. R., Joiner, B. L., &Streibel, B. J. (2003). *The team handbook* (3rd ed.). Madison, WI: Oriel Incorporated.

See, A., &Teetor, T. S. (2014). Effective e-training: using a course management system and e-learning tools to train library employees. *Journal of Access Services, 11*(2), 66-90.

Starratt, R. J. (2004). *Ethical leadership* (Vol. 8). Jossey-Bass.

Shim, J. P., Shropshire, J., Park, S., Harris, H., & Campbell, N. (2007). Podcasting for e- learning, communication, and delivery. Industrial Management and Data Systems, 107(4), 587–600.

Van Hoek, R., et al. (2011). Embedding insights from industry in supply chain programmes: the role of guest lecturers. *Supply Chain Management: An International Journal*, 16 (2), 142 – 147. Wang, R., Mattick, K., & Dunne, E. (2010). Medical students' perceptions of video- linked lectures and video-streaming. Research in Learning Technology, 18(1), 19–27.

Whatley, J., & Ahmad, A. (2007). Using video to record summary lectures to aid students' revision. Interdisciplinary Journal of ELearning and Learning Objects, 3, 185–196.

"The Pandemic Pushed Universities Online. The Change Was Long Overdue." Gallagher, S. & Palmer, J. Harvard Business Review, September 29, 2020

"The rise of the platform economy" Deloitte January 2019

"The Open Talent economy" Deloitte 2013 Resetting Horizons

"Lessons Learned from Decentralised Finance (DeFi)". Meegan, X. &Kones, T. accessed here https://new.ingwb.com/binaries/content/assets/insights/themes/distributed-ledger-technology/defi_white_paper_v2.0.pdf

Lise Hamergren, 2021. Executive Education is Changing For Good, https://www.aacsb.edu/insights/2021/february/executive-education-is-changing-for-good

Prince, Russ Alan, 2015. The Requirements For Success In The Lucrative Executive Education Business. Forbes
https://www.forbes.com/sites/russalanprince/2015/05/27/the-requirements-for-success-in-the-lucrative-executive-education-business/?sh=6ce381957624

"The State of the American Workplace Report," PDF file (Gallup Feb 6, 2020)
https://www.gallup.com/workplace/285818/state-american-workplace-report.aspx

"How the Workforce Learns in 2019," PDF file (PDF file) (Harvard Business Publishing, Corporate Learning, April 2019)
https://www.harvardbusiness.org/insight/how-the-workforce-learns-in-2019/

Kehoe, Mike, 2018. 4 Habits of People Who Are Always Learning New Skills, Harvard Business Review
https://hbr.org/2018/01/4-habits-of-people-who-are-always-learning-new-skills

Gratton, Lynda, 2021. An Emerging Landscape of Skills for All. The Future of Workplace Learning, MIT Sloan Management Review
https://sloanreview.mit.edu/article/an-emerging-landscape-of-skills-for-all/

Gagné Robert M "The Conditions of Learning "1977. Holt, Rinehart and Winston, Inc. 283-313 pp

Ebbinghaus H (1885) "Memory: A Contribution to Experimental Psychology "Annals of Neurosciences" 20(4): 155-156 Translated by Henry A. Ruger & Clara Bussenius (1913)

Collings, David G, John McMackin 2021. The Practices That Set Learning Organisations Apart, MIT Sloan Management Review
https://sloanreview.mit.edu/article/the-practices-that-set-learning-organisations-apart/?gclid=E AlaIQobChMIgbu1_67x8AIVl3ZgCh0HIQLOEAAYAiAAEgLjbfD_BwE

Heredia-Escorza, Y., & Sánchez Aradillas, A. (2013). Learning theories: Definition and characteristics every educator should know.

Tony B. (2014) Learning theories and online learning

Linda H. (2007) Online collaborative learning

Ariella L., Avner C. (2010) Comparing Perceived Formal and Informal Learning in Face-to-Face versus Online Environments

Active Learning, University of Minnesota's Center for Educational Innovation. https: //cei.umn. edu/active-learning

Cepeda, N. J., Pashler, H., Vul, E., Wixted, J. T., & Rohrer, D. (2006). Distributed practice in verbal recall tasks: A review and quantitative synthesis. Psychological Bulletin, 132(3), 354–380. https://doi.org/10.1037/0033-2909.132.3.354
Chin, C., & Osborne, J. (2007). Students' questions: a potential resource for teaching and learning science. https://doi.org/10.1080/03057260701828101

Dempster, F. N. (1989). Spacing Effects and Their Implications for Theory and Practice. Educational Psychology Review, 1(4), 309–330.

Hestenes, D., Wells, M., &Swackhamer, G. (1992). Force concept inventory. The Physics Teacher, 30(3), 141–158. https://doi.org/10.1119/1.2343497

Kane, P. R., & Mattingly, K. The Science of Learning — What Every Teacher Should Know. EdX: https://www.edx.org

Lang, J. (2016). Small Changes in Teaching: The First 5 Minutes of Class. The Chronicle of Higher Education. Advice.

Malamed, C. Chunking Information for Instructional Design.
https: //theelearningcoach.com/elearning_design/chunking-information/

Managing the classroom. Yale's PoorvuCenter for Teaching and Learning. https: //poor vucenter. yale.edu/Beginning-End-Class
Mazur, E. (2012). Confessions of a converted lecturer. https: //www.youtube.com/ watch?v=ZpNjem3p0Ak

Organizing Instruction and Study to Improve Student Learning, Institute of Education Sciences (U.S. Department of Education).
https: //files.eric.ed.gov/fulltext /ED498555.pdf

Rawson, K. A., &Kintsch, W. (2005). Rereading effects depend on time of test. Journal of Educational Psychology, 97(1), 70–80.
https: //doi.org/10.1037/0022-0663.97.1.70

Rowland, C. A. (2014). The effect of testing versus restudy on retention: A meta-analytic review of the testing effect. Psychological Bulletin, 140(6), 1432–1463. https://doi.org/10.1037/a0037559

Weinstein, Y., Madan, C. R., &Sumeracki, M. A. (2018). Teaching the science of learning. Cognitive Research: Principles and Implications, 3(1).
https: //doi.org/10.1186/s41235-017-0087-y

Weinstein, Y., Sumeracki, M., &Caviglioli, O. (2018). Understanding How We Learn. https: //doi. org/10.4324/9780203710463

Anderson, J.R. (1983). "A spreading activation theory of memory". Journal of Verbal Learning and Verbal Behavior. 22 (3): 261–295. doi:10.1016/S0022-5371(83)90201-3. ISSN 0022-5371.

Anderson, J. R. (2000) *Learning and Memory: An Integrated Approach.* 2nd ed. New York: John Wiley, 2000.

Berkley Center for Teaching and Learning https://teaching.berkeley.edu/resources/learn/what-learning (Accessed May13, 2021)

Bouton, M. E. (2007). *Learning and behavior: A contemporary synthesis.* Sunderland, MA: Sinauer Associates, Inc.

Brown, P.C., Roediger III, H.L., & McDaniel, M.A. (2014). Make It Stick. *The Science of Successful Learning, The Journal of Educational Research,* 108:4, 346, DOI: 10.1080/00220671.2015.1053373

Collins, A.M.; Loftus, E.F. (1975). "A spreading-activation theory of semantic processing".

Psychological Review. 82 (6): 407–428. doi:10.1037/0033-295X.82.6.407. ISSN 0033-295X.

Cowan, N. (2008). What are the differences between long-term, short-term, and working memory? *Progress in brain research, 169*, 323–338. https://doi.org/10.1016/S0079-6123(07)00020-9

Crowley, E.& Overton, L. (2021) *Learning and skills at work survey 2021*. London: Chartered Institute of Personnel and Development.

Csikszentmihalyi, M. (1990). *Flow: The psychology of optimal experience.* New York: Harper & Row.

Davachi, L., Kiefer, T., Rock, D. and Rock, L. (2010) Learning that lasts through AGES. *NeuroLeadership Journal.* Issue 3, 2010.

De Houwer, J., Barnes-Holmes, D., & Moors, A. (2013). What is learning? On the nature and merits of a functional definition of learning. *Psychonomic bulletin & review.* 20. 10.3758/s13423-013-0386-3.

Fogg, B. J. (2009). A behavior model for persuasive design. https://endregion.ir/uploads/weblog/persuasive_technology_ref/Fogg%20Behavior%20Model.pdf (Accessed 20, May 2021)

Gobet,F., Lane, P.C., Croker, S., Cheng, P.C., Jones, G., Oliver, I., Pine, J.M. (2001) Chunking mechanisms in human learning. *Trends Cogn Sci.* 2001 Jun 1;5(6):236-243. doi: 10.1016/s1364-6613(00)01662-4. PMID: 11390294.

Hamdan, A; Din, R; Manaf, Abdul; Salleh, Mat; Kamsin, I; Ismail, N (2015), "Exploring The Relationship Between Frequency Use of Web 2.0 and Meaningful Learning Attributes", *Journal of Technical Education and Training*, 7 (1): 50–66

Henry, T., Leufkens, B., Norchet, E., Peiroo, P., Ritsema, E., and Shandal, V.(2021) *Lessons in Corporate Learning for Education Technology Companies* https://www.bcg.com/publications/2021/corporate-learning-in-ed-tech (Accessed 18, May 2021)

Kohn, A. (2014) *Brain Science: Overcoming the Forgetting Curve* https://learningsolutionsmag.com/articles/1400/brain-science-overcoming-the-forgetting-curve (Accessed 20, May 2021)

Lachmnan, S. J. (1997). Learning is a Process: Toward an Improved Definition of Learning. *Journal of Psychology,* 131, 477-480

Mayer,R.E. (2002) *Rote Versus Meaningful Learning, Theory Into Practice,* 41:4,226-232, DOI: 10.1207/s15430421tip4104_4

Meeking, M. (2018). *The AGES model, designing and delivering IL programs* [Paper presentation]. VATL LIT Workshop 2 2018. https://www.vatl.org.au (Accessed 20, May 2021)

Murre, J.M.J, and Dros, J. (2015) *Replication and analysis of Ebbinghaus' forgetting curve.* Chialvo, D.R., ed. PLoS ONE.2015;10(7)

National Research Council. (2000). *How People Learn: Brain, Mind, Experience, and School: Expanded Edition.* Washington, DC: The National Academies Press. https://doi.org/10.17226/9853.

Patterson, K., Nestor, P.J. & Rogers, T.T. (2007) "Where do you know what you know? The representation of semantic knowledge in the human brain", *Nature Reviews Neuroscience* 8, 976-987

Ramratan, W. S., Rabin, L. A., Wang, C., Zimmerman, M. E., Katz, M. J., Lipton, R. B., &Buschke, H. (2012). Level of recall, retrieval speed, and variability on the Cued-Recall Retrieval Speed Task (CRRST) in individuals with amnestic mild cognitive impairment. *Journal of the International Neuropsychological Society : JINS, 18*(2), 260–268. https://doi.org/10.1017/S1355617711001664

Rasch, B., & Born, J. (2013). About sleep's role in memory. *Physiological reviews, 93(*2), 681–766. https://doi.org/10.1152/physrev.00032.2012

Sander, J. (2011) Cognitive Skills. In: Goldstein S., Naglieri J.A. (eds) *Encyclopedia of Child Behavior and Development*. Springer, Boston, MA. https://doi.org/10.1007/978-0-387-79061-9_609

Schleisman, K.B., SelcenGuzey, S., Lie, R. *et al.* (2018) Learning Neuroscience with Technology: a Scaffolded, Active Learning Approach. *J Sci Educ Technol*27, 566–580 (2018). https://doi.org/10.1007/s10956-018-9748-y

Schwartz, B., Wasserman, E.A., & Robbins, S. J. (2002). *Psychology of learning and behavior* (5th ed.). New York: Norton.

Shimamura, A. (2011) Active Learning AND Testing: The Key to Long-Lasting Memories - Arthur Shimamura for the How Students Learn Working Group on March 8, 2011. https://gsi.berkeley.edu/programs-services/hsl-project/hsl-speakers/shimamura/ (Accessed 18, May 2021)

Shuell, Thomas J. (1992), Adaptive Learning Environments, pp. 19–54

Spear, N.E. (2014). *The Processing of Memories (PLE: Forgetting and Retention.* Taylor and Francis.

Statista (2021) *Market size of the gloval workplace training industry from 2007 to 2020* https://www.statista.com/statistics/738399/size-of-the-global-workplace-training-market/ (Accessed 24, May 2021)

The Derek Bok Center for Teaching and Learning https://bokcenter.harvard.edu (Accessed May13, 2021 )

Weissenborn, R.,&Duka, T. (2000) State-dependent effects of alcohol on explicit memory: the role of semantic associations. *Psychopharmacology* (Berl). 2000 Mar;149(1):98-106. doi: 10.1007/s002139900349. PMID: 10789889.

Whiting, K. (2020) World Economic Forum: These are the top 10 job skills of tomorrow – and how long it takes to learn them https://www.weforum.org/agenda/2020/10/top-10-work-skills-of-tomorrow-how-long-it-takes-to-learn-them/ (Accessed 18, May 2021)

Wixted, J.T. (2004) The Psychology and Neuroscience of Forgetting
Annual Review of Psychology 2004 55:1, 235-269

Crisp, R.J., & Turner, R.N. (2012). *The Imagined Contact Hypothesis.* Advances in Experimental Social Psychology, 46, 125-182.

Merrill, D., & Reid, R. (1981). Personal Styles and Effective Performance. Chilton.
Mishra, P., & Koehler, M. J. (2006). *Technological pedagogical content knowledge: A framework for integrating technology in teachers' knowledge.* Teachers College Record, 108 (6), 1017–1054

OECD (2019). PISA 2018 results (Vol III). What school life means for students' lives. OECD

Johnson, D.W., & Johnson, F. (2009). Joining together: Group theory and group skills (10th ed.). Boston: Allyn& Bacon.

Shulman, L. S. (1987). *Knowledge and teaching: Foundations of the new reform.* Harvard Educational Review, 57(1), 1-22.

www.kaganonline.com/free_articles/research_and_rationale/
www.persona-life.com
www.TPACK.org
www.weforum.org/agenda/2020/04/coronavirus-education-global-covid19-online-digital-learning/

Bergmann, J. &Sams, A. (2012). *Flip Your Classroom: Reach Every Student in Every Class Every Day.* International Society for Technology in Education.

2nd Survey of Schools: ICT in Education (2021). [online] Available at https://digital-strategy.ec.europa.eu/en/library/2nd-survey-schools-ict-education-0 [Accessed 06 August 2021]

2021. Expenditure of General Government Sector by Function: 2015-2019 news release no.014/2021. [ebook] National Statistics Office. Available at: https://nso.gov.mt/Home/Visualisation/Pages/Infographics/Public%20Finance/Government%20Expenditure%20by%20Function.aspx [Accessed 25 July 2021].

CEDEFOP (2021) Malta: VET response to the Covid-19 emergency. [online] Available at: https://www.cedefop.europa.eu/en/news-and-press/news/malta-vet-response-covid-19-emergency [Accessed 5 August 2021].

Digital Malta Vision. (2021) [online] Available at: https://digitalmalta.org.mt/en/Pages/Strategy/Digital-Malta-Vision.aspx [Accessed 25 July 2021].

Digital Malta Strategy. (2021). [online] Available at: https://economy.gov.mt/en/ministry/The-Parliamentary-Secretary/Pages/Malta-Digital-Economy-Vision.aspx [Accessed 25 July 2021].

Education Act, Chapter 327

Further and Higher Education Act, Chapter 607
Ncfhecms.gov.mt. 2021. Malta Qualifications Framework. [online] Available at: https://ncfhecms.gov.mt/en/Pages/MQF.aspx [Accessed 26 July 2021].

European Commission (2021) – Internet usage is growing. [online] Available at: https://ec.europa.eu/newsroom/rtd/items/713444/en [Accessed 19 August 2021].

European Commission – Digital Economy and Society Index – Malta Report 2020. [online] Available at: https://digital-strategy.ec.europa.eu/en/policies/desi-malta [Accessed 28 July 2021]

European University Association (2018) - National Initiatives in Learning and Teaching in Europe. [online] Available at: https://eua.eu/downloads/publications/national%20initiatives%20in%20learning%20and%20teaching%20in%20europe.pdf [Accessed 19August 2021]

EUROSTAT – Unemployment Statistics. [online] Available at: https://ec.europa.eu/eurostat/statistics-explained/index.php?title=Unemployment_statistics#Unemployment_in_the_EU_and_the_euro_area [Accessed 8 July 2021]

Eurydice - European Commission. 2021. Political and Economic Situation - Eurydice - European Commission. [online] Available at: https://eacea.ec.europa.eu/national-policies/eurydice/content/political-and-economic-situation-49_en [Accessed 26 July 2021].

Eurydice - European Commission. 2021. Malta - Eurydice - European Commission. [online] Available at: https://eacea.ec.europa.eu/national-policies/eurydice/content/malta_en [Accessed 26 July 2021].

Malta Further & Higher Education Authority. 2021. List of Licensed Providers and Accredited Programmes - Malta Further & Higher Education Authority. [online] Available at: https://mfhea.mt/list-of-licensed-providers-and-accredited-programmes/ [Accessed 26 July 2021].

Malta.AI Taskforce, 2019. A Strategy and Vision for Artificial Intelligence in Malta 2030 [online] Available at: https://malta.ai/wp-content/uploads/2019/11/Malta_The_Ultimate_AI_Launchpad_vFinal.pdf [Accessed 28 July 2021]

National Statistics Office (NSO) 2020. Inbound Tourism: December 2019. [online]. Available at https://nso.gov.mt/en/News_Releases/Documents/2020/02/News2020_017.pdf [Accessed 28 July 2021]

BIBLIOGRAPHY

National Statics Office (NSO). 2021. Labour Force Survey Q1 2021. [online]. Available at: https://nso.gov.mt/en/News_Releases/Documents/2021/06/News2021_112.pdf. [Accessed 28 July 2021]

UNESCO (2021) UNESCO urges all countries to prioritize teachers in national COVID-19 vaccine rollout plans to ensure education can continue safely and schools remain open. [online]. Available at: https://en.unesco.org/covid19/educationresponse/teacher-vaccination [Accessed 06 August 2021]

Enic-Naric. Retrieved 18 August 2021, from https://www.enic-naric.net/

Republic of Estonia Ministry of Education and Research. Retrieved 18 August 2021, from https://www.hm.ee/en/activities/external-evaluation/educational-or-activity-licence

Provider Licences - Malta Further & Higher Education Authority. (2021). Retrieved 18 August 2021, from https://mfhea.mt/provider-licenses/

The COVID-19 pandemic has changed education forever. This is how. (2020). Retrieved 18 August 2021, from https://www.weforum.org/agenda/2020/04/coronavirus-education-global-covid19-online-digital-learning/

Temjournal.com. 2022. [online] Available at: <https://www.temjournal.com/content/94/TEMJournalNovember2020_1669_1674.pdf> [Accessed 10 March 2022].

Temjournal.com. 2022. [online] Available at: <https://www.temjournal.com/content/94/TEMJournalNovember2020_1669_1674.pdf> [Accessed 10 March 2022].

U.S. Department of Education National Assessment of Adult Literacy (NAAL) Survey. (2003). https://nces.ed.gov/naal/index.asp

Montenegro, C.E., and Patrinos, H.A. (2014). Comparable estimates of returnsto schooling around the world. World Bank Group. http://documents1.worldbank.org/curated/en/830831468147839247/pdf/WPS7020.pdf

UNESCO. (2014). Education for all. Global monitoring report 2013/14: Teaching and learning – Achieving quality for all. https://data.unicef.org/topic/education/pre-primary-education/#status

UNESCO. (2014). Institute for Statistics, global databases.
UNESCO. (2012). Institute for Statistics. Opportunities lost: The impact of grade repetition and early school leaving. *Global Education Digest 2012*. http://uis.unesco.org/sites/default/files/documents/opportunities-lost-the-impact-of-grade-repetition-and-early-school-leaving-en_0.pdf

UNICEF. (2014). The state of the world's children 2015: Reimagine the future – Innovation for every child. sowc2015.unicef.org

UNESCO. (2020). From COVID-19 learning disruption to recovery: A snapshot of UNESCO's work in education in 2020. https://en.unesco.org/news/covid-19-learning-disruption-recovery-snapshot-unescos-work-education-2020#

David, R., Pellini, A., Jordan, K., and Phillips, T. (2020). Education during the COVID-19 crisis. Opportunities and constraints of using EdTech in low-incomecountries.https://EdTechhub.org/coronavirus/EdTech-low-income-countries/

EdTech Hub. (2021). https://EdTechhub.org/about-EdTech-hub/

Oberlo. (2021), How many new businesses start each year? https://www.oberlo.com/statistics/how-many-new-businesses-start-each-year

Kastrenakes, J. (June 2, 2020). Zoom saw a huge increase in subscribers — and revenue — thanks to the pandemic. *The Verge.* https://www.theverge.com/2020/6/2/21277006/zoom-q1-2021-earnings-coronavirus-pandemic-work-from-home

Wan, T. (January 13, 2021) A record year amid a pandemic: US EdTech raises$2.2 billion in 2020, *EdSurge.* https://www.edsurge.com/news/2021-01-13-a-record-year-amid-a-pandemic-us-EdTech-raises-2-2-billion-in-2020

The World Bank. (2020). How countries are using EdTech (including online learning, radio, television, texting) to support access to remote learning during the COVID-19 pandemic. https://www.worldbank.org/en/topic/edutech/brief/how-countries-are-using-EdTech-to-support-remote-learning-during-the-covid-19-pandemic

Viewsonic. (February 25 2021). 5 disadvantages of technology in the classroom (and how to overcome them) https://www.viewsonic.com/library/education/5-disadvantages-of-technology-in-the-classroom-and-how-to-overcome-them/

Collis, V., and Vegas, E. (June 22, 2020). Unequally disconnected: Access toonline learning in the US. Brookings. https://www.brookings.edu/blog/education-plus-development/2020/06/22/unequally-disconnected-access-to-online-learning-in-the-us/

Lieberman, M. (March 10, 2021). The big pandemic tech challenge: Reliable, high-quality internet experiences for all. *Education Week.* https://www.edweek.org/technology/the-big-pandemic-tech-challenge-reliable-high-quality-internet-experiences-for-all/2021/03

Lee, N.T. (March 17, 2020). What the coronavirus reveals about the digital divide between schools and communities. Brookings. https://www.brookings.edu/blog/techtank/2020/03/17/what-the-coronavirus-reveals-about-the-digital-divide-between-schools-and-communities/

Federal Communications Commission. (May 29, 2019). 2019 BroadbandDeployment Report. https://www.fcc.gov/reports-research/reports/broadband-progress-reports/2019-broadband-deployment-report

Anderson M., and Kumar, M. (May 7, 2019). Digital divide persists even as lower-income Americans make gains in tech adoption. Pew Research Center. https://www.pewresearch.org/

fact-tank/2019/05/07/digital-divide-persists-even-as-lower-income-americans-make-gains-in-tech-adoption/

Education Superhighway. (2021). Digital bridge K-12 final report 2020. https://www. educationsuperhighway.org/

Thomas, C.J. (April 13, 2020). Coronavirus and challenging times for education in developing countries.Brookings. https://www.brookings.edu/blog/education-plus-development/2020/04/13/coronavirus-and-challenging-times-for-education-in-developing-countries/

Hutton, J., Dudley, J., Horowitz-Kraus, T., DeWitt, T., and Holland, S. (2019). Functional connectivity of attention, visual and language networks during audio, illustrated and animated stories in preschool-age children. *Brain Connectivity.* 9. 10.1089/brain.2019.0679.

Hirsh-Pasek, K., Zosh, J. M., Golinkoff, R. M., Gray, J. H., Robb, M. B., and Kaufman, J. (2015). Putting education in "educational" apps: Lessons from the science of learning. *Psychological Science in the Public Interest,* 16(1), 3–34. https://doi.org/10.1177/1529100615569721

Klein, A. (April 20, 2021). "A year of tremendous growth."
How the pandemic forced teachers to master technology. *Education Week.* https://www.edweek. org/technology/a-year-of-tremendous-growth-how-the-pandemic-forced-teachers-to-master-technology/2021/04

U.S. Department of Education National Assessment of Adult Literacy (NAAL) Survey. (2003). https://nces.ed.gov/naal/index.asp

Montenegro, C.E., and Patrinos, H.A. (2014). Comparable estimates of returnsto schooling around the world. World Bank Group. http://documents1.worldbank.org/curated/en/830831468147839247/pdf/WPS7020.pdf

UNESCO. (2014). Education for all. Global monitoring report 2013/14: Teaching and learning – Achieving quality for all. https://data.unicef.org/topic/education/pre-primary-education/#status

UNESCO. (2014). Institute for Statistics, global databases.
UNESCO. (2012). Institute for Statistics. Opportunities lost: The impact of grade
repetition and early school leaving. *Global Education Digest 2012.* http://uis.unesco.org/sites/default/files/documents/opportunities-lost-the-impact-of-grade-repetition-and-early-school-leaving-en_0.pdf

UNICEF. (2014). The state of the world's children 2015: Reimagine the future – Innovation for every child. sowc2015.unicef.org

UNESCO. (2020). From COVID-19 learning disruption to recovery: A snapshot of UNESCO's work in education in 2020. https://en.unesco.org/news/covid-19-learning-disruption-recovery-snapshot-unescos-work-education-2020#

David, R., Pellini, A., Jordan, K., and Phillips, T. (2020). Education during the COVID-19 crisis.

Opportunities and constraints of using EdTech in low-incomecountries.https://EdTechhub.org/coronavirus/EdTech-low-income-countries/

EdTech Hub. (2021). https://EdTechhub.org/about-EdTech-hub/

Oberlo. (2021), How many new businesses start each year? https://www.oberlo.com/statistics/how-many-new-businesses-start-each-year

Kastrenakes, J. (June 2, 2020). Zoom saw a huge increase in subscribers — and revenue — thanks to the pandemic. *The Verge.* https://www.theverge.com/2020/6/2/21277006/zoom-q1-2021-earnings-coronavirus-pandemic-work-from-home

Wan, T. (January 13, 2021) A record year amid a pandemic: US EdTech raises$2.2 billion in 2020, *EdSurge.* https://www.edsurge.com/news/2021-01-13-a-record-year-amid-a-pandemic-us-EdTech-raises-2-2-billion-in-2020

The World Bank. (2020). How countries are using EdTech (including online learning, radio, television, texting) to support access to remote learning during the COVID-19 pandemic. https://www.worldbank.org/en/topic/edutech/brief/how-countries-are-using-EdTech-to-support-remote-learning-during-the-covid-19-pandemic

Viewsonic. (February 25 2021). 5 disadvantages of technology in the classroom (and how to overcome them) https://www.viewsonic.com/library/education/5-disadvantages-of-technology-in-the-classroom-and-how-to-overcome-them/

Collis, V., and Vegas, E. (June 22, 2020). Unequally disconnected: Access toonline learning in the US. Brookings. https://www.brookings.edu/blog/education-plus-development/2020/06/22/unequally-disconnected-access-to-online-learning-in-the-us/

Lieberman, M. (March 10, 2021). The big pandemic tech challenge: Reliable, high-quality internet experiences for all. *Education Week.* https://www.edweek.org/technology/the-big-pandemic-tech-challenge-reliable-high-quality-internet-experiences-for-all/2021/03

Lee, N.T. (March 17, 2020). What the coronavirus reveals about the digital divide between schools and communities. Brookings. https://www.brookings.edu/blog/techtank/2020/03/17/what-the-coronavirus-reveals-about-the-digital-divide-between-schools-and-communities/

Federal Communications Commission. (May 29, 2019). 2019 BroadbandDeployment Report. https://www.fcc.gov/reports-research/reports/broadband-progress-reports/2019-broadband-deployment-report

Anderson M., and Kumar, M. (May 7, 2019). Digital divide persists even as lower-income Americans make gains in tech adoption. Pew Research Center. https://www.pewresearch.org/fact-tank/2019/05/07/digital-divide-persists-even-as-lower-income-americans-make-gains-in-tech-adoption/

Education Superhighway. (2021). Digital bridge K-12 final report 2020. https://www.educationsuperhighway.org/

Thomas, C.J. (April 13, 2020). Coronavirus and challenging times for education in developing countries.Brookings. https://www.brookings.edu/blog/education-plus-development/2020/04/13/coronavirus-and-challenging-times-for-education-in-developing-countries/

Hutton, J., Dudley, J., Horowitz-Kraus, T., DeWitt, T., and Holland, S. (2019). Functional connectivity of attention, visual and language networks during audio, illustrated and animated stories in preschool-age children. *Brain Connectivity.* 9. 10.1089/brain.2019.0679.

Hirsh-Pasek, K., Zosh, J. M., Golinkoff, R. M., Gray, J. H., Robb, M. B., and Kaufman, J. (2015). Putting education in "educational" apps: Lessons from the science of learning. *Psychological Science in the Public Interest,* 16(1), 3–34. https://doi.org/10.1177/1529100615569721

Klein, A. (April 20, 2021). "A year of tremendous growth."
How the pandemic forced teachers to master technology. *Education Week.* https://www.edweek.org/technology/a-year-of-tremendous-growth-how-the-pandemic-forced-teachers-to-master-technology/2021/04

[1] A. Ng, "Deep Learning Specialization." 2017, [Online]. Available: https://www.coursera.org/specializations/deep-learning.

[2] G. Kasparov, "Deep Thinking: Where Machine Intelligence Ends and Human Creativity Begins," *RevistaEmpresa y Humanismo,* vol. 23, p. 139+, Dec. 2020.

[3] "Schools hit by 17% rise in exam costs, new price guide shows," Sep. 05, 2019. https://schoolsweek.co.uk/schools-hit-by-17-rise-in-exam-costs-new-price-guide-shows/ (accessed Mar. 23, 2021).

[4] "Teachers spend more time marking and planning than in the classroom, Ofsted survey reveals," *The Daily Telegraph*, Jul. 22, 2019.

[5] S.Weale, "'An education arms race': Inside the ultra-competitive world of private tutoring," *Guardian,* vol. 5, 2018.

[6] M. Du Sautoy, *The creativity code: Art and innovation in the age of AI.* Cambridge, MA and London, England: Harvard University Press, 2020.

[7] S.Joordens, "Memory and the Human Lifespan," *PsycEXTRA Dataset.* doi: 10.1037/e526772012-001.

[8] L. Polgar, *Raise a Genius! (neveljzsenit!).* Gordon Tisher, 1989.

Abioui, M., 2022. [online] Link.springer.com. Available at: <https://link.springer.com/content/pdf/10.1007/s40889-020-00100-4.pdf> [Accessed 10 March 2022].

Cdn.ihs.com. 2022. [online] Available at: <https://cdn.ihs.com/www/pdf/IHS-Technology-5G-Economic-Impact-Study.pdf?source=post_page--------------------------> [Accessed 10 March

2022].

Holoniq.com. 2022. [online] Available at: <https://www.holoniq.com/EdTech-unicorns/> [Accessed 10 March 2022].

The Financial Express. 2022. Edtech in 2021: How e-learning will move beyond K-12 segment for startups in post-Covid year. [online] Available at: <https://www.financialexpress.com/industry/sme/cafe-sme/EdTech-in-2021-how-e-learning-will-move-beyond-k-12-segment-for-startups-in-post-covid-year/2163359/;> [Accessed 10 March 2022].

Grandviewresearch.com. 2022. Education Technology Market Worth $377.85 Billion By 2028. [online] Available at: <https://www.grandviewresearch.com/press-release/global-education-technology-market> [Accessed 10 March 2022].

Hibbi, F., Abdoun, O. and El Khatir, H., 2022. [online] Available at: <https://www.researchgate.net/profile/Fatima-Zohra-Hibbi/publication/346647753_Coronavirus_Pandemic_in_Morocco_Measuring_the_Impact_of_Containment_and_Improving_the_Learning_Process_in_Higher_Education/links/5fcb5d54a6fdcc697be0b6dd/Coronavirus-Pandemic-in-Morocco-Measuring-the-Impact-of-Containment-and-Improving-the-Learning-Process-in-Higher-Education.pdf> [Accessed 10 March 2022].

IHS Markit, The 5G Economy. How 5G will contribute to the global economy, November 2019, available online here: https://www.qualcomm.com/media/documents/files/ihs-5g-economic-impact-study-2019.pdf

Google.com. 2022. India Today. [online] Available at: <https://www.google.com/amp/s/www.indiatoday.in/amp/education-today/featurephilia/story/major-EdTech-trends-of-2021-you-should-keep-an-eye-on-1748999-2020-12-12> [Accessed 10 March 2022].
Google.com. 2022. Redirect Notice. [online] Available at: <https://www.google.com/amp/s/EdTechmagazine.com/higher/article/2020/01/how-5g-will-advance-educational-technology-campus%3famp> [Accessed 10 March 2022].

Tauson, M., 2022. EdTech for Learning in Emergencies and Displaced Settings: A rigorous review and narrative synthesis | Save the Children's Resource Centre. [online] Save the Children's Resource Centre. Available at: <https://resourcecentre.savethechildren.net/node/13238/pdf/EdTech-learning.pdf> [Accessed 10 March 2022].

Terrisse, A., 2022. How has the pandemic changed the face of edtech?. [online] EU-Startups. Available at: <https://www.eu-startups.com/2020/09/how-has-the-pandemic-changed-the-face-of-EdTech/> [Accessed 10 March 2022].

eLearning Industry. 2022. Top Educational Technology Trends In 2020-2021. [online] Available at: <https://www.google.com/amp/s/elearningindustry.com/top-educational-technology-trends-2020-2021/amp> [Accessed 10 March 2022].

Whittaker, F., 2022. Gibb wants 'resilient education system' with 'firm digital foundations'. [online]

BIBLIOGRAPHY

Schools Week. Available at: <https://schoolsweek.co.uk/nick-gibb-the-ed-tech-convert-schools-minister-wants-strategy-for-more-resilient-education-system-after-covid/> [Accessed 10 March 2022].

Printed in Great Britain
by Amazon

18754361R00160